No Regrets

No Regrets

Adventuring Through Life

a memoir by
Linda McDermott

No Regrets: Adventuring Through Life

Out There Again Books, Tehachapi, CA

© 2018 Linda McDermott

All rights reserved. Published by Out There Again Books. No part of this publication may be reproduced or distributed in any form or by any means, or stored in a database or retrieval system, without the prior written permission of the publisher.

Editing and design by Indigo: Editing, Design, and More

Illustrations by James McDermott

ISBN: 978-1-7325027-0-3

LCCN: 2018956185

For Helen, Aunt Bertie, my parents, and all free-spirited souls on the planet, including my friends and travel partners and, of course, my children.

Contents

Prologue 1

Chapter 1: First Big Adventure 11

Chapter 2: Costa Rica 33

Chapter 3: Mexico 43

Chapter 4: Dog Sledding I 55

Chapter 5: Dog Sledding II 71

Chapter 6: Spain 81

Chapter 7: Scotland 89

Chapter 8: Tour du Mont Blanc 103

Chapter 9: Dolomites 123

Chapter 10: Patagonia 137

Chapter 11: Peru 151

Chapter 12: Antarctica I 163

Chapter 13: Fiji 179

Chapter 14: Nepal I 185

Chapter 15: Nepal I, Continued 201

Chapter 16: Bali 209

Chapter 17: Antarctica II 221
Chapter 18: Australia Alone 229
Chapter 19: Alaska — Driving the ALCAN 237
Chapter 20: Africa 251
Chapter 21: Greece 265
Chapter 22: Mongolia 279
Chapter 23: Nepal II and III 301
Chapter 24: Croatia 323
Chapter 25: Driving in Italy 329
Chapter 26: Spain — The Camino 341
Chapter 27: Camino, Continued 353
Epilogue 369
Acknowledgments 373
About the Author 375

Prologue

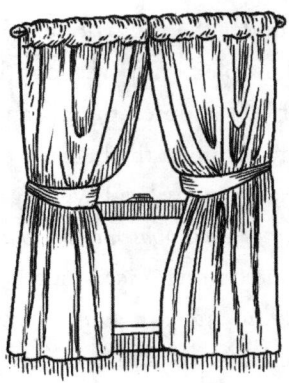

ORIGINALLY MY WORLDVIEW, MY UNIVERSE, WAS VERY SMALL—AND I WAS very small in it. Rules, both spoken and unspoken, left me full of self-criticism and fear, which often led to avoiding risks and change. It has taken more than sixty years to soften the ever-present negative chatter in my head and to grow comfortable in my own skin. It didn't come easily, getting out of my tiny universe, and sometimes I still crawl back toward it, darn it.

In the 1950s my vision of my future life was get married, have children, feed the husband, raise the children, and play bridge eternally during long afternoons with friends. I wanted to be as dependent on someone as my mom was on my dad. When I asked my mother once if she was Democrat or Republican, she replied, "Well, I guess I'm Republican because that's what your dad is."

This vision came from the culture of the Midwest, and from my family structure, something I didn't recognize for a very long time. At a young age, while I gave the impression that I was happy and outgoing, inside a battle ensued. My mother offered me money to lose weight and to stop biting my fingernails, which translated into the message that I was fat and biting fingernails was unsightly. My eating disorders were born, and I never entirely stopped biting my fingernails.

I grew up in small-town Ohio, in a time-warped place, much like any rural place, USA. It was idyllic but held its own set of underlying problems: people swept problems under the rug without really dealing with them. Secrets abounded, as did people's whispers about their friends' actions that they deemed unacceptable. I adopted those standards too, and none of them prepared me for my future in the bigger world.

Then there was the chatter in my head. My negative mental voice would tell me, *This is the way things are supposed to be, so accept it*. Meanwhile, the other more positive and questioning voice would quietly tell me, *Don't listen to the ordinary. Rise above it—you can do it!* I had to learn that when the negative chatter in my head started talking to me about my shortcomings, I needed to recognize it and deal with it.

The windows in my bedroom provided a view of an outside world, something beyond my small world in a house called home. I got the prettiest room, the one with curtained windows, which looked from my world to the streets and trees. My parents always wanted the best for me—*their* best for me. I was expected to succeed, by their standards, and I accepted their standards for a long time, but they never were natural to me. My bedroom was home to smudges of an after-Easter hard-boiled-egg fight with my brother, and to hiding places for my cooking mistakes such as fudge that would not harden.

My brother always got the last bedroom available. His windows didn't reveal the outside world like mine did. He was younger, the boy, so I got the better room. In the summer evenings, we'd meet up with our neighborhood friends to play kick the can or hide-and-seek until our various mothers would call us in long after darkness fell. We'd be hot and sweaty in the summer heat.

Once in a while, my parents would abandon their instincts to protect me at all costs. One time, they let me sit on the back of an alligator at a

Florida alligator farm. There was nothing to keep its mouth from opening and eating me. I was about ten. For my parents to allow that was not normal, though, and for all I know, the experience may have been what planted the adventure seed in me. For the most part, I was shielded from danger.

My youth was a time of incredible innocence and joy, with no relation to real life. As a child, I read fairy tales voraciously, and I wanted the "Once upon a time, in a land far away, she/he/they lived happily ever after." I've been in search of "happily ever after" for a lifetime.

In the 1960s, as a teen, I prized a series of Margaret Keane prints I had of a little girl with huge, sad eyes. I remember my mother questioning me, "Why do you like those pictures? They are so sad!" I couldn't really tell her why I liked them, but I knew I liked them for some reason. There was something in the eyes and dark picture that spoke to me, as if the picture described the real me and the way I thought about myself at the time. I was popular in school, but the true way I thought of myself was completely different from the external shell I showed everyone else. Outside, I appeared to be larger than life. Inside, I felt helpless, small, and stupid. It took a great deal of time for the two characters to catch up with each other and to reach peace.

My father decided it would be good for the family to see more of the western United States, so he planned a two-week trip when I was about twelve—a trip to California. In the 1950s, the only thing on my bucket list was newly opened Disneyland. I distinctly remember my mother telling me to announce that I was eleven years old at the ticket counter so I could get the child ticket price.

My father, with his engineering background, had booked every hotel or motel needed daily for the entire trip. It would all depend on no car trouble—and thankfully we didn't have any. The trip was an immense success, except for my mother, who cried during most of a guided horse ride in Wyoming. She was used to a life of comfort, and all this was beyond her comfort level. The ride was too long for her, and she hurt all over. She took a long bath as soon as possible, trying to regroup for the rest of the trip. I gave her credit for trying.

It was during this trip that I not only developed a respect for what my father had accomplished by mailing checks to each motel or hotel, but I also vowed never to preplan anything to that extent. My love for traveling, and my ideas for how I would do it, started running around in my brain. I was still struggling with many expectations, mine and my parents', but I knew I loved this kind of experience, the kind that had always waited outside my bedroom window.

The next trip out west wasn't as successful. I was sixteen years old, very much in love with my boyfriend, and I didn't want to be anywhere except in my small hometown in Ohio. To prove it, when my family and I stood gazing at amazing mountains in Wyoming, I said something terrible to my parents about not wanting to be there, and I ran into the unfamiliar forest. My hormones took over. My father ran after me, and we both returned safely. Reflecting, I think the beautiful mountains were enticing, an unknown world, but my need to be loved was at odds with the pull to explore the bigger world of the west. My parents, while they loved me, were not able to provide the warm and fuzzy environment I craved. Their love was often conditional: if I did this, then I would get that. Frequently I second-guessed what they were saying. But I didn't have the skills and self-confidence to explore on my own yet, and the Midwest was known. As I ran toward the forest and its symbol of freedom, I simultaneously missed my safety nets.

I was expected to go to college, and I did after high school. Once there, I decided my major should be either home economics or teaching. In the mid-1960s, it wasn't customary for women to have loftier goals than to be a teacher or homemaker. My college career was interrupted for about five years before I returned to college again. During one art class, I was given eight blocks of wood and told to do something with them. I stared at them, turned them over, and tried to see a bigger picture than eight small blocks of wood. Eventually I glued them together to make some shape, thinking I was doing well. The next day at class, I saw that some students had glued them and sanded them to make a ball, or drilled holes in them and joined them to make something interesting. Those students were discovering more than eight pieces of wood. I wanted to be able to do that also, to see possibilities, to leave my limited world behind and enter a universe of the unlimited.

But I still had the vision I'd been raised to pursue: marriage, children, work, card games with friends. Then life happened, and the vision I had been holding for so long shattered. It took even longer for me to actually embrace the change and say to myself: "This is really a great thing because it has enlarged my world and allowed me to see beyond my cocoon, to see something that's larger than me."

My mission over the years became to fight the limiting expectations I had been given. Heck, we all face our childhood demons in one way or another. As life passed, and hallmarks were reached, I embraced traveling. My way to break out of the mold I was given was to travel. And travel, I did.

It never was my intention to go to third-world countries. Even going to Massachusetts from Ohio was a shock to the system. I'm not sure I even knew that avocados or bagels existed until I was in my twenties and moved to California. Just by making the move to Boston and then Los Angeles, my world grew immensely in the early 1970s. I was beginning to see a bigger world than that of the Midwest. And with each new trip I took, my world grew and grew.

Still, I got "lessons" even when I was in my fifties about how I was "supposed" to behave. In the Midwest, the cultural habit is not to say what you really mean. This all led to second-guessing myself and not being secure with myself. Mom would ask me, "Wouldn't you feel more comfortable with your shirt tucked in?" Interpretation: *You look like a slob. Tuck in your shirt!* Another example:

Me: "What is that bag of peanuts for?"
Mom: "That's for your brother."
Me: "Are they from my bag?"
Mom: "Yes, I just gave him some from yours."
Silence. Finally I asked, "Why did you give him my peanuts?"
She: "Because I don't want you to get fat."

Message: You weigh too much now = I just want you to be perfect = you are not perfect as you are = the answer to a lot of my problems.

After I'd become a world-traveling adult, my mother advised me to relay my adventures to her once I returned, not before. She worried way too much to have that burden on my (or her) shoulders while en route to a third-world country, or even to a local camping trip or mountain climb. Although she was afraid for my safety, she was also proud of me. She told me once that a friend asked her, "What's that maverick granddaughter of yours up to these days?" She would reply, "It's not my granddaughter, it's my *daughter!*" I think secretly she was not only proud of me but was also rooting for me, in her own way. A granddaughter was expected to be young and stupid, but a daughter in her fifties was not.

Note to self: Mom will never accept you for who you are. Rise above it, but accept her for who she is.

MY DAD, ON THE OTHER HAND, WAS MORE PASSIVE. WHEN I WOULD ASK him, "What do you think of this haircut?" he would answer, "Does my opinion really matter? If not, I'm not giving it."

Over the years I came to realize that paying attention to serendipity is important to me. It was serendipity that brought an answer to me in one of my many life searches. I boarded a bus that would take me to the Hollywood Bowl in Los Angeles to meet a friend for a Mozart concert. Next to me, a lady close to my age was wearing outrageous shoes for her age. I admired that about her. I said, "I like your shoes!" She smiled, turned toward me, then with a sparkle in her eyes, thanked me.

We continued our conversation awhile, and I mentioned my need/desire/goal of writing a book about my experiences. I had been toying with the idea of writing my experiences for years, and my children begged me to record them. I realized some of the outrageous experiences I'd had by this point in time were worth recording. Sometime later during the conversation, she revealed that she was a reviewer for the books featured in the *Los Angeles Times*.

"Just write," she implored. She told me to write about what I know, the key to my independent nature. "What started it all?" she asked.

It took a long time for me to understand the importance of that question.

You are living the travel life that I fear.

—R. Schroeder, Friend of the Author

CHAPTER 1

First Big Adventure

WHEN I MENTIONED TRAVELING TO MY FRIEND BARB, SHE IMMEDIATELY raised her eyes from her dinner at a local café, stunned. "Oh, I don't know, Linda" was her first response.

The idea was to take five months off work in the mid-1980s, giving up the apartment we shared and traveling around the country in a converted van—and it was crazy. I'd considered the idea of a long van trip for several years as my children were growing, and the idea had simmered so long, I couldn't stand it anymore. It wouldn't be an easy undertaking, and it was decidedly a huge unknown, but the possibilities for adventure were endless. I just had to convince Barb and Rosie, our dog, to go with us—but Rosie needed no convincing, of course.

Aunt Bertie—or as I called her as a child, Aunt Birdie—would be proud of my decision. She had been my favorite aunt, the one who got her nickname from the parakeet she sent me in the mail. The cage fared better than the parakeet did in the postal service. At Christmas, my brother and I always saved Aunt Bertie's gift boxes for last because she traveled all over the world and had very exotic things to give us. One year it was a hand-carved German nutcracker (it actually worked), and other times we got small dolls from foreign lands like Egypt and Turkey (I didn't understand their head coverings at the time). Aunt Bertie never married or had children even though men lined up to date her and she'd gotten many offers of marriage. It was hard to ignore her presence. She talked easily to everyone she encountered, as if she had known them for years, and her dark-brown hair spoke volumes when she brushed it away from her face. You just knew she was one of a kind and could talk with anyone, including the king of a foreign country.

Aunt Bertie taught elementary school on military bases in countries including Japan and Greece. During her time off, she traveled all over Europe and other foreign countries whenever she could. She never seemed to have a care in the world, and whenever she came to our house, she blew in like a tornado. My mother was usually upset whenever Aunt Bertie came because she would show up out of the blue, with no warning.

Aunt Bertie was the one who let me try cigarettes at the young age of ten, the one who would encourage me to go on snake hunts with her and my brother. Her boundaries were nonexistent, and I could talk her into doing anything I wanted. My brother and I loved it when she would come to visit because she would do things like take us to a dirt road and let us drive the family car. Aunt Bertie was the person I wanted to become, even though I didn't have a clue how to get from where I was to where her larger-than-life persona existed. Already the conflicting values were mounting.

Note to self: Huge influence here. Pay attention.

WHILE AUNT BERTIE WAS ONE OF THE FIRST TO INFLUENCE ME TO LOOK beyond my Midwestern life, she was certainly not the only one. As an adult, I moved to Los Angeles and worked at a local bank, where I grew close to my supervisor, Helen. She was as old as my mother, and I considered her to be my Los Angeles mom. As kind a soul as they come, she was never one to step on anyone's toes or to upset anyone. She had never married because the man she was in love with had died in World War II. The pain of that experience was so deep that she never fell in love again. Helen and her sister, who also had never married, lived together for a long time.

After she retired, it was easy for me to see that Helen was getting older and more frail. I would take her out to dinner or lunch when I carved out the time from my work schedule. She relished any time I could give her.

Once, at dinner, I asked her, "What should I learn from you? What would you tell someone new to the planet?"

She raised her eyes to the ceiling and thought for a minute. Then she lowered her eyes and said, "Don't have any regrets. That's it. *Just don't have regrets.*" I think she said that because she did have regrets. She loved to travel and had recounted to me every day of every trip she ever took. Her trips were all in the Southwest, mainly because she had never flown on an airplane.

Note to self: Never forget those words. *No regrets.* Follow Aunt Bertie's footprints and Helen's advice imprinted indelibly on your brain, and have no regrets for your time on the planet.

WHEN I FINALLY CONVINCED BARB THAT OUR TRIP WOULD BE THE EXPErience of a lifetime, we decided to take back roads, those roads that wouldn't involve highway traffic and interstate driving. We read William Least Heat-Moon's bestseller *Blue Highways* as a guidebook for what we wanted to do. He suggested stopping at restaurants only if they had three or more calendars posted somewhere in the restaurant. His book implied that restaurants with many calendars were generally dives that were hidden gems. We generally planned not to stop at restaurants at all because of the expense. Those restaurants we would stop at, we promised, would have at least three calendars on the walls.

While Barb and I had gone on many weeklong adventures including backpacking and camping trips with and without my children, this five-month van trip was a plan off the map. Like nothing any of my friends—or heck, anyone I knew—had attempted. Why us, now? I couldn't stop thinking about how the past eighteen years had gone so very differently than I'd imagined they would.

In my late 30's, I remembered a day that should have been my most glorious, eighteen years earlier. It should have been a life-changing, *defining* moment in my life, and it was—but not in the way I thought it would be. I recalled coming home with my new baby, only a few days old. In those ancient days, new mothers stayed in the hospital for several days to recover from the ups and downs of childbirth. Because of obligations of my family members, a friend picked me up from the hospital and brought me home with my daughter.

At the front door, my friend asked if I was all right, clearly not wanting to come inside. I said yes and more or less gave him permission to leave. I remember opening the door to a very sparse but adequate apartment. It seemed so very cold, with its squares of vinyl on the floor and the limited furniture from the thrift store. No one was there but my baby and me.

This wasn't the happy occasion I had imagined. My fairy-tale brain had envisioned many family members and friends welcoming me and the new little life, someone offering me a cup of tea and a comfortable place to sit, plus continuous *awww*s over the baby. None of that existed on this day, one of the most important days of my life. There was only silence in the cold apartment.

I let the feelings envelop me, the whiteness and silence, the absence of anyone but the two souls in the room, the bursting of my fairy-tale imagery, and the fear that was creeping into my brain. I was tired, and I couldn't sit anywhere because of hemorrhoids. I was hungry, and I held a brand-new baby in my arms.

For years before that first big road trip, that scene had played over and over in my mind, and it still does. I've finally come to understand why it is so imprinted on my brain: It was the first time I truly understood that I was alone in the world—that the only person I could count on to make sure I landed on my feet was *me*. Then I had a little baby who depended on me to land on my feet also. I had to learn quickly to be strong for both of us.

I gently laid my little sleeping girl in her crib. Then I lay on the large bed beside her and started crying, only a little at first until huge swells of sobbing started. I was finally forced to acknowledge that I was not Cinderella and to let that fairy-tale image fade away. No one was there to watch my back, to make sure I had a soft place to land, to help me. It was then that I began to toughen my skin.

Note to self: Take care of yourself instead of expecting your knight in shining armor on a white horse. Appropriately, your daughter's name is Vanessa, "butterfly" in Greek. You will both emerge from your personal chrysalis stages and spread your wings.

A WEEK BEFORE BARB AND I STARTED THE TRIP, WE HAD JUST TAKEN MY precious daughter to settle into her dorm—and the rest of college life. It felt as if I had done my job. I had raised her, and it was okay to give myself permission to take a short break. I'd spent almost twenty years making choices in regard to other people—whether partners, bosses, or children—and now I needed a break. I knew Aunt Bertie would agree. For now, I could see the country. We'd see how that went and then move on to the world.

My young son was with his father, and I trusted that he would be all right during this time. I promised to communicate constantly. When I returned, he would be my priority once again.

Barb and I were both scared and excited at the same time. To quit our jobs and take off in our thirties, knowing we would have to return to work for many more years after this trip, was an oddball thing to do. It took convincing for both of us, but gaining the courage to do it was amazing.

We started out in September, meaning that we'd be traveling in winter in the northern part of the country. We didn't know it yet, but this meant we would have three snowstorms in Wyoming in September and would be camping behind a city library in subzero temperatures in Vermont, but we were prepared for it—kind of.

It was about four weeks after the trip had started that we took our first showers in Brookings, South Dakota. We'd pulled into a park area with a bathroom. Finding things to explore was always at the top of my list because of my curiosity. I walked into the bathroom to find a shower in the totally concrete building. This meant that wherever our feet would touch the floor, they would be cold. Because it was late September, it was darn right cold outside and inside, so we had to weigh the advantages of a free shower versus the cold temperature. The need for a shower won, and we prayed for warm water. I was able to shower first, and I promised Barb that I would be quick so she would have warm water also. It all worked fairly well. At least we didn't smell anymore.

We wove along the blue highways to the Upper Peninsula of Michigan in October. We were becoming brazen enough to wash our hair in gas station restrooms, ignoring the station attendants' stares when we came from the bathrooms with our hair dripping or wrapped in a towel. Luckily we had just washed our hair before we saw a sign that read *Fish Fry at the American Legion*.

It was a Friday night in the Midwest, so finding a fish fry was not uncommon. I pointed the sign out to Barb, and we decided to follow it to see where the event was being held. We pulled into a dirt parking lot lined with trucks and older vehicles plus a small wooden building at the far end. So far, it seemed fairly harmless. There were people standing outside because the line was so long to get inside the wooden structure. We finally spied a sign that said *$5.00*, so we figured that was the cost of the meal.

We got in line and slowly advanced to the long table that held a variety of dishes. While in line, I expected to remain anonymous and not have conversation. From my youth, I remembered that unless you knew the people in the area, in general, people didn't talk with new people until they felt comfortable with them. That was just the Midwestern way.

When we got to the table, I saw not only huge trays of fried fish but also corn, potato salad, coleslaw, fries, pies, and everything else in between—like the Midwestern meals I was used to. We filled our paper plates and decided to sit at the far end of a long table with a vinyl tablecloth near the pine-paneled wall. One by one or two by two, other people sat beside us with their friends, and quickly the table was filled with about twelve people dressed in cotton dresses or casual jeans and flannel shirts. These locals all knew each other, and the conversation centered on so-and-so being sick, another so-and-so's crops not coming in very well, and so-and-so's grandson getting into trouble again. It was all polite conversation, with little of substance revealed about anyone's life.

I sat there and then began to eat slowly. Barb did the same thing.

As we ate, I glanced up from time to time to see people look away from us when our eyes met. We were dressed in used clothes, but we didn't smell badly, to the best of my knowledge. Barb and I were never addressed, and we used that as an excuse to say nothing. I mean, we said nothing to our neighbors at the table during our whole dinner. In response to our silence, they said nothing to us. We were outsiders—we didn't invite conversation because we were too scared, and they probably didn't know what to do with two hippies in their midst. We didn't look like off-the-wall hippies, just girls in jeans and flannel shirts who, maybe, were up to no good. The entire meal seemed to last an eternity, even though every bite was homemade and absolutely delicious. When we finished, Barb and I stood up, nodded to indicate silently that we were leaving, smiled at our anonymous companions, and left quickly.

I felt uncomfortable with the whole situation and thought about the fact that I had let my fear and insecurity get in the way of hearing the stories of the area directly from the people who lived there. At some point during the night, I made a decision: I would never let an amazing situation like that escape again. I would never again be silent, not smile, not invite conversation, or miss an opportunity to find out who the people of the area are and what makes them tick. I may never get to know their innermost thoughts, but I would know how they dealt with strangers.

It is my nature to talk with people and to put my vulnerable self out there for others to see so they also feel comfortable to let themselves be known. I needed to unwrap my skin a bit, like the layers of an onion. I had always equated people who were afraid to let their true selves be seen with an unpeeled onion. But looking back on that dinner, I realized maybe I was closer to an onion than I was able to admit. I needed to look at myself closer. And I probably needed to let my Midwestern inbred culture go.

A week before, in upper Minnesota, we'd had amazing colors of fall. We'd also encountered trouble. Not much in the category of trouble happened on the entire trip, but upper Minnesota was a problem. Because we were traveling in late fall, it was getting colder. It also meant that fewer people were traveling at this point, and we would find ourselves camping alone a lot of the time. Apparently when we were examining a spot in a national forest campground to camp for that night, somebody saw us.

We were in bed by nine, having chosen a site that was well sheltered on three sides around our van. At ten p.m., car lights shone through the van curtains. We were the only ones camped at the campground. Two other factors played into the scene quickly: it was a weekend night, which meant drinking on Friday or Saturday nights and getting into mischief was a likely pastime for locals, and we had pulled straight into our site, with the three sides of shelter now feeling like barricades. The only way we could get out was to back up.

Our eyes were glued on the lights coming in the back window, and we parted the curtains a bit. The car with the lights came closer, and before we could do anything, it had stopped behind us, shining the lights inside our van and blocking any exit. Rosie did nothing. Neither did we.

We had decided not to bring a weapon on the trip, figuring we would probably be hurt more with it than we would hurt someone else. The only things we had were our wits and a wimpy dog.

Two men got out of the car and came to where we could see them in front of the van. By this point, I was in the driver's seat and Barb was in the passenger seat. We just wanted to leave. The men, however, wanted something else. They demanded that we open our doors and show our faces. As long as they had shotguns in their hands, we weren't going anywhere. And, I thought, they appeared drunk.

The two men told us we were there illegally, that the *Sierra Corp* didn't allow camping. We yelled back (windows and doors unopened), that we had stopped at the ranger office and were told it was all right. Additionally, we didn't know any "Sierra Corp" organization. My heart was in my throat. I was trying to think my way through this mess. The conversation went on for a while, but we didn't back down. It must have been ten minutes when all this happened, but it seemed like an eternity to me.

Eventually another set of headlights appeared at the entrance to the campground. *OK, universe, my prayers have been heard*, I thought. The headlights came closer to the van, and mercifully the men got back into their car and pulled away, no longer blocking us in.

I quickly put the car into reverse, stepped on the gasoline, and headed out through the trees to the main road as fast as I dared. By this time both Barb and I were sobbing and didn't know what to do. I kept driving. We made it into town after about fifteen minutes, where I searched for the sheriff's office. Once we found it, we told our story to an officer, between sobs, until he shrugged and said we could park in the back lot near the station for the rest of the night if we wanted. We really wanted acknowledgment and sympathy, but we settled for the safe place for the rest of the night, promising ourselves we'd be more careful about where we stayed on weekends. I chalked this up to being a character-strengthening lesson I apparently needed.

We progressed from Minnesota to upper Michigan and then down to Cincinnati, Ohio, where the weather was warmer and the woods were hopefully not as isolated. Going through Kentucky was warmer yet, although wetter also. One of our trip objectives from the beginning was not to pay for campsites so our money would last. In Kentucky, we pulled into a wet, misty national forest campground with almost manicured campsites. It was unusual to find such well-kept sites in a free campground. There were even a few split logs there at the campsites, so we were able to start a fire and cook our potato-and-onion meal in our cast-iron Dutch oven. It wasn't long before a man in a camouflage shirt and pants started to approach us. He asked if the dog was friendly.

"Maybe" was my reply. Rosie started to growl. My thoughts of the Minnesota experience flooded in, but the lost Michigan opportunity trickled in too. The Michigan event won, and I started talking with the fellow. Barb and I relaxed when we understood him to be just a fellow who wanted to talk with Californians "for a spell." We were in the South now.

The next morning when we looked out of the van, two men were sitting with rakes on a picnic table at the next site over, but were obviously not camping there, and we didn't know what to do. With the gloom of the rainy day and the Minnesota experience fresh in our minds, we conjured all kinds of scenarios about who they were and what they wanted, and I figured all this was just another test of my intuition. I finally decided I would take our pee pot that we had used the night before to the bathroom to dump it. I walked out of the van with a determined gait, piss pot in hand, and made my way toward the outhouse. One of the men yelled out, "Got lunch for me there?" I started laughing, and so did he. It was kind of disarming.

I couldn't help but talk with them after I poured out the pot. They remained at the table, and I found out that they were local workers employed by the US Forest Service to keep the campgrounds clean and well managed. It was a mutually beneficial arrangement: locals got jobs, and the Forest Service got manicured campsites. I complimented them on their fine job, and they commented on our California license plates. I told them, "No, we're not lost. We're really from California." I later sent one of them a California license plate once I got back home, and another friendship was cemented. I was peeling my onion skin, little by little.

"I DON'T WANT TO STAY IN THE MIDDLE OF NOWHERE AGAIN TONIGHT. IT'S the weekend," I was explaining to Barb. "I agree," she said. We were still in Kentucky, en route to the Deep South. We decided to stay in a well-known and hopefully populated place whenever we could on Friday and Saturday nights.

We stopped at a local Forest Service office in one of the small towns we were traveling through. I asked, "We'd like to stay somewhere in our RV for the weekend, someplace safe…and not expensive," I added.

The fellow behind the desk thought for a minute. He then said, "You know, you might think about going on down to the marina a few miles down the road. There's a fellow taking care of things there," he continued, "and I think you could probably park there for free. I think his name is Rick."

Bonanza, I was thinking.

We tootled off down the road in high spirits. After several of our other adventures, this would be a blessing.

It didn't take long to see a sign pointing to a public marina on a road leading to a large lake. Two things Kentucky has are water and lakes. We pulled into a spot, and it wasn't long before a man started approaching us. He came slowly, walking as if something were hurting him a bit, but obviously heading toward our Ford van.

When he got to the van, I said, "Hey there!"

He nodded his head and then said, "Hello! How are you doing?"

We explained that we needed a safe place to camp for two nights; we wouldn't bother anyone and would not leave any trash around. Rick really didn't care about any of that. Matter of fact, he was just glad to have company. It was late fall and no one was around, so he was happy to have someone to talk with. He showed us pocketknives that he had found in the reservoir. It was obvious that he was proud of his finds. I told him I would be making some biscuits later in the afternoon, and if he came back, I would give him some.

We went our separate ways, and I got out my Bundt pan to make biscuits for dinner. I took out my mother's old biscuit recipe and then found the flour, baking powder, and other supplies I needed to put everything together. The Bundt pan fit nicely on a burner that slowly baked the biscuits.

Just about the time I was ready to take the biscuits off the stove, I saw Rick coming up the road. We were camped in a flat spot with a few trees and a road leading down toward the water of the marina.

He came up to talk a bit more about life in the marina. He explained that he ensured the few boats in the docks were safe and how people come down for the weekend to play and to fish. I took the biscuits off the stove and pulled off the lid to show them to him. He stared at them with big eyes. I asked him if he still wanted some, and he said, "Of course!"

I took a spoon and scooped two large biscuits out of the pan, wrapped them carefully in a paper towel, and then handed them to Rick. He looked at them, smelled them, then stuffed them in his back jeans pocket, both in one pocket, and wandered off. My amazing, fluffy, made-in-a-van biscuits were being squished to the size of cardboard in the back pocket of a pair of jeans. After taking a second to understand what just happened, I glanced at Barb, and we both broke out into peals of laughter. We left the next day, and were sad to leave our safe haven and Rick.

I TRIED TO KEEP THE MICHIGAN LESSON IN MIND AS WE TRAVELED FARTHER on our road trip. I seemed to need to learn it again and again. It was in Berea, Kentucky, that it once again came to the forefront.

I remembered as a child coming to Berea, where there was a college in town that traditionally charged no tuition. The students who came to Berea at that time in the early 1950s were from the very poor areas of Appalachia, and the college recruited them so they could learn better skills and bring them back to their areas. In exchange for their education, they were required to work in some capacity to support the college. There was a hotel in town with a huge historical base, and it was almost completely staffed by students. In addition, students made crafts such as brooms, wastebaskets, games, and other such things to sell for additional funds. I wanted to see the town again.

Barb and I arrived in Berea in October on a Friday morning. I was driving the van with California license plates on it. At the time of our trip, the world was still small, with no internet and only television to give a glimpse of the outside world. While traveling through small towns in Kentucky, often there was just a used bookstore because no one could afford new books.

At this point, Berea was still small, even considering the college. It was raining when we got there, so we found the college library, took off our outer clothes to dry them, and sat down to do some research on future destinations for our trip. We had learned to find libraries throughout our trip and were often very grateful for their hospitality no matter where we were in the country.

After an hour or so, we wandered back to the van. It was there that we encountered the town kids. Our California license plates didn't go ignored. As we walked closer to the van, kids started crowding in to see us, as if we were aliens arriving via a vehicle with California license plates.

A young woman, obviously a student at the college, approached us and said, "Are you *really* from California?"

I smiled broadly. "Yes, we *really* are!"

The questions implied we were truly something *special* and must know all the movie stars that the townspeople could name. It was hard to explain that Los Angeles is very big and movie stars usually don't shop at regular grocery stores.

It didn't take long for one tall, thin, blond girl to invite us to her house that night. We could park in the driveway of the house she was renting and come to Bible study that night. It was a reflection of the times, and we were in a small southern town that was deeply religious, curious about the outside world, and very welcoming. We declined the huge-hearted offer, and then we were told we *had* to come to the square dance in the streets that night. We asked where to go and were told, "Just come back here and you'll see!"

We parked on a side street, trying not to be noticed. That night, after a very quiet and private dinner in the van, Barb and I got out to investigate the square dance we'd been told about. About seven o'clock, we noticed that the main street near the hotel was shut down. Any cars in the area would have to detour. This seemed a little strange to us, but then, we weren't really sure what to expect. As we stayed in the area, more and more people came. Eventually I saw a fiddler or two coming into the area. Most of those with an instrument were jovial; they were smiling and seemed to love beer or, at the least, good food.

Sure enough, soon the music started up. I looked around to see what was up and found that the musicians were standing at one end of the road closure, right in the middle of the street. It was Appalachian music, some songs I recognized and many I didn't. But the beat was unmistakable and easy to strike up a square dance to. Barb and I stood around, just watching in amazement at all the people forming foursome squares and dancing to the calls made by an announcer somewhere.

It wasn't long before Barb and I had men coming up to us, inviting us to dance. I protested loudly because I didn't know all the calls. Protesting was in vain, though, as I was pulled out to the street to dance. Everyone was so happy, so friendly, and so inviting that I couldn't say no! So we danced and danced for hours, smiling all the while, not really knowing what we were doing, and having the time of our lives in this tiny Appalachian town. I was shaking the Michigan experience from my mind, or rather, maybe allowing myself to learn from it.

Continuing our journey, we headed through Virginia and crossed the Chesapeake Bay Bridge-Tunnel and were safely in Maryland. We were cruising around, looking for a place to stay for the night, and found a beautiful small white church on a very flat piece of land in this part of southern Maryland.

We pulled into the gravel parking lot of the church and were grateful that no other vehicles were around. We figured that churches welcome everyone, so we'd be allowed to stay in the parking lot. We slid the van door open for ventilation, hoping for no mosquitoes, and started cooking and getting ready to stay for the night.

Everything was fine for a while, until about five thirty. It was then that cars started appearing in the parking lot, one by one. It piqued my interest and also my fear that we would be ousted. I looked at the arriving cars, trying to figure out what was going on. In the meantime, no one came to ask us a thing—not "What are you doing here?" and not even "Who are you?" We started feeling more secure as people walked past us, just waved, and went into the church.

After a while, I couldn't hold my curiosity any longer, so I went inside the church, leaving Barb in the van. There, I saw people filling up the choir loft behind the pulpit. Well, of course, this was choir practice, and here I was able to witness it.

I went up to the ruddy-cheeked man I identified as the choirmaster and asked him hesitantly, "Is it okay if I sit here in the pews and listen to the choir practice?"

He turned around and stared at me with a twinkle in his eye. He said, "No, absolutely not." I started to slink away, but he continued, "If you are going to be here, you are going to sit in the choir loft *and sing with us!*" Well, that was a surprise, to say the least. He pointed and said, "Sit down here in the front, and here's some sheet music to follow."

Needless to say, I had the time of my life. Everyone gave me warm smiles, and the young teenagers in the choir would talk with me between songs, much to the frustration of the choirmaster, who was trying to maintain control.

The teens would ask, "Do you *really* live in California?" and "Have you seen any *movie* stars?" and "What is it like to *surf* on your beaches?" I would nod, give short answers, and smile at their curiosity. They were just babes starting out, and here I was, twice their age, having the experience of my life. It was stunning conversation.

When the practice ended, the ladies of the group promptly asked if I could stay until Sunday morning and sing with them at the church service. They had an extra choir robe for me, so there would be no problem on Sunday. Sadly, I had to decline so Barb and I could keep moving.

We heard little news on the trip, but we did hear about the *Challenger* blowing up and Rock Hudson's death. Another thing we heard about was airline tickets to Europe on a supercheap airline. Barb and I decided to hop over to Europe for a week in the middle of this trip. At this time, we only had library books to research the trip to Europe. We had to use libraries to find out about the Eurorail, the train system in Europe. We researched as much as we could and then purchased the cheap airline tickets.

This would be my maiden voyage to anywhere overseas, and it was a special destination: Europe. For some reason, maybe because we had been on the road for about three months at this time, I felt little apprehension about going on this trip, even though we had only airline tickets, train ticket information, and a general idea of where we might go. Slowly, I was growing into the comfort zone of travel.

Barb and I flew to Brussels and immediately found the rail system right beside the airport. We bought Eurorail passes for the week so we could hop on and off trains as we wanted, and we had maps of the area copied from library books. Our first stop, we decided, would be Dinant in Belgium.

The town of Dinant was totally medieval and gave me an introduction to a much older history than I had ever encountered in the fairly young US. We found a hotel in the area, not too expensive, found a pub, and also found an incredible bakery where I bought a special gingerbread cookie. It was large, about six inches across, shaped like a heart and had amazing designs in the top, as if someone had taken a year to carefully carve out the designs. I kept that thing for about ten years, using it as a Christmas decoration, until the bugs in the house found it and ate it for me.

On a Sunday we got off the train in St. Goar, along the Rhine River in Germany. Talk about eerie—this town was downright like a ghost town. There were no tourists anywhere and not even locals to be found. We bought a twenty-five-cent chocolate bar at a dispenser in the train stop when we got off. That was the only normal thing in this town.

We passed gray buildings. Except for a few flowers here and there, the entire town was gray. It actually matched the weather: gloomy, dark, and moisture laden. We kept glancing at each other, trying not to be scared. Had a natural disaster come and we didn't hear about it? We walked down the main street, peeking in stores, bars, anything that might have life.

Eventually we turned a corner and heard music. We glanced at each other and then turned our heads to the direction we thought the music was coming from. We went down a side street and came to a tall church building. It was Sunday; this was a church—and all of a sudden, it all made sense. We opened the side door to the church and peeked in stealthily. Much to our surprise, the music dwindled and all eyes turned to us.

It took no more than a minute for the people, all the people of the village, to realize that two strangers who were dressed like hippies, wearing gray wool sweaters and jeans and carrying backpacks, were invading their town. The townspeople stared at us while we stared back as the music came to a stop. We quickly sized each other up. Then the townspeople started talking very quickly in German and motioning for us to come inside. Because the church was already totally full, several people pushed others down the rows so there would be two seats for us. It struck me like lightning that here was an amazing venue, with amazing music, and the entire town of St. Goar was welcoming us to enjoy the concert.

We went in, sat down, and listened to the most beautiful chamber music concert I will remember in my lifetime. My only regret was that I didn't understand German, because each time the players stopped, I couldn't understand the introduction to the next piece nor what I imagined was the historical explanation of Mozart and his growth. I also felt a little ashamed that I didn't know the language of the country we were visiting. Of course, that wasn't stopping me from being there and making the best of it.

Note to self: You are growing.

BARB AND I STARTED TALKING WITH THE OWNER OF THE PUB WHERE WE were staying, telling him we enjoyed the room and the coffee. We asked if there were any castles around that we could visit.

His eyes lit up, and he said, "Oh yes! There is a castle up on the road here, and if you follow it up, you'll find the castle, and they rent rooms. You may have to search for someone to let you in, but it is wonderful!"

We were instantly buying in. Much as we enjoyed the pub room, it would be more of an adventure to stay in a castle. So we packed up our things in our backpacks and headed up the street, to the left, where the pub owner indicated. Eventually we saw gray walls and the rocks of a fortress. We walked around the castle, and it seemed deserted. Apparently there was a restaurant at the entrance, and although no one was there, we were able to go inside and see what was around. We went down the halls, saw the rooms, and then came back to peer into the restaurant some more. Like St. Goar when we first arrived, the place was deserted. We could have helped ourselves to an entire meal, including wine, at the restaurant.

Eventually, however, someone did come in, and we found ourselves talking with a very kind German woman who, in broken English, told us we could stay in the castle for ten dollars each. We could have any room we wanted, and that sounded good to me.

Barb and I went to bed early so we could get up early and be on our way the next day. About eleven o'clock that night, we heard the first noise. We both sat up in our beds when we heard it—a ping reverberating through the castle. We stared at each other, as if saying, *Did you hear that too?* My first thought was ghosts. I had no idea what Barb was thinking. We both listened for the longest time. It sounded like someone was hammering on a pipe somewhere distant in the castle. The sounds were regular, about one or two seconds apart, and truly did sound like a metal pipe being hit by a hammer.

I finally whispered to Barb, "What do you think that is?"

She replied, "I have no idea, but it is freaky."

After a few rounds of the hammering, I listened more closely. The sound started often very near us, seemed to get farther away, and then returned to our neck of the woods—well, castle. I finally decided it was the metal pipes in the castle and that they were rattling on the wall or something. Maybe air bubbles in the pipes were causing the rattle. One way or the other, the rattling started near us, made its rounds throughout the castle, and then returned to us, only to repeat its journey again and again.

We finally got up, dressed, and decided to go down to the restaurant to see if we could find someone to help us. We were the only ones in the place.

Once we assured ourselves we were safe and the clamoring was probably just old pipes in the castle, it all made sense and was more like a known entity. We'd simply have to deal with the pipes and try to sleep. The lesson for me was about known vs. unknown events.

Note to self: Once a rational mind can process information, it all makes sense. Before then, fear of the unknown takes over.

After we returned to the US, we started heading farther south, into Florida. Barb and I checked the map for a small town in Florida's panhandle. "You've got to try Del's Diner," Sandy, my friend from work, had told me. "It's a dive, but you'll love it! The food is *great!*" Now, Barb and I walked up to the front door. It creaked open, and we immediately saw about six people looking at us. We were strangers in the small town. There were also three calendars on the walls, we noted.

Glimpses of our fish-fry adventure passed by in my mind, so I smiled broadly and said, "Hi!" to everyone. I got an immediate response of smiles back, and the townsfolk went back to what they were doing.

The server, obviously a bit harried, came over to us and asked us to sit down wherever we wanted. She handed us a one-page menu and told us she would be right back. I wondered what "right back" meant in Florida panhandle time. Meanwhile, I took a look around the restaurant to soak in the local culture. The three calendars had pictures of fish, flowers, and food on them, ordinary calendars. It was a small restaurant, with about six tables, and the kitchen was a stone's throw from me. The entrance to the restaurant almost spilled onto table number one. I saw a whiteboard with *Specials* written on it and put on my glasses to see what was listed.

I saw *Roe* listed at the top of the specials list, and I thought fish sounded good and I should definitely try it since we were in such an unusual place. I looked at the rest of the menu and then decided to just order the roe and take my chances. It was unusual for Barb and me to purchase a meal anywhere, so I wanted to spend my money wisely. I took a third glance at the menu and then decided to order the roe. My final decision.

The server came over to our table quickly, and I ordered the roe, asking if it was good. The server quickly stared me in the eye and said, "Well, of course it is—it's our special, and we don't have it often." Barb ordered something else, and we agreed to share anything that was good. While waiting for our meals, we glanced around the diner to see more about it. The locals were all sharing beers or French fries, going about their business and ignoring us.

It wasn't too long before our meals came. They were definitely full meals, each a plateful of food that was hot and steamy. The server placed mine in front of me, and I noted that I didn't see the piece of fish I had ordered. As the server was putting Barb's plate in front of her, I asked, "Where's the fish?"

The server glanced up at the ceiling once and then back down to me. "You ordered roe."

I replied, "I know. Where is the fish?"

"Right on your plate!" I think she would have added "you idiot" if it had been appropriate. She waited a second and then pointed to a pile on my plate. "See? There it is."

I stared at the pile, which seemed like a bunch of tiny marbles, small and round, dark and a bit glossy. I looked up at her. Everyone in the restaurant was staring at our table at this point because there was obviously a communication gap.

I finally said, "I thought I ordered fish, the special, roe."

The server smiled at me, and I heard a gentle laughter throughout the diner. "You don't know what roe is, do you?"

I had to shake my head.

She started laughing, as did everyone else around. The locals were getting a good laugh at this. The server continued, "Roe is *fish eggs!* It's a true specialty around here!"

I lowered my head in embarrassment and started eating while enduring the smiles and under-their-breath amazement of the locals. It was a delicious meal.

AFTER FIVE MONTHS ON THE ROAD, OUR ADVENTURE ENDED RATHER QUIetly as Barb and I pulled back into Los Angeles one evening. It was early February, cold in Los Angeles, and hard to be enthusiastic about returning. We spent the nights on the streets in the van until we found a place to live a few days later. It wouldn't be easy to reintegrate into life in a large city, but our adventure had cleared our minds and slates to begin careers and take on family responsibilities once again. Barb and I looked at each other with mixed emotions, knowing that we had experienced something amazing. I was happy to be in familiar territory and with my children again. The plan was to enter the world of business for a long time, but the things we had experienced were indelible in my brain and only made me want to travel more.

CHAPTER 2

Costa Rica

A YEAR OR TWO AFTER BARB AND I RETURNED FROM OUR ROAD TRIP, I jumped at a chance to see Costa Rica for a week. I was fat at the time I went to Costa Rica. I hadn't intended for that to happen—it just happened. *Fat* was a relative term to me. I had never been morbidly obese, according to some medical dictionary somewhere, but I sometimes gained weight because it was the one thing in my world I alone could control. I understood that my fatness, with each bout of weight gain, was an indication of an imbalance somewhere in my life. This time, it was probably unhappiness because of the lack of control of my life. I was back in Los Angeles, bound to work for many more years, and I didn't like the tediousness of work with its lack of personal freedom. I also knew it was the responsible road to be on. I had to be the *responsible* Linda again for many more years, and at times, that was hard to accept. I was not able to fully seize the reins and take control of my happiness yet. However, I was starting to grasp them loosely—I was considering foreign trips. Part of me was unsure of the entire idea of going to Costa Rica, since I would be going to a foreign country alone for the first time. I wanted to see a rain forest so I could understand the dilemma about losing it, and I didn't know anyone who might want to go with me.

I looked in a magazine for tickets to Costa Rica and found a cheap trip, one with a guide meeting me at the airport in the capital city, San José. The trip cost was under $1,000 for airfare, guided trip, and all hotel and meal expenses. This was in the mid-1980s, so trips were inexpensive. I was a cheapskate at the time too, so it had to be cheap for me to go anywhere. I heard that Costa Rica was safe and tourist friendly, and their businesses wanted the American dollar. Plus, it was being "discovered." I couldn't pass it up—I wanted to be ahead of the discovered-ness. In order to understand a rain forest, I wanted to see it and experience it. I hadn't yet learned that the best way for me to experience another country was to take long walks, backpacking trips, and to leave guided and supervised, "safe" excursions behind. At this point, I made big strides just to go to each destination. The trip had been advertised as a river trip, floating down three Costa Rican rivers: the Sarapiquí, the Pacuare, and the General (or Reventazón). At this point in my life, I had run many rivers in the US, but this was my first experience outside the States. I wanted a guide and a safe boat for sure. I would make the trip as safe as I could so I would not end up bowing out from fear.

When I arrived, I was met at the airport by a fellow with a sign. This was new to me and would become my beacon of safety when I went to third-world countries—someone with a sign so I felt recognized in a foreign country. He led me back to a van that held two other people, a young woman and man from Boston. She worked at Harvard's library, and he was an entomologist from Harvard, a "bug guy," who was particularly interested in the ants of Costa Rica. Over the course of the trip, he would regularly collect ants and doom them to death in a tiny vial of formaldehyde so he could study them later. His girlfriend and I learned to collect different ants and take them to him, asking, "Do you have this one yet?"

As the guide drove us to our hotel, I looked out the window to see flowers everywhere in San José. Through the open windows, I could tell the city was alive with smells of plants and freshness. In other words, it rained all the time there. Costa Rica is famous for its rain. I was fascinated. The freshness of everything seemed to open my senses and make me smile.

Our guide sat down with us in the hotel, explaining that we would run the Sarapiquí, a class I river, the next day. It would be a very easy river to run in a raft, and that would get us more used to the climate and rivers of Costa Rica. The day after that, we would be on our own, and the third day we would head to the Pacuare, a class III river. The higher the class, the more likely we would be to be thrown out of the boat in rapids. Great.

Running the Sarapiquí was an education. The river was dark and muddy, with no chance of seeing the bottom. The day was rainy, but it didn't really matter if it was raining or not. The temperature of the air, the water, and the rain was all the same. It was like being in a huge three-dimensional swimming pool with your clothes on. A large lizard would sometimes plop from a tree limb and crash into the water, sounding like a tree falling into the water each time. There was little sound, so the entire scene was rather eerie. I loved it and embraced the new experiences it gave to me.

I decided the next day would be a day of total exploration. The guide had told us we could go wherever and do whatever we wanted for this free day in San José. The other couple was off exploring, so I had to decide what to do with the day. I loved having control of it, with no expectations or requirements. I considered taking the train from San José to another city and then heading back, but luckily I decided not to. I found out later that there was some concern that I had taken the train or bus to Limón by myself. Limón was not a safe place to venture in the 1980s. Today, apparently it hosts cruise ships, and I assume has been made safe so more tourist dollars flow into the country.

Instead, I walked around San José exploring the *mercados* (marketplaces) and tourist shops. It was in one of the mercados where I was pickpocketed. I learned quickly never to wear a daypack on my back in a third-world country. On this particular day, I had a small daypack with a large pocket and a smaller one with a zipper on the back. Apparently, the person who targeted me went after the small zipper pocket and was in the process of unzipping it when the owners and customers of the market started yelling at the young woman to stop. They understood the importance of preserving tourist confidence. The woman took a small change purse from my zippered pocket and ran as the merchants followed her. She got away, but my loss was minimal. I will never forget the kindness of the Costa Rican people as they tried to help me. I was learning about the universal kindness I would come to know worldwide.

After that incident, I wandered the streets more. I passed several highrise buildings and many street vendors along the way. My heart went out to a legless man who sold sewing needles, so I gave him what I could for his small package. I ate some coconut-and-molasses candy made on a tiny street vendor's stand—it was delicious. I was always careful about what I ate from vendors' stands because of the worry about waterborne illness there. I was especially vigilant about avoiding salads, even from restaurants, because they might be made with lettuce washed with tap water. Juices were to be avoided also because they might be diluted with tap water. Coming in contact with tap water usually meant instant bowel problems. Everything I drank came from a bottle, and everything I ate was hot.

I made the decision to see the active volcano, Poás, in the nearby mountains. The next challenge would be to find a way there. If I took a bus, it would be an all-day trip, and the bus schedules could be sketchy. I decided to take a taxi.

At the time I had very little money for anything other than the trip itself. In other words, I was cheap and had to make my money last. Finding an appropriate taxi would be hard, so I got creative. I flagged down the first taxi I saw, a black Mercedes. Mistake. I started negotiating.

In broken Spanish, I asked how much a round-trip to Poás would be. "*Cuanto cuesta Poás?*" I asked. The Mercedes driver understood my question, mercifully, and told me it would be one hundred dollars. That was too expensive for my meager funds. I shook my head, and he turned away with a little shrug.

Next, I flagged down a newer Ford taxi and asked the driver what the cost would be for the mostly all-day trip. He quoted me a rate of fifty dollars. I let him go. *Good thing my friends don't know how cheap I'm being today*, I thought. Most of them already knew just how cheap I was.

Lastly, I flagged down a man in a really old, beat-up jalopy. He smiled at me as he pulled over and I asked about the trip to Poás. He said he would make the trip for twenty-five dollars round-trip. I jumped in his car as soon as I trusted he would wait for me at the top of the volcano and actually bring me back down. We started a conversation, as much as was possible between us. He was a man trying to feed his family by taking his taxi around town. Everyone in Costa Rica was simply trying to make enough money to survive.

As we passed the small shack houses, I could see huge trees standing in the yards. I knew the large trees were hardwoods, probably very valuable trees, a part of the rain forest that is so dear to our existence as human beings. I asked my driver about the trees.

"Yes, lady, these are the trees on our land in the rain forest," he replied.

I asked if the trees were cut to make furniture and other items.

Again, he answered, "Yes, lady, these people need the money from their trees to survive, to live."

Lesson from the universe: It became very apparent to me that it is hard to judge a family for their right to survive versus the right for the tree to survive. The need for people to live should really supersede my right to cry for the tree that gives us the oxygen we need to live. I had a higher standard of living in the US, and I felt like Big Brother (or Sister, maybe) from George Orwell's *1984* telling others what they had to do for the world to survive. On a very small scale, a family living in a twelve-by-twelve shack has a right to live in the world. With this simple exchange, I understood more about the dilemma surrounding our rain forests.

We made our way up the huge volcanic mountain, Poás. More signs in English were posted as we neared the top: *Beware of toxic fumes* and *Do not stay for more than 15 minutes*. We were entering a really toxic zone. In the US, tourists would not be allowed anywhere near the top of an active volcano. When we got to the parking area, the smell was very much like rotten eggs: sulfur. My driver stopped and began to talk with the other taxi drivers parked there. It was "old home week" to him—I was sure he made this trip often. He nodded to me and pointed to signs in English as I left the area for a trail.

I hiked to the top of the mountain and looked down on the volcanic mess. There were smoky clouds all over, the smell of sulfur, and several molten bubbly areas with bright orange at the base. This truly was an active volcano, complete with current eruption activity, and I was very close to it. I was fascinated. However, I reminded myself not to stay more than fifteen minutes. No one else was at the site to save me if I had a problem. Once I had viewed the volcano, my taxi driver was still there, waiting for me in the parking lot. He took me safely back to San José, where I paid him well for his generous taxi rate, had a great dinner, and went to bed.

The next day our guided group was off to raft the Pacuare, a very wild and scenic river. It didn't occur to me at the time that it also was particularly remote and if something happened, there wouldn't be much help. I had a guide and would be totally safe, or so I thought. It was then that I started asking about the snakes of Costa Rica. Apparently, this Central American area has a number of poisonous snakes that can kill you within minutes. Great. So here we were, miles from anywhere, camping out, and I was among some of the world's deadliest snakes, including the coral and fer-de-lance snakes. In reading about it now, information says that the snakebite is much less fatal than before. That is, if you have the antidote and help is nearby.

I hadn't thought too much about snakes as we'd glided through the Sarapiquí landscape the first day in the raft. The scenery was beautiful, with small streams joining the main stream throughout the journey. Now on the Pacuare, there were some rapids, unlike the previous float trip. At one point, the guide stopped the boats and started jumping off some cliffs and playing in the streams. He must have picked up on my thought process at some point, though: *Here is our guide playing in dangerous territory, and we have no other guide. What if he does something really stupid and hits his head? What if we can't find our way to safety? What if…?* Many scenarios were entering my mind. Just then, he said, "I guess I shouldn't play so much in case I get hurt." Thank goodness, a reality check swept in. He got us back in the boat, and we proceeded down the river.

That night, we camped near a small thatched home of a farmer. There was a riverbank safe for us to camp on, and we took advantage of it. As dinner was being prepared, we sat on raised logs, an inch or two from the ground, and watched the fire. Telling stories and laughing, we were oblivious to the snake that was crawling from the space between the ground and the log where my friends were sitting.

I was the first one to spot it. An orange, black, and white snake stuck its head out from under the log and started flicking its tongue. When it started to lick the leg of one of my friends, I spotted it. Adrenaline started flowing, and I tried to tell the group about the snake. I could only point.

Everyone jumped up to safety, and we let the leader take charge of what happened next as we huddled together. The snake slithered on the ground, and the guide called to the owner of the farm to come quickly. The farmer brought his machete with him and quickly pinned the snake's head to the ground with it so we could determine if the snake was a deadly coral snake or not. After a little banter back and forth, the guide and farmer decided it was a harmless king snake and not the deadly coral, so the guide picked up the snake and tossed it into the raging stream, where it quickly swam to safety downstream.

A discussion of the snakes of the area ensued, and I quickly went to my tent to be sure it was totally zipped up. The fer-de-lance snake was nocturnal, and I didn't need nor want company that night.

The third river we were to raft was at flood stage, dangerous, and after this Pacuare adventure, neither the other two clients nor I were up to it. So we decided to go to a hostel on top of a mountain where it would be cooler and we could rent bicycles. It was there that one of the helpers on the trip propositioned me.

After dinner I was sitting outside, enjoying the view of the valley and rain forest below. A big man, our assistant guide for this part of the trip, had become accustomed to drinking beer and had a beer gut. He approached slowly—I assume so I wouldn't be scared—and sat down beside me. He spoke no English, and I barely spoke Spanish. He talked about how beautiful it was up here while surveying the view over the trees. He asked about how I liked the trip, and I answered the questions quickly. Finally he started pointing to the little cabin where I was staying, his eyes scanning my body and motioning to go over there. I had never been propositioned before, and I wasn't thinking too highly of myself or my weight just then anyhow, so I didn't recognize it right away. I was astounded and had to use my brain quickly when I realized what was happening. I was being the nice American who smiled a lot and didn't want to offend anyone. I still needed to learn to honor my intuition and sense of danger.

At that point I was still naïve, still thinking I had to please people and not hurt them. It was very hard for me to just say no. I remembered being told by my mother to change my outfit because it wasn't appropriate for church, for dinner, for anything. Back then, saying no was not an option. I had to toe the line because I would be spanked if I reacted. So I continued to listen to the man but kept my gaze on the ground while shaking my head. He kept pointing, and I kept shaking my head. I didn't have the courage to look him straight in the eye and make myself clear. Finally I got up and left for my cabin, shaking my head more vigorously. I opened the creaking door into the cabin, shut it quickly, and made sure there was some kind of internal locking mechanism on it. Then I put a chair in front of the door too. It was an unsettling night, this lone girl traveling in a Central American country. I envisioned hordes of zombies or horny men hovering outside. Inevitably, I survived the night and became stronger for it.

Shortly after our stay at the mountain hostel, we made it to the Caribbean coast. Our dusty van pulled up to a two-story building that must have been white at one time and had an open-air eating area and bar. At this time in the afternoon, everyone was taking a siesta, so our guide had to scrounge a bit to find help. Eventually a robust man came out to greet us and show us to very basic, but adequate, rooms in the sleepy two-story hotel. The beaches were volcanic black sand, absolutely pristine except for a coconut here and there. We were about fifty miles above the border to Panama. This was a completely different Costa Rica from the adventures of the prior few days.

The restaurant owner asked us what we wanted for dinner, and would lobster be all right? Well, of course it would be all right. He had to send out some local fishermen to get us our dinner, so it was important to ask early. It was easy to slide into the lifestyle as I drank Corona beers and enjoyed the gentle winds.

The shabby white hotel was the only commercial building in the area. There were a few shacks, where the locals lived, but not much else. This would be our world for a day or two. It would be easy to get used to, and I was glad we'd changed the itinerary away from the flooding river. I was also grateful there were only three of us on the trip so we could make easy decisions.

That afternoon we rented kayaks to go on a trip in the gentle Caribbean Sea. We bobbed around, following each other like ducklings, able to see everything on the ocean floor because the water was so clear and not too deep. I noticed something sticking out of the water and went over to investigate. Quickly, I realized I was floating directly over a man who was snorkeling. He was a very tanned local who eventually popped out of the water.

I asked, "What are you doing?"

He pulled a husky, struggling, two-pound lobster out of the water and said, "Catching dinner."

Astounding! To peel back all the layers of job, cars, people, and problems and instead drink Coronas in the afternoon until deciding to catch dinner was incredible—one of many lessons.

We eventually had to leave this idyllic place and make our way back to San José and on to our homes, but the simple lessons of the beautiful country were impressed upon me forever. It was a beginning.

Note to self: Life can be so very simple if I let it be.

CHAPTER 3

Mexico

"You might get shot," a friend told me.

My brain started saying, *You're an idiot. Don't go*. But I had already sent money for the adventure, and my cheapness would not allow me to cancel the trip. Mexico didn't seem to be a foreign country, just a large neighboring state. That is, a neighboring state full of new adventures, some of which could be dangerous.

I had signed up to backpack in Copper Canyon, an area in northwestern Mexico in the state of Chihuahua. In itself, backpacking in Mexico wasn't such an uncharted adventure. However, my friends told me that the area I was stepping into was famous for illegal drugs. This explained the danger they were worried about. Nonetheless, I had spotted an ad in a magazine about a backpacking trip in Copper Canyon and signed up. It was only $700 for two weeks and sounded like a deal to me in the late 1980s. I was going.

I flew to Texas where I met the rest of the group. I arrived for the Copper Canyon trip fat—like, really fat. I was even bigger than I had been when I went to Costa Rica. Just stepping out of the airport, I started sweating in the humid Thanksgiving air. I had thought Thanksgiving would be cool enough to do the trip, but I'd guessed wrong. It would be hot and humid in Mexico, and to make matters worse, this was a backpack trip.

I had not physically prepared for the trip because of an earlier surgery. Medication for the surgery had made my weight go up and down like crazy, and unfortunately most of the weight was up and not down. I had not resorted to past eating disorder behaviors at this point to correct the "problem." I was sweating like crazy and no one else in the group had that problem. I started feeling sorry for myself.

Note to self: Victim mentality here, kid.

BESIDES BEING FOUR TIMES LARGER THAN THE US GRAND CANYON, Copper Canyon is the homeland of the cave-dwelling Tarahumara Indians, an indigenous people who adapted to this harsh environment in Mexico. I wanted to see them and to understand them. The Tarahumara are world-class long-distance runners because of all their trips up and down the canyons on dirt trails. Their trips are made mostly without shoes.

Our general trip plan was to take the local bus to Chihuahua, Mexico, the Copper Canyon train to Creel, local transportation to the bottom of one canyon where Batopilas is located, and then to backpack up, over, and down a hill to the other town at the bottom of the adjacent canyon, Urique. It was a guided trip, so all I had to do was to follow directions and hike. At this point in my life, that was welcome because I had not yet gained the confidence to go alone.

When I arrived in southern Texas, I found a group of four. Our group included two men who seemed kind enough and about my age, the leader, his girlfriend, and me. We sized each other up and then boarded a local bus to Chihuahua. We only spent one night in Chihuahua, and although the accommodations were unremarkable, there was a *terrific* restaurant with *incredible* margaritas. I bought a denim shirt embroidered with *Chihuahua Charlie's* on it so I could never forget the restaurant as I swaggered with help to our hotel that first night.

From the beginning, I knew I was the weak link. The two male customers were obviously in shape. Their strong, muscular legs showed all those details. The shorter man smiled a great deal of the time and was a great conversationalist. The girlfriend was beautiful. She was blond, had a bronze-tanned body, was strong but thin, and she talked with us as if she was with her best friends. She also often wore shorts, something that was frowned upon in this very conservative area of the country. The machismo culture of the area, and in Mexico in general, said that women were expected to be virgins when they married, which meant that they should be modest and were usually protected by the men in their families. The men in the villages ogled the girlfriend, and the women scoffed. I secretly thought she probably should have known better than to wear shorts.

The leader was a piece of work. He was average height but thin and very strong. His body was tanned from the sun in Texas where he lived, and he loved this area of Mexico. He often acted as if the weight of the world were on his shoulders and we were just a little band of idiots that he had to round up and take care of for a week or so. We followed him like ducklings.

The next morning, the train ride was epic. I'd been looking forward to it. We were in an open-air car, which meant the only air-conditioning was the open window. The seats were wooden, with no cushions, and everything was rickety. As it pulled out of the station, the train moaned and groaned under its load, but once it built momentum, it sounded like wood creaking and pulling apart as the train expanded and contracted around turns. We motored past many small homes with gardens and a few animals as well as some sawmills, probably the only ones in northern Mexico because this area was at a high enough elevation to have trees. The sawmill buildings were old and used antiquated machinery to mill the few narrow trees they harvested from the somewhat forested area. All the wild animals in the area had been eaten years ago, so there was little evidence of any wildlife, not even squirrels or lizards. We passed several Mennonite villages successfully surviving in northern Mexico too.

I walked to the open-air space between the cars where people unload and board the train, the area where train cars are connected. People were allowed to congregate there if they wanted. It was the only place to get a major breeze and better than in the overcrowded cars.

When we pulled into small towns where the train stopped momentarily, the locals would push towel-covered trays of tamales or other handmade foods up to the train windows and into the open areas between the railroad cars. They also sold water and any other type of food or drink that would keep all day until each train's arrival. Coca-Colas in bottles had to be rapidly consumed so the bottle could be returned to the vendor for a refund. We could buy anything we needed for the journey from these people, so food was never a problem. Besides, we were probably the only gringos on the train, therefore a particular target—we had money. It broke my heart that I couldn't buy something from each vendor, but my cheapness and the fact that my body could not hold all the items in my stomach forced me to only buy an item or two. Most everything purchased had enough lard or shortening to make the food really good, and fattening.

The train continued its journey toward Creel, winding past incredible depths, tunnels, and bridges. When we got to Creel hours later, our guide took us to a small hostel-type facility with common rooms about a block from the train station and right off the town central square. We were welcomed there by a kind Mexican woman who hugged our guide because he frequented the hostel regularly. I felt somewhat comforted, especially after my friends' warning about possible dangerous situations had been echoing in my mind. It felt safe for me to walk around town alone, so I explored as much as I could. In the middle of town, near the railroad station, people and emaciated dogs were walking through the dusty, unpaved streets. People here were living life as well as anyone else in Mexico, I supposed.

It took me a minute to recognize the famous native people of the region, and then I began to see many of the Tarahumara in the area. They had beautiful black hair, brown eyes, and a gentleness and shyness to their nature. According to our guide, they preferred not to be noticed, to blend into the scene. I tried to be discreet when I watched them.

Back at the hostel, I was still sizing up the situation and determining my comfort level. The hostel was fine. That is, it had beds, good food, and a very welcoming owner. No one spoke English, and there was never an expectation for them to do so since our Spanish-speaking guide was in charge. I still knew some of my high school Spanish—enough to get into trouble, I would joke—but I never did manage to get into trouble on my own on this trip.

I wandered around town and into the local hardware store, a favorite place to visit for me. I had been taking woodshop classes for years now, and I enjoyed seeing how tools might be adapted, or handmade, in areas not as prosperous as the US. I found a wooden saddle for hauling freight on a burro, and I wanted to buy it. Then I decided it took up too much room and the leader would probably not be happy having it along. Once again, I was not bold enough to think that I should push for what I want. In my eyes, the saddle seemed like a perfect magazine holder. Here in Mexico, it was a necessity for the donkey owners.

The next morning we had breakfast and boarded a very old, dusty van to drive to the bottom of the canyon to the tiny town of Batopilas. The trip was death-defying because the road was dirt and must have had a thousand very narrow U-turns down the canyon. Several turns involved stopping and backing up to safely navigate them. There were so many twists in the road that I couldn't see where the snake road ended. I worried about the brakes on the van, which often smelled. Heck, I worried about everything! The mountainside dropped thousands of feet from the top, from the safety of Creel, and we could see it most of the way down. More than once, I turned my eyes to the sky to see if the universe, a departed friend, or anyone might be watching over me. It was a lesson I would learn time and again.

Note to self: Trust the universe!

EVENTUALLY WE SAW A FEW TREES AND SHRUBS AND THE LIFE-GIVING RIVER flowing into Batopilas. We arrived without fanfare, but at least we were alive. In Batopilas I felt as if I were in another era—a time warp, like an Old West town in the US in the nineteenth century. Buildings were old, adobe or some kind of brick, and in various states of disrepair. Concrete fences were topped with various colored broken-bottle pieces so intruders couldn't jump the fences. The array of colored glass was actually kind of pretty, but it had to be deadly for anyone pushing their luck to get over the wall. Batopilas had electricity but not much else going for it.

We stayed in rooms in a wooden one-story hotel of sorts with several horses tied to a log in front. The rooms were small and dingy, yet they had beds. That was about it. It all was a throwback to the US western era.

I had to remember not to drink any water from this area. Even a swallow from the shower water could spell disaster from Montezuma's revenge—diarrhea—for the rest of the trip. I couldn't rinse off my toothbrush with tap water because it could mean a lot of unhappiness, especially on a backpacking trip.

Our group walked down the main street looking at old structures, houses along the way, and restored buildings. It was then that I started noticing huge, brand-new Ford and Chevy trucks once in a while, alongside old jalopies on the same main dirt road. It seemed strange to see new trucks in such a poor, dusty, dirty town. Then it dawned on me that this probably was a prime drug area. It was.

Marijuana and much more was grown throughout the entire region. I realized very quickly that we needed to be careful, to look like tourists, and to not stray from the main trails and roads. I clung to the guide, staying right beside or behind him. This would become more critical as the trip progressed. We could see dried plants in a few open doors in town, in the restored buildings—where the new trucks were parked. Turns out, we were walking in one of the kingpin drug areas in Mexico.

A shot rang out, and I stopped in my tracks. I tend to second-guess myself, so I had to consider if I had truly heard a gunshot. The others searched my face and verified my thoughts. We didn't quite know what to do. We had been making our way back to our Wild West hotel and were walking in the middle of the street. Behind us, there was some kind of commotion, and just as we started to turn around to look, more shots rang out.

What do you do in a Wild West town, on the main dirt street in town, when shots ring out nearby? *Quickly get out of the way* was my only answer. At the sound of the second gunshot, we ran into an alley, seeking cover of any sort, and tried to evaluate the situation. I could only hope that the shots were aimed somewhere else in town and not at us, the only gringos. The folks who had been running behind us stopped running, the commotion stopped, and there were no more shots. Unreal, absolutely unreal.

We returned to our hotel quickly, still shaking our heads in disbelief. I survived the night, unscathed by gunshots or bacteria-laden water.

The next morning we walked out of the hotel, and our guide motioned us to a place beside the hotel where we saw several donkeys and their owner. The donkey owner was a slight man with a very weathered face, a mustache, and a wide-brimmed hat—the kind with a leather braid around the crown. Life had worn him down, and it was obvious. He seemed tired of leading these donkeys, tired of tourists, and maybe tired of life in general. In the end, I don't think I heard him speak more than seven or eight words during the trip. Still, he seemed glad to get the business from our leader. He would be guiding his six donkeys loaded with our stuff from Batopilas to Urique.

After he put our gear and food on the donkeys, we started out. I carried only a small backpack with some water and a jacket in case of rain, although even those few things felt heavy on my back. Things went fairly well at first, though as we started uphill, I was melting fast. I wilt in high temperatures no matter what my weight, but fatness made it worse.

At one point our perturbed leader turned around and said to me, "If you had lost some weight for this trip, you wouldn't be having as many problems."

Problems to me usually meant slowness. I held my tongue even though I really had a few choice words for him. I had to spend several days with him, trusting him with my life, and I couldn't make an enemy just now. He didn't know or care about me. Often I just sat with perspiration running down my face as if I had taken a bath in a nonexistent stream, wondering what I had been thinking when I'd signed up for the pain of this trip.

We started slowly, and I continued slowly. I was as stubborn as the donkeys.

The donkeys were taking my pack, mercifully, and my only job was to get my body up the steep hill, around the top on a trail, and then be ready to descend. I stopped often, probably seeming like I was taking my last breath, and tried to appear pitiful to the leader so he might take more breaks or go slower. He truly didn't care how I felt, so that wasn't working. Some of the others in the group had some sympathy, but they weren't in a position of power. I knew once we would be on our way downhill, things would improve for me.

The trip was booked to include Thanksgiving, and we discovered on Thanksgiving Day that the tall fellow hiker had never tried Cheez Whiz. We all sat around him as he raised the plastic container with the orange goo in it to his lips. My eyes were glued on him for his response. He squirted a glob of the goo in his mouth, thought about it for a moment, and then smiled. Soon he said, "Pretty good." Well, anything out in backpacking country tastes relatively good. Cheez Whiz was our treat for Thanksgiving, along with canned chicken. I declined the orange goo treat, thinking that not even a backpack trip could make Cheez Whiz taste good to me. On most backpacks, *any* food usually tastes great.

We were warned repeatedly not to stray from the path. As we passed small farms and families with children, we usually got stares. It was uncommon for them to see gringos from the States in this area. We'd wave and say *hola* to them as we passed by, and the children would generally break into a smile at our greeting, but their elders were understandably wary. It was hard not to notice differences in reception, and I could only imagine that those who greeted us were just trying to live their quiet lives while the others were guarding secrets.

The trail had been used for years, probably hundreds if not thousands of years, so we were just visitors to the area. Once we got down into the water-filled canyon before the town of Urique, we started seeing the Tarahumara Natives who lived in the canyon. Often there were men clad only with cloths for underwear, no shirts or shoes, carrying hundreds of pounds of dried cornstalks on their backs. The stalks protruded above their heads as if they had huge headdresses as they walked up the streams. I didn't feel comfortable taking a picture of one man from the front, so I took one as soon as he passed us, silently, as if we didn't exist. Or maybe he didn't want any acknowledgment.

One day, as our group was savoring the water of the stream by wading in it, we pulled out a simple lunch and started eating. Some sat on the sand, others on rocks, and some in the shade of the few trees along the river. From upstream toward the village, a young man with a large machete walked toward us very slowly. All of us, including the donkey owner, were instantly aware of this stranger and kept watch like alerted animals as he walked closer.

Eventually he was in our group's range. He was a young man, husky and rather short, with a bronzed body and not much clothing other than a pair of jeans and an old T-shirt. With a scowl, he walked over to one of our male friends who was sitting on a rock in the sand.

For what seemed an eternity, this fellow stared at our friend, advancing toward him with piercing eyes. When he got within a few feet, the Mexican raised the machete to shoulder height and threw it downward defiantly into the sand, letting go of it at the last second. He waited a few seconds, pulled the machete out, and then tossed it again with its sharp end into the sand with all his strength. It was a strong thrust, and the machete landed solidly in the sand each time.

The message became clear very quickly: *I don't want you in this area. You are in an area that I am protecting. If you cause any trouble with me or take my drugs, you will pay dearly.* His nonverbal message made a huge impact on me, and I just wanted to tell him, "We're just passing through. Please let us through." I would have added quietly, "This is not the place I want to die. It's too damned hot." Each of us was totally involved and terrified while this was going on. Finally the donkey owner slowly went over to the young man to talk with him in Spanish. At first, it didn't seem to help because the young man seemed to dismiss him. The donkey owner was a slight man, someone who just wanted to do his job and be left alone. But the situation had to end, to have some kind of outcome. I secretly said a prayer for our humble donkey owner. I couldn't hear the conversation, but I was encouraged to see him finally engage the young Mexican in conversation.

Eventually the young man walked away, taking his machete and scowling at us over his shoulder to be sure we got the message. I have no idea what the gentle donkey owner told him, but luckily he convinced the young man that we were not there to cause trouble. We were able to turn off our internal alarm systems eventually. We had escaped yet another bullet.

Note to self: It is not your day to leave the earth.

WE MADE IT TO URIQUE THE NEXT DAY, HIKING UP THE RIVER INTO THE tiny, dusty town and arriving in late afternoon. We walked into town amid whistles from men appreciating our leader's girlfriend's legs. Walking around town, we saw a basketball court with no fences. I looked up, and there at the far end of the court was a television up in a tree on a wooden plank. If I had assessed the situation correctly, the people of the town could bring chairs and sit to watch the television, kind of a communal experience. I took that to mean that televisions were a special treat in this poor town. Next, we found a restaurant and went in to have something to eat. The family who owned it apparently lived in a separate room in the back behind the four plastic tables with plastic tablecloths.

It was late in the day, and our guide asked if we were ready to eat. We were eager for a good Mexican dinner—but dinner wasn't ready for us. The owners, a man and his hefty wife, had been smiling at us and nodding up and down until we asked about dinner. They kept smiling and told us it was not possible to have dinner. The guide turned his head quizzically as they told us to come back at seven o'clock. They explained that the generators in town turned on at seven and there was no electricity before then to cook anything.

We started to laugh because nothing was in our control and we had to go with the flow. It was a good reminder to me to forget my Los Angeles behavior and relax. I was happy to have survived the trip, so it was no particular problem to unwind. After dinner, we walked to our hotel, another Wild West outfit, past the children who were gathering to watch television at the basketball court.

The next day we caught a local bus that took us up a winding road to another train station. Going up the new snake road wasn't nearly as harrowing as going down the previous one. Besides, our vehicle was a year or two newer than our other one, and we had survived so much by this point that a ride in a car was nothing. We were out of the Old West eventually, ending up in Texas once more. I felt as if I had entered the twentieth century again.

CHAPTER 4
Dog Sledding I

"Why Paul Schurke?" I asked the young woman who had just given a presentation at a local sporting goods store.

"You want to go with someone who knows what they're doing, don't you?" she replied.

Well, that made sense for someone who had never dog sledded before. Paul Schurke is a North and South Pole explorer who has a dog sledding business based in Ely, Minnesota, and I was considering joining one of his trips.

The fact that I needed an expert guide wasn't so much because I wasn't capable of dog sledding—it was that it was new to me, and I was alone and was considering signing up for the intermediate-level trip rather than the beginning one. I absolutely loved animals and had a variety of shelter dogs at the time. I figured I had knowledge of the outdoors, was a hearty soul, was familiar with dogs, and knew what I was doing for the most part. All that translated into an intermediate trip in my mind.

This amazing woman had been part of a team of women crossing Antarctica on cross-country skis, so I rushed to talk with her after her lecture. Bright, enthusiastic, and young, she was totally enthralled with her adventure in Antarctica. I wanted that feeling too. I'd first decided to come to the talk because Ely seemed alluring, with its summer canoeing and winter dog sledding opportunities. I still had no one to travel with, mainly because my trips were expensive and my friends either didn't have the money to travel with me or weren't up to the adventurous trips I wanted to do. I had to keep my vacations short enough that they wouldn't impact my work schedule in the human resources field or my children, so I searched for challenging excursions. I would go alone on a Paul Schurke trip.

My adventure would be on a much lesser scale than this woman's, though. Antarctica was too scary, big, and unknown to me. I was still in my infancy when it came to feeling confident traveling. I had looked at Paul's schedule of trips and decided that I wanted the weeklong intermediate trip out of Crane Lake. The group would visit an Ojibwa village on Lac La Croix, would stay in the village gym and meet the local medicine man, plus would get to talk with the people of the area. For once, I didn't consider if the presenter who suggested I contact Paul Schurke's office would encourage me to sign up for an intermediate trip or not. I just did it.

I called Paul's organization, and he answered. I explained that I was a seasoned traveler and thought that the intermediate trip would be good for me. No, I had no beginning experience with dog sledding. But the thought of visiting an Ojibwa Native village would be intriguing and fun—it would make the trip for me. I begged him to allow me to come. He did.

I coordinated it with a weekend of studying the wolves in the area at the International Wolf Center in Ely, which I would do before the dog sledding trip. When the information packets for both the dog sledding trip and wolf center arrived, I read them carefully. At this point in the 1980s, books, stories, and information packets were still the main ways to look anything up. The allure of the wild north was strong.

But this trip was not true north. Heck, it was barely out of the lower forty-eight states. The description read something like "Dog sled 80 miles along the Minnesota-Canadian border, visiting an Ojibwa village where you will stay in the village and meet locals."

I read the information further: warm, adequate clothing required along with good boots. I had the good boots, Sorel's high winter boots, and they seemed adequate to me. The clothing was another story, kind of a mystery. Paul's wife had made the clothes for the Antarctic expedition, and they looked great in the sledding advertisement: a big fleece and a windproof anorak that would come down to my knees. As if I needed an excuse to buy clothes, I ordered one of each in a bright red with cute blue trim from her store catalog. I already had one of those sheepskin bomber-style hats that covered my ears. When the gear arrived and I put everything on, I could convince almost anyone that I was a cross between Santa Claus and a very red snowman.

Arriving in Minneapolis was an adventure in and of itself. It was late February or early March, and the weather was very, very cold. I arrived in a snowstorm, the kind that means you can barely see the ground when you peer out the airplane window—or any other window, for that matter. It all added to the drama of getting to an unknown place and doing an unknown expedition. I walked to the gate where the smaller plane to Duluth was berthed. Eager and curious, I got on the plane, sat in my window seat, and looked out the window at the snow blowing by.

Shortly, I noticed a truck pulling up to the wing, and then it started spraying red goo onto the wings and body of the plane near where I was sitting. It was shooting all over the wings, and I stared at it, thinking, *This is not right. I'm going to die.* And then it hit me, the plane needed to be de-iced before it could take off again. It all made sense, and I stared at the goo, hoping it would help make the takeoff successful. It was one of those times when I needed to trust the universe, be in the present, forget worst-case scenarios, and give up my anxiety.

The plane took off successfully, heading for the small Duluth, Minnesota, airport and mercifully landed safely. I was met by a fellow who had a van to take me to the "lodge," which was really a few rustic cabins, one of which I would stay in for the weekend. The place was terrific—homey and just my style. I fell asleep instantly and enjoyed shaking off the jet lag from the west coast.

I woke up and reread the magazine advertisement: "Learn about wolves in their natural environment." I was familiar with the International Wolf Center's founder, L. David Mech, because he and wildlife photographer Jim Brandenburg had traveled to Ellesmere Island in the Arctic where they studied the white wolves. For me, going to Ellesmere Island was like the ultimate place to visit, and anyone who went there was a god. I owned the book they had published together.

The weekend was filled with education at the center, where other curious people and I looked through plate-glass windows at a few captive wolves in an outside yard. They were being trained with skills such as catching food, all with a minimum of human contact, so they could be released at some point in the future. We observed them for a long time while the guides told us about their behaviors. Then we hiked to kill sites in the afternoon and radio tracked them the next day. Looming all the while was the upcoming dog sledding trip. I second-guessed my decision to go for the intermediate trip, worrying I'd presented myself as more brazen and experienced than I really was. At least, that was my internal message.

Finally I left for Schurke's outfit in Ely, where I would be educated on the ins and outs of dog sledding and other details that had probably escaped me when I read the brochure. All I really had were a brochure or two and a contact phone number, so I wasn't sure what to expect.

My welcome to the compound was complete with dozens of barking dogs and the commotion of other newly arriving guests and workers. The facility was on a few acres in the Minnesota woods. When we entered a large building, the new puppies came out from under the deck. These dogs were used to—and actually loved—the cold, so they were quite happy outside. Their mom was nearby, and she seemed grateful for a breather while we petted the month-old pups.

The building was fairly new, and inside was a large wood-paneled gathering area with large tables for common meals with others on the trip. Adjacent to the great room were other large rooms with many bunk beds.

The bunkhouse was clean, rustic, and scary all at the same time. I was quiet, not yet sure of myself after arriving on a de-iced plane and seeing wolves that I now realized might be in the areas where we would be sledding. I was looking forward to hearing them, if not seeing them, on the trip.

I tend to retreat inside my mind when I'm unsure of myself or my situation—especially back then. I didn't really know what to expect, and in hindsight, this was probably a good thing. It avoided disappointment. It would take many trips for me to learn that expecting nothing, embracing serendipity, and wearing a smile are the only necessities for a good trip.

A guide helping Paul gathered us around, and we did group introductions, but I instantly forgot everyone's names. I was told that I would be in the group with the three married couples, and the other group would be all singles. I thought that rather strange but then realized that I was probably the oldest of the singles. Paul came in to introduce himself before dinner, so we were able to meet the legend. He seemed confident, strong, and a leader. Then we were pointed to where we could get a very simple but delicious buffet dinner as we sat down to meet the others in the group. I was quiet and held back my normal talkative nature because, well, I was scared. Actually, I was really scared.

Next, we were ushered into the bunk room. There were at least ten people in my room in the bunkhouse. The beds lined the walls, and I climbed onto one on the second tier. Once up there, I realized there was no easy escape to the bathroom, which added to my anxiety, but it was too late to switch.

We would be getting up early the next morning, so turning in early sounded like a good plan. It *was* a good plan except for the unexpected snoring. It started softly, then graduated to the sound of an angry mother bear trying to corner someone coming after her cub. It rattled the house—heck, it brought the house down. I tried to identify the snorer so I would be sure not to camp next to him or her. He was sound asleep, with no anxiety on his part. There was no possibility that I would sleep at all this night.

Note to self: Remember that you don't do well with no sleep. Watch your actions tomorrow.

The snoring kept me up most of the night. I hadn't thought of bringing earplugs, but believe me, I did on every trip after this one. Lesson learned. My defensive mechanisms were at their lowest level, and I let negative thoughts stream into my consciousness. I contemplated the next day's events, living beyond the present again. Things like, *Oh my God, I'm going to die and there is no one on this trip who gives a crap about me.* The universe and the no-sleep monster were chattering in my head. *Poor me.* Somehow I had to learn to "put on my big-girl panties."

I saw the sun rise and was grateful that it came that cold, wintry morning. The two trucks for the dogs were parked nearby. *Okay*, I told myself. *Today's the day.* I tried to appear anonymous. I was wearing my brand-new duds and did, admittedly, seem either like a pro or a wannabe. I kept observing what was happening around me. I saw a huge burly guy in a traditional French-style eighteenth-century voyager shirt flash a big smile my way. I instantly loved him because he was a replica of the former adventurers in the area. I discovered soon enough that he was a helper on the trip, and I made a mental note to befriend him. If I needed to be pulled out of anything, he would be the one to pull me out, throw me over his shoulder, and then drag me to safety somewhere.

Someone barked out, "Get a dog and take it to the truck," and I stood still trying to figure out just what I was supposed to do. I figured, *I can do this.* I started spying on others to see how they were getting their dogs and taking them to the truck. Paul was somewhere in the mix, helping with the trucks, and I tried to keep out of his view.

I went to the dog yard. These gorgeous creatures each had their own doghouse, were chained so they couldn't reach each other, and were howling loudly. Many of them were the descendants from the last dogs removed from Antarctica when an international treaty banned them from the continent to avoid the spread of domestic dog diseases to the meager Antarctic wildlife populations.

I noticed a dog that was some kind of husky, sported a coat of very thick fur, and must have weighed about ninety or a hundred pounds, although it looked more like it weighed 250 pounds to me. As I would learn later, on a dog sled, there are the lead dogs, which are generally smaller and not as heavy; then there are the freight dogs, which are huge, have weight, and can pull all day. This was a freight dog.

The dog didn't bite me—that was the first good thing that happened. I unleashed the excited ninety-pound dog, held on to its collar, and started for the dog-carrying truck. I later learned that these dogs don't have a great deal of respect for each other but are taught that humans are the alphas. They learn to obey humans. That's all good except that their excitement and size can literally carry just about any human away.

My dog took off, starting to run because it was so excited to be off leash. I was trying to appear as if I knew what I was doing, and I reasoned that it was not a good thing to have a dog running loose here, so held on to the collar for dear life. I tripped and went down, determined to hold on to the dog, and went sprawling into fresh dog poop in my brand-new, just-took-the-tags-off gear.

Big Burly guy came over to me, trying not to laugh. "You want me to show you how to get a dog to the truck?"

I smiled weakly and got up. "Yes, I think that would be good." My disguise of being an intermediate was blown.

He grabbed the dog by the collar, yanked it on its hind feet, and made a beeline to the truck. By pulling the dog up on its hind legs, it disengages its four-wheel-drive-dog-legs mechanism, and the dog becomes more manageable, forced to go where the alpha human leads. Big Burly guy got the dog into the very tiny cage with a hole in it, and the dog was safely behind bars. The holes in each cage are in various stages of size depending on how much each dog had chewed around the hole during transit. The next time I chose a smaller dog and was successful. Meanwhile, I was trying terribly hard to blend in. All the while, my heart was in my stomach and I was starting to get more chatter in my head: *This is scary. You don't know what you're doing. Leave now while the getting's good.*

Eventually the two trucks were filled. I watched from the sidelines as much as I could, trying to deal with my anxiety and lack of sleep. The trucks took us to Crane Lake without incident, with the dogs barking and howling as loudly as they could in the back. Once there, we filed out and were instructed to get a dog and chain it to the harnesses on the sleds.

I was surveying the scene in my demented mental capacity, trying to assess the situation. I started wavering. I watched as other people tied seven dogs to each of the four sleds—one lead and six freight dogs. These critters were barking, jumping up in the air, and trying to do 360-degree turns in their harnesses because they were so excited. The sleds were on the ice, tied to a dock solidly frozen into the lake. Meanwhile, the lake was pristine, like a well-groomed ice-skating rink with smooth ice and very little snow. I envisioned our brave souls flying two hundred miles per hour across the ice-skating lake once the dogs were released and started worrying again. Ice-skating rink + fast dogs + me = disaster.

I wasn't going home with a broken limb—or worse, in a casket. I made the decision to bail on the trip and go home. I was sure this was the right decision. The dogs were nuts, I was going to be traveling at breakneck speed, and I didn't know what the hell I was doing.

I was about to turn to Paul to tell him I wanted to leave with the truck and go home to my nice, safe little house in Los Angeles. I was getting ready to say, "Thank you very much for your trouble," when a stout soul, one of the married fellows, came over to me and said, "You look nervous." Thank God, someone had interpreted my nonverbal language. "Are you okay?"

No, definitely not, I was saying inside. "Well, it does appear to be a little scary," I replied.

"Here, get on the back of the sled, and I'll get behind you when we start out. We'll be fine," he said nonchalantly.

I complied, as my mind reverted to, *I spent all this money to get here to do this, and I'm not going to let it go to waste*. My eternal stubbornness and thriftiness won.

The man introduced himself as Ted, and I noticed he sported a beautiful head of dark hair, a body that told me he could handle anything, and a smile that disarmed me. He continued, "Just stand on the back of the sled, and I'll be on it behind you. We will be just fine."

I started to cry and glanced quickly away from him. Someone in the universe had made him come along just at the right time. For many years, I had fallen into that backing-out habit, but I finally stopped. Over time, I found that other people would use other excuses: "Oh, my husband would never let me go on a trip like that," or "I could *never* do that!" whatever *that* was. I didn't want to be someone who used excuses.

My new friend showed me the brake—a small metal scraper with teeth on the underside. It had some kind of elastic strap on it so when the musher stepped on the scraper, the metal teeth on it gripped the ice to some degree. With enough pressure, it would stop the sled. Ted explained that the dogs would start out fast and fall into a rhythm that would keep them going all day. Our job would be to guide the back of the sled and yell commands.

"These are dogs," he continued, "and they will follow our lead." He turned toward me. "You will not die on this adventure—it's not good for tourism."

I smiled, somewhat weakly.

The sled itself was not for riding on—it was for hauling gear. This trip would be fairly tame, but each sled could haul five hundred or more pounds of gear. Everything was packed in tarps, which were roped shut each morning before travel. There was only room for one or two mushers on the back of the sled, so many of the participants had to use cross-country skis to travel because of our numbers.

The big moment to start came and went quickly. My heart went into my throat when the dogs were unmoored. The sled lurched forward, and I held on to the back of the sled for dear life. There was nothing to do but hold on tight. My friend was behind me, relaxed as could be. The dogs ran fast as they could.

After the initial jolt, the dogs slipped into a consistent jog and the sled trailed behind them with little effort. It should have: the sled runners were on an ice-skating-type lake. We went at a very reasonable pace with very reasonable dogs.

My next question was, *Are we going to stop easily?* I had to trust that the flimsy metal brake could stop a sled with hundreds of pounds of supplies on it. Ted said the next thing we would do was test the brake. He yelled, "Whoa"—that made sense—and told me to step on the brake. After what seemed like five minutes, but in reality was probably fifteen seconds, the sled stopped. I was elated as the dogs turned around for further orders. I was not at the mercy of the dogs—they were at my mercy.

We journeyed for a long time, during which Ted showed me that we could each take a runner on the back of the sled and stand on it, rather than doubling up at the back, so we ended up side by side.

In dog sledding, being able to keep the sled upright is key. If the sled goes over, it results in tangled and pissed-off dogs that are within reach of each other's throats, not to mention a very heavy sled that must be righted. On this lake, there was little chance of spilling over. That would occur on our second trip.

As the dogs trotted along, somewhat obeying commands, the little entourage made progress across the lake. As I became more confident, I was finally able to enjoy my surroundings. At one point we started to slow down, and Ted told me, "Run up there and get the lead dog so the dogs don't get close enough to each other to fight." If I could get the lead dog, I could stretch out their ropes and harnesses, putting more space between them.

Disaster struck. I had on huge, slippery, rubber-soled boots as I rushed to catch up to the lead dog. I fell hard, landed on my tailbone, and couldn't walk. I crawled on the ice to the lead dog where I did what I was told and stretched out the dog caravan. Then I crawled on top of the supplies on the sled for the rest of the day. Ted continued at the back of the sled to be able to bark orders to the dogs to go right or left, and to step on the brake when necessary.

As I started to feel better, I was finally able to look up and enjoy my surroundings from the sled. I could see trucks on the ice in the distance. I mean *big semis* on the ice. I learned they were taking supplies to the village, and this lake was the only way. In the winter, it was an ice road, and during warm months, supplies were taken by water. It was reassuring to see these huge trucks on the ice because it told me that little sleds had no chance of falling in. That is, until we got close to the village.

As we got closer, I could see open water. To the left of the village, the lake fed into a river, and running water brings a lack of ice. Right in front of the town, we could not get across. I was reminded of the trucks. They had to get across the ice somewhere. Eventually we explored to the right of town and found ice thick enough to cross. Never mind that we could see bubbles under the one or two feet of ice that we stood on. I reminded myself that I had a knife around my neck that I could stab into the ice for a hold to pull myself from the water should I take the holy, frigid plunge. It wouldn't have made a dime of difference—heck, my boots would fill with water and take me down immediately—but it was reassuring to me.

The village was fascinating. The small Ojibwa town would host us and feed us for the next few days, and we'd get to visit schoolchildren, observe a powwow, and talk with the local medicine man. I felt welcomed, educated, and grateful for a grand visit.

We were housed in the gym of the school and spread our sleeping bags on the hard floor. One night I asked several of the married folks if they wanted to play cribbage. I'd bought a new little cribbage board before the trip and brought it with me. One friend smiled in amazement. "I *love* cribbage. My wife and I play all the time. Get that board out."

I reached in my duffel bag, trying to find the board by feel. My hand pulled it out, and I raised it in triumph. I was beaming, glad to have brought such a valued item. My friends gathered around, ready to play. As I tried to figure out how to set it up, one eventually asked, "Where are the cards?"

I asked, "You need cards?"

There was silence for a minute, and then belly laughs came in waves. "Yes, you nut, you need cards," my friends were saying. I received several sets of playing cards that following holiday, sent to my home.

We left after two nights, packing the heavy sleds and putting on heavy, daunting clothes once again. We had seven more days on the trip, and from this point on, we would be under our own power, relying on our own supplies and resourcefulness. I had butterflies in my stomach, excited to get started but remembering the open water near the current in the river.

Note to self: Be careful of open water.

THE MORNING WE GOT READY TO LEAVE THE VILLAGE, WORKERS STARTED dynamiting for construction. When the first round went off, I immediately fell to the ground, hugging whatever I could hold on to. My heart was pounding and head was shaking as if screaming, "Not again!" It had only been about six weeks since the Northridge earthquake, and my house was less than half a mile from the center. My body reacted much as it had during that quake, and I immediately felt as if I were in the middle of a washing machine, having zero control of anything. The quake was over, but it would be years before my body would stop reacting with panic or I would be willing to park in an underground lot. Immediately after the quake, I was required to go to the office to call in paychecks for the company employees, while my house was near the epicenter and had broken glass in every room and crumbled cinderblock walls outside.

As I lay on the snowy ground in the remote village, my friends stared down at me, worried. "What are you doing? Are you okay?" I was so embarrassed. I got up slowly and started dusting myself off as I described the earthquake. "I can't handle loud noises now without making a fool of myself." I tried to laugh.

The first day of the true sledding adventure was glorious. Good weather, camaraderie with both the single folks and the married couples, and excited dogs once again. We started our journey at a slow trot, which would become the norm.

I had been to the Boundary Waters area once before, camping along one of the lakes for a day or two. The glaciers from ages past had stopped along the Minnesota-Canada border and formed more lakes than any normal person could fathom. Each lake is usually a lake unto itself, meaning that the only way to get from one to the other is to go over a land barrier. In canoe language, these passages are portages. In dog sled language, I reasoned, they are just plain small hills that the dogs, sleds, and people have to negotiate. I soon learned that often there were no trails and the party had to negotiate fallen trees, brush, and miserable territory until the next lake was reached, where we could mush on the smooth ice again. Any way I looked at it, dog sledding was a full-body workout, particularly on the hills.

I had become comfortable handling the dog sled myself, and Ted went back to his sled with his wife. On the back of my own sled, I learned to lean the opposite way from the direction I wanted the dogs to go. If the dogs were going right, I leaned left and called out, "Gee!" And if they were going left, "Haw!" was the command. Transferring my weight would more or less balance the swing of the sled as it turned.

I was becoming proud of myself for surviving the first day, for surviving the ridicule of the missing cribbage cards, and for learning to keep the sled upright. The first night of the true dog sled trip led to new discoveries. We easily collected wood to start a fire to keep us warm, and Paul hiked out fifty feet on the lake with an auger. Using it like a huge corkscrew, he made a hole in the lake ice, which would become our water source. Apparently it was so cold that giardia and other waterborne illnesses were not a concern in this area. I had to trust that. After a lot of laughter and a dinner of backpacking-type food, we went to bed. The married couples went off two by two, and I, the lone single person in the group, arranged my sleeping bag. I heard howling in the distance, either from wolves or the wind.

We slept outside, in no tents, just on a pad and inside a sleeping bag. In fact, that really wasn't a problem and added to the allure of the North. I hadn't expected it, and I loved it. With my experiences hiking in the US, often I would toss out a tarp and put my sleeping bag on top of it. A tent was a luxury. Although initially cold, I warmed up easily in my sleeping bag and got a good night's sleep. The snoring culprit was out of my range of hearing. Fortunately, someone had warned me to bend the tongue on my boots out that night so I could still get them on in the morning after they had frozen. It was a challenge day after day to get my feet into frozen boots.

Then we were off again, for the rest of the journey. We left the big lake that we had come across and ventured into forested land. The terrain was uneven, tricky, and full of snow-covered tree roots that were out to make us fall. All was going well the next day until worry popped into my mind again. I fell silent. My friends gave me a few inquisitive glances, but that didn't pull me out of it. We were becoming more intuitive with each other.

We all had to navigate a tiny trail beside a large stream—*right* beside it. I clammed up as the trail got extremely narrow and the open water was just beside me. My insecurity was there in full force, and I went inside myself with fear. I was quiet enough that Sam took charge of me. The husband of one of the other women on the trip in my group, Sam was one of my favorites. He had probably laughed the most at my having no cribbage cards. Ted had probably told him and the other fellow in my group to keep an eye out for me after the day-one experience. Sam gave me directions and basically told me what to do. I was appreciative of having no decisions to make right now.

That area was scary enough, but then we made it to a *really* dicey area. This was no ice-skating rink; it was corn snow, the kind that seems crunchy and solid but is actually soft and will let you fall through. Added to that was the fact that the trail was next to the running stream, and although it was frozen, it was apparent to me that the ice was not solid. We pulled the sleds up behind one another. I could tell from the expressions on the leaders' faces and the lack of jovial conversation that this was a dangerous situation.

Paul finally told us that we would go, one by one, across the stream on cross-country skis and, I assumed, hope no one fell in. Of course I hung back in the group until other brave souls got across (or would go in the water before me). After each person skied across, we towed the skis back to our side of the stream by rope. When it was my turn, I put the skis on and then skied as fast as I could across the area, hoping all the while that I was not giving the snow a chance to give way. As I was leaving, I could hear dogs barking and perhaps fighting.

Once I was on the other side, I said a silent Hail Mary, even though I was not religious. I think the leaders held their breath as we each crossed safely. Once the people were all across, the leaders called the dogs to pull the sleds over one at a time, with no one on back just in case a sled went into the icy water. I wondered, *Well, what about the unfortunate dogs on a sled that goes down?* We all watched as each sled crossed successfully. The dogs actually brought them over fairly quickly, luckily.

With the dogs on our side now, someone realized that two of the dogs had gotten into a fight—that was the noise I'd heard as I was skiing across. Apparently, just like people, when one dog keeps irritating another, it is not unusual for the dog being irritated to turn on its tormentor.

Later that night around the campfire, my friend Sam slid over to me and said, "You got mighty quiet today. What's up?"

At this point, I was embarrassed but couldn't avoid the truth. "I was scared shitless going across that river. The ice was really dicey, and we could have fallen in and died."

Sam's eternal optimism spoke. "Well, I thought that might be the problem! We didn't. And you were brave."

Note to self: You put on your big-girl panties, yes, you did.

THE DAYS CONTINUED AS OUR SMALL MARRIED GROUP PLUS ONE GOT TO know everyone and really care for one another. We were easily joking with each other, and my apprehension about the entire journey dissolved with the kindness in the group. The trip was totally successful, totally safe, and totally wonderful. By the end I didn't feel so guilty about signing up for the intermediate trip because of the amazing experience and friends I'd made in the group of married couples. I was sad to say goodbye to them on our last day. Little did I know then that this would not be the last time I would see these companions.

CHAPTER 5

Dog Sledding II

IT WAS ONLY A YEAR LATER WHEN MY MARRIED FRIENDS INVITED ME FOR the *real* intermediate trip.

My first decision was to put my trusty quick-release knife on a shoestring around my neck once again. When I read that we would be "travelling through the highest density of polar bear denning areas in the world," I started thinking about my knife. It wasn't that a tiny (or larger) knife would do anything about polar bears. I was hoping I could cut a dog off the ropes so the bear could eat the dog instead of me. I decided I wanted to be on the sled that carried a gun.

My seasoned friends on the prior dog sledding adventure had planned this trip to the old Hudson's Bay Company trading post at the settlement of York Factory on Hudson Bay in Manitoba, Canada, to happen in March 1995. No one had dog sledded to the old Hudson's Bay trading post for as long as could be recalled, and they wanted to see if it could still be done. I felt so honored to be invited on the expedition, I didn't even consider declining. I was in the big leagues, even though I really only had an inkling of what to do on a dog sled.

Apparently, the Canadian government got wind of our travels and invited themselves along. We were doing something historic, without knowing if we could accomplish our mission or not. But we had a tightly knit group of seasoned dog sledders (well, all but one). There were nine of us plus the leader, Stephen, his girlfriend, and a young fellow from the Churchill area to assist on the trip. The leader was a stalwart explorer, someone who had helped take dog teams to the South Pole earlier in his career. At the last minute, though, the government decided not to send team members for the trip.

York Factory was not a factory at all. It was, in fact, the name for a settlement where a trading post of the Hudson's Bay Company had operated for over 270 years, until 1957 when it closed. The only way to get to this remote building was by boat, small plane, or dog sled. It is located on the banks of the Hayes River, where the Hayes feeds into Hudson Bay. Traders at the post initially purchased skins from the Natives in the area and then sent them to England and other places for sale. Particularly valuable were beaver furs, which were made into beaver hats for the people of England to survive the cold winters of Europe.

Our journey would take us from the small town of Gillam, Manitoba, to the buildings of York Factory and would take ten to twelve days, depending on how fast we maneuvered the five heavily laden sleds. From Gillam, we would head north through spruce forests and snow, lots and lots of snow. We had the key to the Hudson's Bay Company building at York Factory if we were successful, which to me seemed like having the key to New York City. On day twelve, a plane with skis would land on the ice in Hudson Bay to pick us up and carry us out.

I was no longer the greenhorn but a true intermediate this go-round. I now knew to stand the dogs up by the collar so they could only use their back legs to get them into the truck, I knew that my anoraks were no longer new so a little poop wouldn't hurt them, I knew that I could do the trip, and I knew and loved the people who were on the trip with me. What more could I ask for? My confidence and talkative nature showed.

There were two of us on each sled, and the sleds were loaded much more heavily than the ones from the previous trip. Knocking them over would be a monumental event to be avoided at all costs.

I had asked to ride on one of the sleds with a gun. There was a high-powered rifle on board my sled, and Stephen's beautiful girlfriend assured me she knew how to use it. I was told that the mother bears and cubs would stay out of our way as they made their way to the ice of Hudson Bay. It would be the large, single, adult males that we would have to be careful to avoid. Apparently they could be pretty nasty this time of the year since they were just getting out of hibernation and were quite hungry. Everything, including humans, was fair game for bear dinner.

The sleds and drivers were wobbly in the beginning, and then we settled into a nice pace. I learned quickly that it was much easier to put my butt out to the wind while balancing on a blade of the sled runner to balance out a turn than it was to pick up a sled and its gear that had turned over on its side. I became good at the deep lean. My sled tipped over once, and after that I tried my best never to let it happen again. It didn't. I had to giggle when I thought of my paralyzing fear of a non-functional brake and breakneck speeds on the prior trip.

The lead dog was my partner's favorite, and she was grooming her for the Iditarod. For a long time we would be following an old railroad bed, which would make it easy for the dogs—not many downed trees or sharp turns. Our lead dog learned to pick a trail by staying on the most packed snow. If it got deep or too steep, she was able to correct the dogs' path to create an easier trail. Our lead dog was amazing, and the freight dogs were magnificent too. I fell in love with Aurora, a hefty, reddish-white dog.

The snow would pack and freeze into small marbles between the pads in the dogs' feet. We would stop occasionally to pull the ice balls out. For the most part, however, there were no complaints from the dogs. They were just thrilled to be doing what they were bred to do: pull.

We stopped in late afternoon, before the sun went down, to set up camp. Manitoba was a great deal farther north and much, much colder at night than where we'd sledded before at the Canadian border. When we stopped at night, the first task was to hang a long rope between two tall, scrimpy spruce trees, and then we chained our sled dogs to it at such a distance apart that they could not reach each other and fight. We had several lines available, one for each of the five sleds. Next came feeding the dogs. Stephen had connections with a mink farm, and he asked that whatever meat from the minks was not used on the farm to be frozen into a large popsicle for the dogs. We had several of these large popsicles on the sleds, and each night our assistant used a hatchet to break apart a small section for each dog and then fling it to a dog. There was no water for the dogs; they ate snow for whatever water they needed. As soon as they had eaten (a very quick proposition), each dog curled up for the night. The lead dogs were slimmer than the others, so they wore coats, and by morning all the dogs were often covered with snow.

Next came the preparation for our night's survival. Our assistant from Churchill would cut down a live spruce tree and then cut it into small logs. The spruce trees, tall and spindly, were abundant, and even though they were still green, they made great fires in our small stove. In groups of four, we stomped down our tent areas and put up the expedition dome tents, which still had markings on them from Antarctic ventures. I could see latitude readings written on the walls of mine when I lay in it at night, markings to show where the tent had been set up as the expedition it was on moved closer to the South Pole, to 0° south. Meanwhile, we basically froze in the tents. Once the sun was down, the only place we wanted to be was inside the large canvas tent that served as a galley for us and a sleeping area for the guides.

While the small tents were easy to put up, especially with four people on each one, putting up the large canvas tent was an ordeal. It was square with a hole in the top for the vent of the small, collapsible woodstove. Once the walls and top were up, getting the stove together, pushing the vent through the roof, and starting a fire were critical first moves. Then we gathered large kettles of snow and started the process of melting it for lifesaving water. I had a hard time drinking the amount of water I would need to survive because it was so cold. At the same time, I felt the need to scrimp a bit on the water in the evening so I wouldn't have to go to the bathroom in the freezing night air. Snow was everywhere inside the tent, and we used shovels to carve out seats to enjoy our meals.

Meals were always delicious—and always involved butter. We had butter in everything, and everything squished of butter when we ate it. I tried not to think about the butter as I ate it with pancakes and oatmeal for breakfast, and meat at night with lots of carbs. The idea is that the work and the cold really zap your energy, so the more butter you eat, the better. When my skin started getting pimply, I begged for mercy and not so much butter.

I got a bright idea one night. I wanted to see the northern lights yet was leery of going outside the tent for any reason. A bathroom break would make sense, but looking at lights in the cold for no reason was crazy and I would freeze. We had been able to see the lights occasionally as we set up camp in early evening, when they were green and white, but I wanted more. Stephen came up with an idea for me, and I took the bait. He said, "Why don't you sleep on the sled and peek out of the tarp to see the lights? You can see them all night long that way." It sounded like an incredible idea to me, a little crazy, but I was up for it and agreed to do it that night.

My sleeping bag was getting larger by the day because my breath was freezing in it all night long as I slept and it never defrosted during the day. Nevertheless, the bag would most likely keep me warm on top of the sled. I put it on top of the frozen mink meat and crawled in at bedtime, and then I let Stephen tie tarps around me for more insulation. I hoped I didn't have to get out to pee in the night.

I peered from my cocoon, waiting in anticipation of the lights. I was able to see a few green and white lights, and I waited patiently for other colors to appear. I was hoping for the whole enchilada, like the colorful auroras I had seen in Alaska on a prior backpack trip to Gates of the Arctic, or at least a lot deeper green and white. It was colder than hell frozen over, and the hole I peeked through got smaller as I pulled the strings on the tarps tighter.

Then the voice in my head—the loud, fear-inducing one—spoke up. *I'm here, in the middle of nowhere, which also is the largest polar bear denning area in the world. And I am sleeping on top of the dogs' food, primo mink innards, something the dogs love and which is probably very popular with polar bears also*, I thought. *So, I would be the snack on top of primo polar bear food if they happen to smell this stuff, and they have extremely keen senses of smell.* Now I had something new to worry about, so I kept up most of the night just waiting for the first polar bear nose to meet mine. It didn't happen, of course. Although the lights never got brighter, and I got very little sleep, the experience was magnificent.

Note to self: About time to cross the bridge to face your fears.

Our lead dog kept doing her thing, and the rest of us followed. On the long days' journeys, we found interesting things to do such as turn our water bottles upside down when carrying them so the lids didn't freeze, and to enjoy the Top Ramen noodles we had with tepid water at lunch. Mercifully, the days were not miserable at all, sometimes overcast or even clear, though we still wrapped up in our layers of fleece and wind-resistant anoraks.

We held meetings every night, looking at maps and a compass to figure out where we were. GPS was nonexistent back then. At one point we were told we would have to put in more hours if we were to meet our plane at York Factory on time. This meant that we would have to get up earlier to prepare and leave earlier every day.

We finally made it to Port Nelson on Hudson Bay, where we applauded ourselves as we gazed over the expansive waterway, but we weren't done yet. The most critical part of the journey was to cross the Nelson River at this point. The ice was starting to melt in the spring weather, which meant there might have been open leads on the river. An open lead is a channel of water in an ice field, in our case a river, making the section impassable. We could go upriver to see if it the conditions got better, but if the ice was too unstable, we would have to go out onto the Hudson Bay ice in order to skirt around the mouth of the river. My mind lingered on the deep water in the ice-covered bay—they would never find our bodies if we went under.

Either way, we would be on ice with either a lake or river about a foot underneath our very heavy sleds. Our allotted time for the trip was almost up, and we had to make a decision and go for it. We decided to go upriver, cross it if possible, and then advance back along the other side to continue south to our destination. I held my trusty (but probably worthless) knife close to me and made sure I could get to it.

The open leads at the mouth of the river going into the bay were treacherous and unstable. I was grateful to go up the river because in my pea brain, I thought at least I would have a chance to survive, whereas any accident on the bay would be fatal. That is, if the polar bears didn't eat us first.

I'd heard the more experienced sledders talking about pressure ridges along the way, but I didn't understand what they were talking about—yet. As our sleds traveled on the river, we had to navigate—and usually go over—large blocks of ice that had been pushed together and fused because of the pressure of the river and ice. The strength of nature was on display. Often, the top of the pressure ridge was a sharp point even taller than we were, making it impossible for the sleds to go over the top.

My eyes were glued to the open leads. All I could see was open water beyond the ice in the river. We were traveling on the ice at this point. As I looked down, I saw bubbles floating under the ice and could hear an occasional crack as the ice moved. I asked how thick the ice was there and was told, "Oh, it's fine. Probably about twelve inches." Twelve inches didn't sound like a lot to me, and the bubbles were not reassuring. If I fell into this cold water, my limbs would quickly freeze and be useless. I could die any number of ways on this trip.

I was in charge of the sled for this adventure. My partner was on foot on the ice with her rifle, looking for polar bears coming after us. Stephen was in front of us the entire time, walking with a long-handled axe. He would toss it, releasing the end of the long handle, and let the metal fly into the ice. How the axe struck the ice and sounded when it landed would determine how sturdy the ice was. The plan was that he would walk while the fellow handling his sled would follow close to him. His sled had a rifle on it, and the fellow on the sled was told that he had probably just a few minutes to use the rifle should the guide encounter a bear while he was walking. There was a lot of ice on the bay and on the river, so the bears most likely were farther out on the ice floes, but there were no guarantees. I glanced at my tiny but trusty knife. I have no clue why it made me feel comfortable.

I guided the dogs up and over several two- to three-foot-high pressure ridges, and as I did so, it took my mind off the danger. I felt like a second-class pole explorer, but it was, admittedly, fun.

It was also slow going. The sleds stayed together, or at least in sight, as each one maneuvered the pressure ridges. My sled would come across a pressure ridge, climb it slowly, and then swoop down the other side. The trick was not to allow the sled to hit the dogs or bounce me off the back with its manic moves downhill. Worst-case scenario stuff bobbed around in my head. *The sled must not turn over, not in the middle of this godforsaken frozen stream.* Most of the time, everything went fairly well. At least the open channels were a hundred feet in front of us.

After hours of travel, we had gone far enough upstream to cross, about five miles. The river was getting narrower, and the leads were less visible. I felt a little better about the situation. Maybe I would live. We crossed successfully, and on the other side of the river, we all hugged each other because we knew we would be able to make the rest of the journey. We were able to stay near the shore of Hudson Bay as we guided the dogs and sleds toward the trading post. After a few more hours, we ran into a few small fishermen's cabins that were used in the summer by the hardy souls who make it there by boat or small plane.

Then we rounded a corner, and there in front of us was a magnificent two-story building, painted white with green trim and sporting a Hudson's Bay Company sign across the front. We were ecstatic, jumping up and down.

Note to self: Your confidence level is rising!

We embraced each other as if we didn't believe that we had arrived. I gave my partner a huge hug and a big smile, and she hugged me as if we had just reached the top of Mount Everest. We took pictures of each other in front of the building, with the top of the doors and windows beneath our feet because the snow was so deep.

The current Hudson's Bay Company building was not the original building from the 1680s, but it had been built in the 1830s on the permafrost at the mouth of the Hayes River, which provided a pathway for goods to be delivered from the interior. Having a building on permafrost means that the ground, and everything on it, expands and contracts with the outside temperatures. We soon found a second-floor entrance in the back that we could reach due to the snow level, and best of all, the key worked in the door.

We entered and were struck by artifacts. All kinds of artifacts had been left in the building, and each one had a label on it to be included in some unknown researcher's book. The building contained everything that was needed for survival in the brutal land, including an area on the second floor for a church. The yellow windows of the church were in full display, with the sun shining through them. I silently lifted my eyes to the ceiling and thanked the universe that I, and our entire group, had arrived safely.

We wandered through each floor and looked at each of the artifact displays. The most interesting item to me was the fur press. Apparently, when the trappers brought their furs to York Factory, the pelts were pressed to be as compact as possible for shipment on boats back to England. It was a space-saving compactor of the era. Furs were placed on top of each other in this machine of sorts. It acted like an apple press—when one turned the large wheel with a screw-type mechanism, a large board squeezed the furs as much as possible. More furs on the ships equaled more sales, money, and profit.

We celebrated our journey that night by eating caribou steaks, brought by our assistant from Churchill since only Native people are allowed to hunt caribou in the area. It tasted like a good steak to me, but it probably would have tasted good one way or the other. It still was very, very cold, and I was glad to know the plane would be coming for us the next day, landing on the ice on Hudson Bay.

The plane was tiny and only held a few people and gear, so I was on the second load. I wasn't sure about the dogs' future destination, but I knew they were going on another trip. I was sorry to leave this land, flattened by massive glaciers so very long ago, and so full of polar bears that we mercifully didn't encounter. But, heck, I lived to tell about it.

CHAPTER 6

Spain

By the spring of 1999, I had traveled on guided trips in the US as well as North and Central America, with one very short, unguided trip to Europe with Barb. I wanted to branch out at this point, and I wondered if I had the courage to go on my own to some of the places I was dreaming about. I was gaining courage, like the lion in *The Wizard of Oz*. I figured I wanted to see the rest of Oz, that is, the rest of the world.

One of the things I had learned quickly was that traveling was defined by who I was traveling with, even when I traveled alone. Good friends and laughter were the goal, and I usually found someone to travel with at this point in time. Eventually I traveled a great deal by myself, once I became a friend to myself, but sometimes I felt sad when I couldn't share the laughter and experiences with someone.

Slowly, as I was getting older, I realized that I had reached milestones in my life. I had finished my jobs of being a child, a student, a housewife, a worker, and most importantly, a mother. For many reasons, including lack of time and money, during those earlier years, travel had mostly been restricted to short trips in the US. Now I could give myself the gift of my passion, international travel. My prior short trip to Europe had enticed me, and the guided trips were fairly predictable, so I was hoping for more unplanned trips.

I was honored when my friend Susan said she'd go with me to Europe. I worked with Susan at this time, and we had a good friendship. She seemed to roll with the punches, and we would laugh when we talked.

Because I hadn't traveled with Susan before, I felt I had to tell her the rule that my mother had taught me years before: I don't care what you bring as long as you are able to handle your bags yourself. I told her I carried very little and had learned to wash out clothes instead of bringing a daily change. Susan did not have the same perspective, though, as I realized when I saw her very large bag.

Note to self: You may be hauling this around.

WE LANDED IN MADRID, SPAIN, AFTER SEVERAL VERY LONG FLIGHTS AND were exhausted, really exhausted. We rented a car and I asked Susan if she wanted to drive or wanted me to drive. We decided I would drive, and in my mind, that meant Susan would be the navigator. Mistake. I needed to spell out that one person drives and the other one navigates. Susan put her luggage in the trunk, as did I, and we drove off en route to Toledo.

After an hour I finally acknowledged that I was so tired that it was dangerous for me to drive. I asked Susan to look on the map and tell me how to navigate the last bit to Toledo. It was then that she told me she didn't know how to navigate using a map. The realization sunk in quickly that I would not only be responsible for our driving but would also have to conquer the map.

The roundabouts were of particular concern, especially since I had never seen one before. Instead of traffic lights, there were large circles that you could eternally drive around until you found the particular street exit you wanted. Often most roundabouts had four intersecting streets, so if you entered the roundabout on one street, continued halfway around and exited, you'd continue on the same street. If you wanted the perpendicular street, you would have to exit the circle a quarter of the way or three-quarters of the way around. It was truly all very confusing until the roundabout became a normal part of driving for me. Another thing that could be confusing was if there were more than four exits, like when six streets intersected. Together, Susan and I would panic when entering the roundabout until we saw the sign for our exit out of the circle.

Near Toledo, we stopped at a pension along the route for the night. A pension in Spain is like a hostel; however, we had our own room with access to a shared bathroom down the hall. We had agreed to stay in local places like this to save money along the way. I still often worried about not having enough money to last my lifetime, a fear that was both helpful and not so helpful. The room was painted white with two twin beds and white curtains that blew in the wind from the fan in the room. Basic but adequate. The bathroom was clean, and there were very few people to compete for it, so for the most part the room and bathroom were great. Susan hauled her large suitcase up the two flights of stairs, and we settled in to get the sleep we needed.

Another thing I hadn't counted on was time frames. When I get up in the morning, it takes me about fifteen minutes to be out the door and on to the next adventure. With Susan, it took a good hour to be ready. I learned to take a walk in the morning once we'd negotiated a time to leave. It was all an exercise in negotiation and understanding—for me to learn to chill. I needed the lesson anyhow.

The adventures kept coming our way as we found more and more pensions in small, out-of-the-way towns. We were able to find castle ruins here and there where we could clamor around the old walls and staircases with the absence of *No Trespassing* signs that would have been plastered all over the States.

There was one night, however, that we ran into a problem. We usually waited until mid- to late afternoon to find a place to stay for the night. That way we could follow our adventure wherever it took us and then spontaneously book a room when the time was right. No planning everything out like my father had on those old cross-country road trips.

On this particular afternoon, each place we stopped told us, "No, we have no vacancy—there is a festival nearby, and all accommodations are taken. Sorry." We were turned away time after time. This was a hitch in our plans, and something we had to deal with one way or another. My mental chatter was starting up: *What are you going to do? We can sleep in the car, if needed, but that's a last resort.* I still wasn't trusting the universe enough quite yet to understand this was just an interesting hiccup in our plans.

Eventually we found a pension that said they had a no-show and we could have that room. Susan and I hauled our stuff up two flights of stairs and went into the room, closing the door behind us. At least, we tried, but it only kind of closed, and its lock was broken. We were settling in when the manager came in to tell us we had to leave immediately. In my broken Spanish, I asked why, but I couldn't understand the reason he gave.

He repeated that we must pack and leave, sounding like we were criminals, or at the least, unwanted. Shortly thereafter, some people showed up, shoving their way into the room, and the situation became more clear: the *no-show* was now a *show* and we had to give up our room or do battle. Susan was already repacking her suitcase and preparing to carry it down the stairs again. Forget squatter's rights.

We traveled farther, stopping at barns and farms to see if we could get a room with someone along the winding road. Eventually we came to a turnoff to a town and asked the first person we saw if she knew of anyone who rented rooms for the night. We truly were begging, and anyone could have detected the panic in our voices. She was a very kind, large, middle-aged woman who smiled and said in Spanish, "Yes, I think that Rosa rents rooms. It's possible she might have one." Then she showed us with hand gestures how to reach Rosa's house. It was just a few turns from where we were. I was pooped from driving.

We walked up to the door of a house in the neighborhood and hoped it was Rosa's home. It was an active neighborhood, with people walking on the street, carrying their groceries for dinner. In most of the small towns we experienced, the market was the primo spot in town, and everyone with produce was there in the mornings and sometimes after siesta in the afternoons.

We knocked on Rosa's door and waited. The door was wooden, the house painted white, probably over adobe. We waited longer. When we were turning to leave, the door opened wide enough for us to see a stout, aged woman standing at it with a cane in her hand. I tried not to look too pathetic, simultaneously attempting to send the same signal to Susan telepathically. It really didn't matter. We'd be sleeping in the car soon if we didn't find a place. Susan was discouraged by the whole thing.

I asked Rosa if she had a room we could stay in for the night. Rosa nodded and let us in. At this point the cost wasn't really a concern, and I wouldn't ask until later. She told me there was only one bed and we would have to share it, but we would have welcomed anything. Rosa told us that she had just had surgery, pulled up her blouse to show us her scar, and then quite jovially showed us all around. The one issue I hadn't expected cropped up when Rosa pointed to the ceramic pot under the bed, which was to be our chamber pot if we had to go to the bathroom at night. I found it endearing. Susan hadn't counted on that at all, but she took it in stride.

We were grateful to have the bed, and were most grateful for Rosa's hospitality. We'd eaten, so we went to bed early, vowing to see the town in the morning.

When we got up, we walked down the main street. It was like entering a medieval world—something I had not expected at all. The town was off the main road and was not much of anything on the map. The streets were cobblestone and had a water channel running down the middle of them as well as water along the sides. It quickly dawned on me that in medieval times, those channels were probably the main sewer system, and for all I knew, they probably still were.

Winding around a corner down a hill, we encountered the main water source for the town. It was a carved lion, with a stream of water pouring from its mouth. Several of the village women were collecting water in jugs, probably for daily use. Walking farther, I started seeing small metal containers with fire in them on the street in front of people's doors. This probably was where food was prepared outdoors, for everyday consumption. I guessed it avoided carbon monoxide poisoning.

The streets were narrow in this part of town, and all the houses were connected in rows. The houses were two stories high, which made the narrow streets dark and almost foreboding. Often the second story protruded a bit into the street. Apparently it allowed for more room on the second floor. There was no color along the streets, just a gray-yellow glow that permeated the entire town.

Occasionally we saw some graffiti, but most of the town seemed to be from an era long past. When evaluating everything, I could only think that we were experiencing the remnants of a medieval town that was somehow still present—not particularly desirable to live in but inhabited by people who had nowhere else to go. For the most part, it was depressing, but it gave us Rosa, an amazing place to stay for the night, and the experience of a town and way of life that had been forgotten.

Susan and I got back in our rental car, and our trip progressed to the larger towns of Spain. I had to drive through them, much to my chagrin. I was a nutcase driving in these towns, especially after we saw a motorcycle accident where the young driver had probably died. Fortunately, we made it to Granada. I had seen information on the Sierra Nevada mountains southeast of Granada, and I wanted to go there. We were able to travel on the winding roads with no middle lines into the mountains. Before long, we saw small mountain towns on terraced land just as I imagined Nepal would be like. I made a mental note to be sure to go to Nepal once I gathered more courage.

We stopped and walked around the small towns and often found the local markets. Women would be lingering as they talked, caught up on gossip, and did whatever local women did during the day. At one produce stand, I picked up a head of lettuce. From their immediate stares, I thought the ladies of the market were going to whack my hand or, at the least, scold me. I didn't know what I was doing wrong. Through hand gestures they told me that we were not to touch the produce. That was the job of the vendor, to pick out what we wanted, to weigh it, and to put it in a bag. All we were supposed to do was point.

Eventually the trip was coming to a close and we had to find a place to stay for our last night before our flight from Madrid the next day. We drove past towns, asking each other for agreement. We passed one hotel with a lot of graffiti all around it, and Susan was tempted. I gave her my *Are you crazy? Do you see the graffiti?* stare. We drove on until I saw a pension with three flights of stairs, and Susan immediately said, "No. No more stairs, we are staying in a motel or hotel tonight." Although she had been good about taking her suitcase up the stairs most of the time, I had helped a great deal as it went in and out of the car every day. She was done.

It wasn't long before we found a more or less decent-appearing hotel. We pulled in, and Susan's first question to the manager was "Can we have a room on the first floor?" He nodded yes, and that sealed the deal. Susan wheeled her large suitcase into the room and asked me a legitimate question: "What do you want to do for dinner?"

"Well, if we go to the restaurant here in the motel, it won't give us much of an experience of the town. But if we walk around town, we might get lost."

Susan, in her very direct approach, turned her head quickly, peered straight at my eyes, and said, "You never answer my questions. You answer my questions with possibilities but don't tell me what *you'd* like to do. That was my question—what do *you* want to do?"

Her comment stunned me. I was taken aback and didn't know what to say. It had been a long time since anyone had used such honesty with me. *Oh my God*, I thought. *I do this all the time, trying to guess what the other person wants instead of just plain saying what I want.* Now here I was being told that it was okay, actually preferable, to state what I'd really like to do.

Note to self: Apparently people actually care about *what I want*. I don't have to second-guess *their* needs.

I DECIDED THAT WE WOULD WALK AROUND TOWN. AT FIRST THERE WERE no people anywhere to be seen. I figured it was because it was a Sunday. Then, little by little, a few more people showed up, all seeming to go to a common destination. We fell in behind them and, when we rounded a corner, saw the most incredible sight ever.

The city opened up in front of us, with hundreds of people milling around the town center. It was a large square with a big open area in the middle and many shops all around it. Many townspeople were there visiting with friends, going into the shops, watching their children play and feed the birds, drinking beer or wine at restaurant tables, and just enjoying the Sunday afternoon in a common place.

The warmth and camaraderie washed over me as I was drawn into it with strangers' smiles, and I felt a pang of regret that there was so little of this in the States. Susan and I ate at a small restaurant, smiling as we people-watched for hours before we found our way back to the hotel. We slept soundly that night before leaving Spain the next day. This trip had taught me about spontaneity, but it had also taught me about interacting with others, whether friends or the locals in a foreign land. I was learning a great deal about traveling.

Note to self: You are *not* the center of the universe. There are wonderful people in the world, and they are waiting out there to meet you.

CHAPTER 7

Scotland

Judy came into my life just when I needed a friend like her. Maintaining romantic relationships wasn't my strong suit, so I'd stopped looking. I had been married for fifteen years, from the time I'd had my beautiful daughter at my young age. The marriage didn't last, but two of the most beautiful things ever came from it: my two children. Although I was able to find good people to be in relationships with after my marriage, and traveled in the US with them, I never found the right fit.

Note to self: Embrace yourself.

Feeling sorry for myself had come naturally since I was a child. Add on the adulthood relationship struggles, and eventually I began to think of myself as damaged goods. During the years I was married and after, the call of the outdoors and mountains beckoned. In the mountains, I wasn't "damaged goods," but capable, worthy, and lovable. I had to be in the present, watching where I put my feet and not worrying about the past or future. Daily problems had to take the back seat to my next footstep.

I usually stayed away from touristy large cities, preferring the outdoors, so as opportunities to climb mountains came, I embraced them. I considered the mountains my main escape from my daily life in Los Angeles, and I always had a trip planned. In February of any particular year, I could tell you what I had planned for November. The mountains meant that much to me. I kept climbing after my divorce and through future relationships. Going to the outdoors was my retreat and way to center myself.

Along with climbing mountains came vast opportunities to meet people. I had joined the Los Angeles chapter of the Sierra Club's climbing sections and started participating. I learned quickly that the "tiger" type A folks were out of my mountain-climbing league because I am slow and scared on rocks, where a fall could be fatal. They wanted to push forward, faster than my comfort zone, so I avoided them. Likewise I avoided the people who were too dependent on me—the ones who could not make decisions on their own. They were the type to ask anyone around them which way to go. My personality was somewhere in between.

Then I met Judy.

Judy was a hearty 5'2" woman who captured my heart, an immediate friend. She came on many trips with her friend Gary, who also became my friend. At first, whispers went around the climbing group that Judy and Gary were having an affair. Eventually I had to ask her, and she whisked her hand in front of my face saying, "I don't care what anyone else thinks. We're just friends. My husband doesn't want to do this stuff, and I do." Turns out, her husband only liked to accumulate footsteps on golf courses, but Judy liked to see the world, so she was always up for any adventure, just like I was. It was refreshing to see someone who knew herself and was committed to having no regrets. Judy and her husband respected each other enough to honor the other's needs.

As our friendship grew, I found that Judy was an amazing friend. The knot was secured on one particular climb in the California desert in 1997. I really wanted to do Maturango Peak. I arranged a small group of five for the climb, including four men and me. I was always the organizer, never the leader, because I had the initiative to get us out to the location, but I questioned my navigation skills and was basically a wimp about scary stuff when climbing. I'd decide where I wanted to go, recruit a good leader, and find others who wanted to go along.

This climb would take all day, so we started off about six in the morning. One member of our group opted out almost immediately and gave his food to another participant because he had an injury and was too slow to complete the hike. We had to be fast and strong to complete it in one day. Judy and Gary had decided it was chancy that we would get to the peak, so they climbed another nearby peak and said they might meet us back at the base afterward.

We forged ahead on the hike, mostly off-trail, but at one point we encountered a gate blocking the way we'd expected to go, so we detoured, adding six miles to the trip. By about seven that night, thirteen hours into the hike, we still weren't back to the base. We'd hiked twenty-six miles, with seven thousand feet of gain, and it was lengthy to say the least. Weary and exhausted, our small group would be getting out in the dark. I was near tears. It was a Sunday night, and going to work the next day loomed.

I was slow, but nothing hurt. I didn't have the stamina of my friends. Nonetheless, I had climbed up the mountain and was now on a rather flat trail in the canyon leading back to the dirt access road. Still, the climb had tuckered me out. I was known to whine, so I was trying my best not to say anything. Once in a while, I couldn't help it. "Will this *ever* be over?" I would say under my breath. One of the fellows would turn back and say, "What?" He probably didn't really want an answer. We were all wiped out. Out of fear of being reprimanded and adding to my reputation, I shut up. Eventually, with the dark all around us and still no sight of the car, I was starting to say something again when I saw something moving in front of us.

I kept my eyes glued on what I thought was a light. Had I interpreted it right? Yes, it was moving a little and then more up the canyon toward us. Our small group rounded the corner and there, in the distance, were two headlights. As we got closer, we realized it was Judy and Gary coming to check on us, to make sure our bodies weren't out in the desert somewhere rotting. That's when I knew that Judy was just the right person to travel with. We'd watch each other's backs.

Over and over again, Judy proved to be the stalwart friend and trekker I knew she would be. Still, I approached her carefully, trying out my ideas slowly. We climbed many mountains together over the years, but I liked the idea of adventuring with her abroad too. Traveling with anyone for a period of time is always an adventure. I had been across the country with Barb and to Spain with Susan, and it had been eye-opening to understand what I had to consider when traveling with a friend. Adding an overseas component, especially, is another layer of complexity. Basically, you're stuck with the other person for whatever length of time you are abroad, so it's best to be sure beforehand that you'll complement each other well under those circumstances.

Judy is a point-A-to-point-B person. I'm not. She is very goal oriented, accomplishing any amazing thing she decides to do. I'm kind of that way too. As it turns out, we complement each other very well. She gives me a push and shove sometimes, and because of me, she gets to see the points C, D, E, and F that I happen to see along the way. Her personality is more analytical, and mine is more artistic. She makes sure we make the right turns, and I strike up conversations with the locals as we go along. It all blends fairly well, even on lengthy trips.

Many times over the decades, when Judy and I would finish a trip, I would look her in the eye smiling and say, "There's no one else I would rather have done this trip with!"

Our first foreign trip together was a grand adventure. After many conversations, Judy and I decided to venture to Scotland. We reserved airline tickets and a rental car, then would make the rest of the trip serendipitous. The car and our ambitions would take us wherever we wanted. The only thing I really wanted to include was a visit to my namesake castle, Dunvegan Castle, on the MacLeod estate on the Isle of Skye in the Hebrides. That would become our first mission. Scotland was, after all, the land of my heritage.

We decided to go in October 2000, despite warnings that it might be cold and rainy. The airfares were good, we were both available, and it truly would be very wet in Scotland. Heck, it would be wet no matter when we went. Scotland in October should be a piece of cake—however, we bought waterproof boots just to be safe.

The trip almost ended in disaster because of airports. Judy and I booked separate flights since I was leaving from Los Angeles and she lived in San Diego. Her trip would route through LAX, but we'd be on different flights the whole way. She worked carefully with the AAA automobile club travel department so all the details were covered for her portion of the trip. And I—well, I dialed in my airline miles from my credit cards and scored a free ticket from LAX to Aberdeen, Scotland. We could count on our tickets being booked correctly, but we couldn't count on all of our various flights being on time.

Judy's husband dropped her at the San Diego airport and she went in to catch her flight to LAX. The flight that was delayed. And delayed.

Meanwhile, I was learning new airport techniques. At the international terminal in Los Angeles, there were a ton of stations for the myriads of airlines serving the international patrons. I was just one of those patrons. I looked around and saw more ticketing agencies than I had ever seen in my life. There were numbered gates for particular airlines, and there were huge billboards to find which gate was serving each particular flight. Eventually I discovered the ticketing agent lines for my airline and was able to check my bag. It was a relief, giving up my backpack, but I silently wished the bag, *Good luck*, as it left on the conveyor belt, hoping it was going to show up at the other end of the trip.

I made my way to the gate and had to undergo the scrutiny of air travel. In reality, it was just all an extension of the regular domestic travel I was used to, but I still carried my fears with me, extra mental baggage.

Unbeknownst to me, Judy was having her own challenges at the same time. Her plane from San Diego to LAX had been canceled, and she was put on the next available flight. Her flight arrived just a few minutes before her connecting flight overseas was to take off. Frantically, Judy asked where her connecting flight was. She was told it was across the airport and that her best bet was to leave this terminal and to run through the parking garage to the terminal on the other side.

With her backpack strapped on, Judy sprinted out the door, across streets, holding out her hand to stop traffic, across the parking lot, and across another street, finally reaching the other terminal. She raced in, waving her ticket in her hand, and ran to the gate. Because this was pre-9/11, airport security didn't stop everyone outside the gates for screening and bag checks. Good thing because Judy would have missed her flight were those systems in place at the time.

Meanwhile, I was also leaving LA on a later flight. My flight was uneventful once I boarded, and I leaned against the side of the plane from my window seat. It was grand that I was off on such an adventure. I left the States with butterflies in my stomach—heck, in all of my body—because I was leaving the hallowed ground of home for a foreign country. I could think of the most unbelievable things when I was worried. I would think about the past, about my inaction or stupidity or blunders. I tended to gather all my past sins in one basket and evaluate my missteps in each of them. My mind cycled on worrying about them all, though I knew I had absolutely no control over changing any of the outcomes. I remember worrying once at work when I had not been able to make a change in health care plans that I was requested to do. Embarrassingly, I told my boss that I couldn't make it happen, and then I *started crying.* How unprofessional! My boss laughed at me and said, "You know, in a few weeks this won't even be on your radar."

Then I would start agonizing about the future. I'd worry about not finding Judy, about the plane not landing on time or at the right place. I'd fret that we wouldn't be able to get our car or that they would run out of cars just when we got there. I realized that it was my norm to worry when the trip was starting.

Of course, all this worry was for nothing in reality because all such events lay in the future. On the plane that day, waiting for takeoff, I told myself to pull back and get perspective. I remembered my father's advice when I'd asked him one day, "What advice would you give me if I were a new person on the planet?" He told me, "Put all your troubles into two baskets. Separate out the things that you have control over and those you don't have control over. Worry about the things you have control over, and toss aside the things you don't have control over. Life will be ever so much easier for you." He was right, but I couldn't always see it. It's hard to give up ingrained practices, especially when my mind was telling me to hold on to them. I guess that's called growing up. Some of us take more time than others.

When we landed, all I could think about was Judy and whether everything was going according to plan. We were two souls, taking two vastly different routes, hopefully meeting each other somewhere in the small Aberdeen airport in Scotland.

When I got off the plane in Aberdeen, I sensed that I was alone, but I was too tired to feel scared. Judy was supposedly going to be at the gate to meet me because her flight was to land before mine.

Somehow, the universe was with us. I got off the plane and Judy was there, feet up on an adjacent chair, smiling and saying, "Glad to see you!" I started talking nonstop, as if I needed to get all my demons out at once. I told her about my flight, that I'd been worried that she wouldn't be there, that I hoped I'd made the correct reservation for the car, and that I hoped all was well with the world.

She listened patiently while I jabbered about this and that. Then she slowly started her story about her delayed flight, having to run across the huge Los Angeles airport, and how she almost didn't make it. I finally was quiet for a while as I evaluated her troubles against mine. Mine paled in comparison.

Meanwhile, in my nervousness, I started rambling on about planes, cars, family, and any other subject that came to mind. That's what I tended to do when I felt anxious, just start talking about anything that came to mind. Getting the car required that we take a shuttle from the airport parking lot to an off-site parking/ticketing office. The shuttle drove several miles to what felt like the middle of nowhere, and I didn't feel comfortable with it. We got to the entrance of a very small shack with a very small door, and we asked the shuttle driver to wait. The door slowly creaked open, and we found no one inside. It was getting creepy in my opinion. I didn't feel good about the whole thing, and eventually we decided to go back to the airport and try another car rental place.

That's the best thing about having few plans—we could change directions ninety degrees or even 180 degrees if we wanted. We found an agency that had a car for us at a fair rate and seemed to want our business. That made all the difference for me—they actually wanted to work with us. Looking back on the situation with older, wiser eyes, everything would probably have been fine, though I chose to listen to my intuition, which was good.

We found that all the cars in Europe were tiny. Good thing, because the *roads* in Europe, especially Scotland, were tiny also. We were happy to be on the road, me as driver and Judy as road guide/navigator. No on-the-job training here for this navigator.

We drove off in our rented Renault, finally smiling and hoping to find someplace to stay for the night since it was getting late in the afternoon. Not only were we tired, but also I was having problems driving on the opposite side of the road from what I was used to. People in Scotland drive on the left side of the road, and I was only used to driving on the right side. I anticipated no problem but forewarned Judy that it would be fine with me if she quickly screamed at me if she saw a hazard or realized I was driving on the wrong side of the road.

This car was also a stick shift and was set up differently than any other car I'd driven. All this overwhelmed me. Within the first hour, I pulled over to the side of the road and tried out all the gadgets to feel more acquainted. We were smiling with each new trick—until I tried to get the car in reverse. It was impossible for me to get it in reverse, which bothered me. I looked at the gearshift, I searched for the manual, and I tried to interpret the instructions on the gearshift handle. There was nothing that told me how to get the darned car in reverse. So I took things into my own hands.

I drove only forward, around the block, until I could drive into a gasoline station, where I pulled up to a pump and got out. I walked toward other pumps and tapped a middle-aged man's shoulder as he was filling his car with gasoline.

He turned around abruptly, staring at me while he evaluated me and the situation.

I sheepishly glanced at him with what I must say was an endearing look, and said, "Excuse me, sir. Could you please tell me how to get this car into reverse so I don't hurt someone because of my stupidity?" I pointed to our tiny car.

My target started howling with laughter. He couldn't believe what he was hearing and stared at me as if to ask if I were for real. "Really?" he asked. "You really can't get it into reverse? Where are you from?"

I shrugged. "We just rented this car, and I've tried everything. We're two friends from California."

It was hard for him to contain his laughter, so he burst into belly laughs as he walked over to the car. We profusely thanked him as he peered inside. He glanced at me and said, "See this gearshift?"

"Yes," I replied.

"All you do is pull up on this ring below the top of the gearshift. It goes into reverse then."

So simple, and I'd had no idea. He shook his head as he left the scene, but I figured he'd never see us again, so why feel embarrassed? That was probably the instant that Judy and I knew we'd travel together forever. Every time we made stupid judgment calls on our future trips, we always got each other's attention and, with a laugh and a shrug, said, "They'll never see us again." We were on our way, both forward and reverse, and our motto was born: *They'll never see us again.*

Getting into the next small town was easy. Finding a place to stay was not. We were tired after our flights, so we stopped at the first small two-story building we saw with a *B&B* sign out front. The very gracious hostess told us there was no room in the inn for us, but mercifully she gave us the name of a farmhouse outside town that might have a room available. My first impression of Scotland was that the people were friendly and helpful.

We drove out in the country, as instructed. The large farmhouse was tucked back on a gravel road. As we approached, we could see that the two-story farmhouse was filled to the gills with farm equipment and comfortable, used furniture. It was immediately welcoming. The lady of the house brought us in, showed us where the tea and cookies were, and left us to get a feeling for the place. Our beds were on the second floor in a bedroom sporting two beds with flowery comforter tops. After our long journey and worries about the car and finding a place to stay, it was a reward. The tea and cookies were amazing.

We had picked Aberdeen to begin and end our journey because it was north of the intensely large and intimidating Edinburgh and had an airport small enough to navigate easier. The general plan was to drive a large circle from Aberdeen, going to the west coast of Scotland, to the Isle of Skye, north to Cape Wrath, east to see the Orkney islands, and then back to Aberdeen.

We started sampling scones all over the country. There were cheese scones, currant scones, berry scones, and plain scones. At one bakery, we pointed to two scones and the young lady behind the counter said, "You may not like those scones. They have sugar on top." We bought four.

At the local thrift stores, I would buy woolen scarves to take home, cut up, and make braided chair seats from. We also found wool sweaters in almost every thrift store we visited. The women of Scotland did an amazing job of knitting. After experiencing their rain, I could see why.

We zipped past the watering hole of the Loch Ness Monster, past pastureland and the Highlands, and eventually to the Isle of Skye in the Hebrides, a famous set of islands to the west of the Scottish mainland. We drove across a small bridge onto the island, stopped at the obligatory tourist shops, and eventually drove to Dunvegan Castle, where my heritage rested. We had passed other castles that had been remnants of the past, some with only the ground bricks left. This castle was not only intact but also had a sign showing times (and admission) that it was open to the public.

Note to self: Don't tell anyone you are a MacLeod. The organization operating tours of the castle might get your maiden name, and you will be forever on their donor request list.

WE FOUND A SMALL, QUIET BED-AND-BREAKFAST PLACE JUST OUTSIDE TOWN. From the one-story house that rented out an extra bedroom or two, the view looked out on the serene inlets from the ocean. There was hardly any traffic on this part of the island, and the village was extremely small. At this early evening time, all was deceivingly quiet on the ocean and in the sky. I noticed two mountains that seemed cut off at the top, and when I asked the proprietor about them, she told me, "Those are MacLeod's Tables." Apparently, these large hills are flatter than a pancake on the top, maybe pushed by up Mother Nature to show off her power. We asked if we could access them and climb them.

"Of course" was her reply. Nothing was really sacred around here as far as private property, and it was all right to tramp through someone's property without permission. The mentality of the people in Scotland, throughout the country, was one of peace and understanding. So the next day, we climbed one of MacLeod's Tables with our high boots on, slipping and sliding all the way up the hill because of the ever-wet terrain. When Judy and I reached the top, I turned and looked at her. I knew my ancestors had loved these hills and had come to trek and hunt here. This was my heritage. I closed my eyes and was grateful to understand my ancestry. I hoped my daughter and son would someday understand it also.

Next on the agenda was to visit my castle and not let anyone know I had a close connection to it. We signed up for a tour and found that the castle was in top shape for castles in Scotland. It had several floors, and all were usable and furnished. I took a picture from a window, looking out to the green surroundings. Apparently taking pictures was generally not allowed—I guess we were supposed to buy them at the little souvenir shop in the basement. I discreetly snapped one anyhow, perhaps to show my confidence. I looked in each room, seeing the starkness of the heavy stones that made up the building. These building materials were all that had been available to the people of the time, beginning in the 1200s, and most of the castles were of stone in various states of disrepair. My castle was holding up well, probably from all the MacLeod donations from all over the world.

Not long after the visit to Dunvegan, we drove through the Cuillins, magnificent barren mountains of the area. I told Judy, "I'm going to pull over for a minute." I got out of the car and soaked in the surrounding scenery. Once again, I let the wind and fogginess of the air surround me. I looked at the hillsides and noticed a sign commemorating where someone had died while hiking because of the relentless terrain and weather. I glanced at Judy once more and said, "Now I understand who I am. I love coldness, the winds, the fog, and the barrenness. I finally know where I came from." Judy smiled, apparently in approval. I stood there for several more minutes before getting back in our tiny Renault, driving down the little one-lane road with pullouts, in the country that is my heritage.

One particular stay encapsulated the friendliness of the Scottish people. We'd made it to the Cape Wrath area in the northwestern corner of Scotland. It was the weekend, near the end of our trip. And, as usual, it was raining. We had hiked almost every day, and this day was no exception.

We got out as much rain gear as we could and hiked several miles toward Cape Wrath. The clouds kept accumulating and becoming darker as we walked. With rainbows around, we didn't think too much of the weather coming our way from the ocean. We got to the end of the cape and started celebrating our adventure, proud that we'd made it. By then, the series of gray clouds gathering in front of us could no longer be ignored. Mother Nature takes her own course. Finally it dumped. I mean, the rain came at us at an angle, blasting the left side of our bodies with winds and a wicked force. We'd been foolish to be out in it in the first place, and now we needed to come up with a plan.

Our immediate plan was to turn around once we realized our predicament. Now we were being lambasted on our right side, with the rain still coming at an angle because of the winds. We hiked as quickly as we could back to the little rental car and got in after I fumbled with the keys a bit. We were totally soaked and had no place to stay for the night even though it was dinnertime. Predicament.

I started driving down the small country road for several miles, but we found nothing. We went farther as we tried to find towns not far from our location since we were totally wet and somewhat hungry. This was October, and many of the summertime rentals were closed for the season. Not many braved Scotland in October, and fewer still visited this northern, remote area.

I saw a sign, *Room to Let*, at an intersection with a dirt farm road. I squinted to see if I could see the house, but it wasn't in sight. I looked at Judy, and she shrugged her shoulders—it was all right with her.

She asked legitimately, "What if we go all the way down there and don't like it?"

I shrugged because I had no answer for her. "I guess we'll just turn around and come back—remember that they'll never see us again, so what's the harm?"

I drove for what seemed an eternity, but in reality was just a mile or two off the road. We came to a few barns then a big, authentic farmhouse, two story. Through the screen door we could see a mudroom, necessary for obvious reasons, and when we opened the door, the squeaking gave away our presence.

"Hello!" a voice from within yelled out.

"Hello," I replied back. We stayed in the mudroom, dripping from all the rain like drowned cats. A robust lady with a dress and apron appeared, and immediately we felt at home.

I was worried about the cost of the room since we were so far from civilization. "We'd like to stay here if you have room."

She laughed at seeing our sorry state of affairs. "Take your wet things off there and come on in. I'll start a peat fire."

Still no discussion of room price. Judy and I went in after taking off our dripping raincoats.

Peat is used throughout Scotland to cook and keep warm. The entire country must be sitting on a big peat bog. The woman brought in large pieces of the ground and put them in the fireplace. She started burning the peat, and we sat on the floor to get as close to the fire as we could. It felt amazing. Then the kind proprietor brought us the afternoon cookies and tea, which again, were totally amazing.

We talked with her for a while and then asked if there was a pub in town where we could get some soup. We had more or less become pub connoisseurs, having soup (usually tomato) and maybe chips (fries) and a beer on almost a daily basis (with a few scones worked in).

"No," she said, "nothing really close. But why don't you let me fix you some soup. My husband and I have had dinner, and I have some leftover salmon also."

I nearly kissed her. I didn't care what her room rate was. "Oh my goodness, that would be so wonderful and appreciated!"

It wasn't long before she came out with a tray of hot soup and handed it to us, still sitting on the floor. It was most definitely the best soup anywhere in Scotland. We would have given her a million dollars for the experience and her kindness if we'd had it. Turned out, the room cost the same as any other room we had stayed in, but the kindness of the housekeeper was immeasurable.

And so our Scotland trip ended, after all the barren landscape, daily hikes, amazing hospitality, and finding our travel skills becoming more finely tuned with each day.

CHAPTER 8

Tour du Mont Blanc

AFTER SURVIVING AND RELISHING THE TRIP TO SCOTLAND, JUDY AND I became more adventurous. We were still doing a great deal of local mountain climbing together and were in decent shape. I was starting menopause when we decided to tramp around Europe. The menopause thing caused only a few problems. Somewhere along the way, we had heard about a trek around Mont Blanc, the highest peak in the Alps in Europe. We picked one of the most difficult trips, the one that the book said was "amazingly beautiful." We didn't really have a clue as to what it would involve; we just knew we wanted to go. It sounded good to take our hiking skills and focus on a hiking trip.

In the mountains there, we found kindred spirits. Europe has an amazing set of trekking routes, called GR routes. It stands for *grande randonnées*, which means "grand routes" in French. The treks are days or even weeks in length and often have refuges available at the end of a day's trek. Ideally, one could carry just a sleeping bag and a jacket plus a few odds and ends to hike from refuge to refuge. But no, not us. We carried about forty pounds each, with every provision for disaster. Tent camping is discouraged along most of the routes, with the exception being near the refuges.

My mother scolded me for wanting to stay in refuges, thinking they were for poor people, until I explained they were just for folks hiking trails—although Judy and I appeared and acted poor. We didn't know much beyond that, though, except that they were along trails and cost money. As it turned out, refuges are absolutely magical places, often high up in the mountains and below a glacier or mountain meadow, available for trekkers to sleep in. They are often accessed by foot or helicopter, with a few having dirt roads.

After doing a little research, I discovered the Cicerone Press book series. These guidebooks give very specific directions, such as "Go to the big church on the main street and turn right just after it." When I found *The Tour of Mont Blanc*, specifically, it told of red-and-white markings on rocks as trail markers. That sounded like my kind of guidebook. This series would become our bible for this and future trips.

According to the guidebook, the trip would take nine and a half days to accomplish. As usual, I didn't do too much research, assuming we'd figure it out when we got there, whereas Judy had religiously figured out all the daily mileage and elevation gain and then converted it from kilometers and meters to miles and feet. I just knew the book said the trip would total about 120 miles and thirty-five thousand feet of elevation gain over the nine and a half days. We had Judy's daily information guides plus distances and elevation gain charts, something to look at in our hands. This would be our first time doing something like this overseas, so she really took the time to know what she was getting into. We would have to fly to Geneva, Switzerland, and transfer somehow to Chamonix, France. The Cicerone Press books gave limited information on getting to the trailhead, but it was enough information to get started.

When we landed in the Geneva airport on a weekday afternoon, we searched for whatever information booth was available. Kind of global, the big *I* sign showed us the way. We walked to the booth and waited for a person or two to finish. We went up to the booth, and fortunately the attendant spoke broken English.

"Is there a bus or transportation to Chamonix, France?" I asked.

"Yes," she replied, offering no more help.
"Do we pay here for the bus?"
"Yes."
"Can we get two bus tickets?"
"Yes."
"How much?"
"Seventy francs each."
"Where is the bus?"
"There." She pointed.

It was a simple conversation, but still hard, and we got through it question by question.

I dared to ask one more question, trying to be sly, using my Midwestern style (which meant that you never ask a direct question). "Is the airport closed at night?"

The older female clerk was not fooled. She replied quickly and tartly: "If you are asking if you can sleep in the airport at night, the answer is yes. The airport is closed and they lock you in, but you can sleep here if you are already in."

Hmm. No fooling her. She saw right through me and addressed our concern just fine. Our return flight would leave at five in the morning in a few weeks, and we knew we weren't going to want to pay for a hotel then.

At the information station, the annoyed lady allowed us to purchase tickets for the bus that went to Chamonix, and we went outside to wait for it. We saw a young couple who looked to be backpackers. They had the normal worn clothing, used backpacks, and cheerful attitude, so we started talking with them. Most people who love the outdoors are willing to share information and experiences, so we started grilling them with questions once we saw a more or less green light to ask.

"Do you know if the water is safe to drink?" was my number one question. We found that the water was all right to drink anywhere along the trail, and often we would find watering holes in different shapes and contraptions along the trail too.

Clutching our backpacks to us, we boarded the bus to Chamonix when it pulled up. It was hard for me to contain my excitement en route to a real adventure in the Alps. This mountain range had held a mystique for me since I'd seen *The Sound of Music* years ago, followed by *The Eiger Sanction*, in which a young Clint Eastwood climbs the hallowed Eiger peak. My quest to experience the Alps had been thriving for decades at this point. Judy and I each took seats near a window so we could soak in the journey—until we were told that we had assigned seats and to look at our tickets. We moved to the back.

The bus took us through the streets of Geneva and by the lake near the center of town. Tall gray buildings lined the litter-free streets. The place reeked of opulence, wealth, and cleanliness. People on the sidewalks included men in three-piece suits and women in dresses and fashionable shoes. I imagined that the people walking the streets looked at Rolex watches on their wrists. The bus went slowly, allowing us to savor the sights.

We'd planned the trip for mid-July for two reasons: the guidebook warned that before July 1, the snows might prohibit passage on the higher passes and some of the refuges might not be open. Additionally, most Europeans take their vacations in August; therefore, the spaces in refuges might be fewer and more valuable if we waited to go later in the summer. As usual, we had made no reservations and planned to wing it.

Eventually the bus made it to the countryside. This early in the summer, and at mountain elevations, the landscape was amazingly green, with wildflowers peeking out here and there. We saw homes that were like none in the US. They were small, wooden or stone, with roofs occasionally made of slate, built on small plots of land. Unique as they were, the most beautiful thing about them was their boxes of flowers in the windows. Usually made of wood, the boxes held begonias, petunias, and other flowers in a multitude of colors. It was truly a feast for our eyes, and a reminder that there was probably a lot of water (as in, *rain* we might have to dodge) in the area.

Having no place to stay in Chamonix turned out to be somewhat of a problem since we arrived on a Saturday. We roamed the streets for almost an hour, wandering into brightly lit, obviously expensive hotels. The prices were more than we wanted to pay, and we probably didn't appear to be their regular customers because of our backpacks and hiking pants. Eventually we located the information booth near the center of town and walked up to it.

The young woman in the booth glanced at us, appraising the situation quickly. We asked for inexpensive hotels or hostels in the area. She told us that it would be hard to find something inexpensive, that the booth mainly dealt with three-, four-, and five-star hotels. We were expecting more help than we were getting. Of course, in hindsight I had to picture us: two older ladies, appearing homeless, with backpacks slung on their shoulders. Then, for whatever reason, she opened up a bit. She told us to try to spot stars as we searched hotel signs and directed us to the back streets of Chamonix. Those hotels with one or two stars were probably what we were searching for. Turns out, she was spot on.

We followed her directions, wandering a bit and exploring the back streets of Chamonix. The town itself is not very large, so wandering the streets was not difficult or dangerous. There were no rats in the back streets of town, as one might imagine when hearing of "back streets." We eventually spotted one star on the front of a hotel that seemed perfectly fine to us. It was not large, appeared clean (instant criteria), and proudly displayed its one star. We walked up to the front desk and asked about a room for the night.

Luckily, they had one, and we were happily surprised when we saw it. With the cheap price we paid (about twenty dollars), we expected less than we got. This room had a window and a nice view, was large, and had its own bathroom. I had heard that in Europe, no one thinks anything of sharing bathrooms. In the States, a communal bathroom would usually be a deal-breaker with travelers. Judy and I learned to be humble and go with the flow as our travels expanded.

The next morning we walked into the restaurant on the first floor of our one-star hotel and waited for breakfast. Breakfast on our Scotland trip had included eggs, toast, stewed tomatoes, juice, and coffee, basically enough for breakfast and lunch. Not so in France. That breakfast never came. The server brought a small plastic basket with about four small slices of a stale baguette plus two cups of coffee. That was it. We ate the bread and sipped our coffee as we waited for the rest of our expected breakfast. Nothing came, *nada*. Eventually I turned around and asked a couple nearby if this was breakfast. Nonchalantly, they simply said yes, but their body language said something more like "Well, of course—what else are you expecting?" Hmm, a quick initiation to a French breakfast.

We finally realized that this was it, breakfast in full. We left the hotel that had befriended us the night before, excited to start our journey, even if a little hungry. We had probably expected too much from our one-star place. We searched for a market to purchase a few things and to eat more before our long hike. Outside, on the cobblestone street, Judy spied a tomato that had just fallen off a produce wagon.

"Pick it up," Judy said.

"Me?" I took a second to make a decision. I gave her a glance, knowing she meant it, shrugged, and walked to the middle of the cobblestone street to retrieve the delicacy. We stuck it in the back of my pack while still trying to find a place to buy yogurt.

The produce stands were small and full of good-looking produce. Oranges, apples, carrots, and even tomatoes were at their best. We bought baguettes, cheese, and small containers of yogurt. These three things would turn out to be staples not only on this journey but for many future journeys too. Often friends would question the yogurt and cheese, because they need refrigeration, but we had discovered that in mountainous areas, these products would last days with no problem. The last thing we needed was to be sick, so we were wary, but adventurous.

Our next step was to get to Les Houches to start our journey for the GR 8, the start of the Tour du Mont Blanc. When we asked questions at the hotel, people directed us to the train station. There was a small-gauge railroad that could take us from Chamonix to Les Houches, or we could also take a bus. We decided to take the train because it was so European. We waited at the station, and thoughts of a Disneyland ride floated through my head.

Both trains were small, on small tracks, and yet here I was on the other side of the world on a similar train. The trip was short, less than half an hour with a stop or two, and we hopped off at the tiny station with a large *Les Houches* sign above it. There were two other passengers who also got off the train, so we begged them to take a picture of us as we started our adventure.

Judy and I were all smiles as we left for our ten-day trip. We were in excellent shape, having climbed many mountains together during the winter season in California and neighboring states. Not even all that mountain climbing had prepared us for the trails and elevation gain and loss of this trip, though. The first day nearly killed me.

As predicted, the weather was rainy, actually drizzling. I had put on a Gore-Tex jacket and rain pants by the time we found the red-and-white sign veering off to the right on a stone wall. Our guidebook told us the first leg of our journey was uphill, and uphill it was. It didn't take long for me to peel off my rain pants. Although it was raining and slippery, it was also fairly warm. Quickly, my Gore-Tex jacket was becoming a tent in which I was roasting. Occasionally the rain was only a mist, so I would take off my jacket and try to dry out. If this was a prelude to our journey, I decided I would suffer and whine silently, if possible.

Note to self: It's hard for you to suffer silently, but maybe it's a lesson you need to learn.

According to our book and Judy's calculations, the first day would involve over five thousand feet of elevation gain if we made it. This was not too much out of my league, but I had a heavy backpack. Judy was always ahead of me, although I caught up to her regularly as she waited for me. We climbed first through small farms with stone houses here and there. The green landscape remained that way as we kept going uphill. The farms became more infrequent as the muddy path led ever higher. We hiked, and we hiked.

We plodded onward and upward, taking breaks when needed. The joy of walking with a friend and not a group is that you can make your own rules. If you want to stop, stop. Judy and I had hiked together a great deal, but it took us a while to figure out our system: Judy, although much shorter than I, hiked faster than I and would often hike ahead then wait for me. Her comforting Tilley hat was often in sight as I rounded most corners.

The trail went past small houses that advertised beer and colas and had small round tables and umbrellas. The table umbrellas seemed to advertise a brand of beer that the stand carried. Each one seemed more and more welcoming as we climbed higher, especially as we subsisted on only our baguettes and coffee. Then they disappeared as we climbed more or less straight up. We stopped on a rock to eat one of our yogurts and some cheese.

After a very long day, we got to the top of the first pass. The trail down was very slippery and steep, not using many switchbacks like we were accustomed to from trails in the US. Eventually we came to a small house with picnic tables, wooden planters with summer flowers in each window, a spring water spout and trough, and inviting Coca-Cola signs. The owner begged us to stop for a drink, and we drank not only water from the spout in front of his house but also a soft drink. Taking off our packs for a short time was heaven. I was pooped, but we were not as far as the book said we were supposed to be by this time in the day. We looked at the book again and decided to do the next five hundred feet of gain to a plateau we could see in the distance. Trekking that last five hundred feet was grueling—more like torture.

We decided to collapse for the night. We had packed a tent that we could share in case there were times when we couldn't make it to the next refuge. Because it was nearly nightfall, we pitched our tent, vowing to get up at daybreak and take it down quickly because camping was generally discouraged. We would beg for forgiveness if we were found.

The next challenge was acknowledging our meager food supply. We made a mental note that night not to forget to pick up more food at the next available place. We ate our stolen tomato, a yogurt, and a little cheese and bread for dinner. I watched Judy as she spooned the yogurt to make sure she didn't get any more than I did. We split the tomato. It was not nearly enough to recoup the calories we'd spent to get there. We could have stayed at our Coke place for the night, but we'd decided not to spend the money. We could hear laughter not too far away, and peeked over a rock to find a refuge only a stone's throw from where we were. We decided to stay camped where we were—although we were very curious about our neighborhood refuge and what it meant to stay there, we were too tired to explore and immediately went to bed in the chill.

The next morning, we were starving. According to our book, we had a four-thousand-foot elevation loss to the next village. We quickly learned that the Tour du Mont Blanc was a journey that traversed seven major valleys as it circled the mountain. Translation: uphill seven times, downhill seven times.

After stealthily stowing our tent the next morning, we passed the refuge we'd heard the night before and then descended into our first little village. The trail was good as we descended into Les Contamines. From a very high elevation, we could see the town below. We knew that there was food there, and we were ready for it.

Eventually we got to the quaint town, sat in the first small outdoor restaurant we found, and ordered the absolutely best club sandwich I have ever had in my life. It was one of their largest sandwiches, filled with wonderful pleasures from the eating world. Round bread (like a small loaf), tomatoes, lettuce, meat—it was great! I almost ordered a second one, but we decided to go into the small grocery store across the street first. We bought more yogurt, cheese, and large loaves of bread.

Most of the grocery stores in these small towns were locally owned and contained fresh bread, produce, and cheese. No large chain stores here. The people of the town were used to buying locally on a daily basis, cooking fresh food. When we walked out of the store, I immediately turned around, went back in, and purchased another loaf of bread. Although I needed to make no apology, I said to Judy, "I can eat an entire loaf of bread before we get out of town." And I did.

Having food helped our journey. We walked outside of town on a small road and then veered off toward another high pass. There were donkeys at the beginning of the uphill portion, available for hire to haul our stuff up the hill. Apparently we could turn them around at the top and tell them to go home. They would come back on their own. It was all very inviting to me, but when I glanced at Judy, she gave me a look that said, *Really?* We lugged our own packs up the pass after I sulked a bit.

We passed a refuge that was bursting with activity and laughter. Why we didn't stop there confounded me, because it was the second stop in the guidebook. Instead, we hiked on down the hill and eventually into a small farm at the bottom. There was water in a small stream, and it looked very inviting. We decided to ask the people in the house if we could set up our tent in their nearby pasture.

I asked the fellow who was sitting outside the farmhouse if he spoke English. He shook his head but called to his wife, who came into the doorway, ready to answer our questions. She spoke very little English, so I used universal sign language. I pointed to Judy, then to myself, put my hands together next to my ear and laid my head on them, and then pointed to the pasture. They got it immediately and burst into laughter. She continued laughing and, with her hand, told us to go ahead and pitch our tent.

The next morning we walked into a tiny town with an *albergue*, like a small bed-and-breakfast. European accommodations are much different from those the States. There is a hierarchy, but we were still discovering that.

After an upscale albergue there are *gîtes*, which are like refuges but usually don't include dinner. Typically, the gîtes are located in towns instead of on the mountainside, as refuges are. Next are *dortoirs*, or hostels with dormitories—bunk beds and nothing else. These are about at the bottom of the list for cheap places to stay in towns because usually no food is included. Next are mountain refuges. These usually have rooms with maybe four to eight bunk beds and a communal bathroom for both men and women. A night at a refuge up in the mountains can include dinner and breakfast. Last, of course, there is camping. We had done that for the first two nights. We typically looked for signs in the town for dortoirs or hostels first, then gîtes. In other European or even South American towns, there may be a sign saying *Room to Let*, which means there is an extra bedroom in someone's house available for a night or two. Also, a pension is an inexpensive place to stay; they are common in South America but can also be found in parts of Europe.

By the third night, after two nights of tent camping, I was ready for a refuge. As we descended a steep trail high in the mountains, we saw the end of a huge glacier and several people on the trail. We could see the refuge at the bottom of the glacier and asked the people we saw if they thought there might be room available for us. They weren't sure because apparently it was crowded. The advantage of traveling with just the two of us was that we didn't require more than two beds. I begged Judy to stay at the refuge, even though it was a little early to stop hiking. It was nestled in the mountains, above the timberline, and the view was spectacular, absolutely breathtaking. We stopped to ask about availability, expecting to find nothing available with all the people milling about.

We were lucky to find accommodations. Two bunk beds were available in a room with two other bunk beds. Soon after we walked into our room for the night, two young women from France opened the door, and we met our roommates for the night. Over the next week, we would pass and be passed by these two amazing French ladies until we ended in Chamonix again.

I took a very welcome shower. There was a stall with a dispenser for money, and showers were about one dollar for three minutes, but they were so worth it. We found out that dinner was served about seven o'clock typically, and this refuge was no different.

We'd basically had nothing to eat for the past two days, had hiked up about ten thousand feet on empty stomachs, and were therefore exceptionally hungry. The dining hall had about five very long wooden tables with benches to seat as many people as possible. Well before seven, all the seats were taken. I could hear many languages being spoken as people from all over the world gathered at the common tables to eat together.

We passed jugs of wine around, and each person was to keep a tab on what they owed for the free-flowing wine. At about three dollars per glass, it was a bargain. When the first course arrived, Judy and I each took a huge helping of spaghetti with marinara sauce. We ate voraciously, completing the plateful quickly. Then the main course arrived: pork chops. Then came vegetables, potatoes, salad, and even dessert. We quickly learned that refuges produced the most amazing meals of all time, and we adapted our eating methods in the future so we always had room for dessert. Or at least I did.

The next day our spirits soared as we left the little compound and hiked down the trail. With food, sleep, and new friends, all was well with the world. Wildflowers were sprouting all over the high country, and I had to restrain myself from collecting them.

That day we hiked over the highest pass on the trip, one dividing France and Italy. As usual, we gathered friends along the way and we passed them at our turtle pace, then they passed us as we stopped beside small streams, and so on. We were lucky to have lunch at a junction with a view before we turned off to go over the pass. At the pass, we met a band of young folks, mostly teenagers, who were on an adventure with a leader. The leader was a handsome young man who had worked in the deserts of Arizona with young people who were on the wrong path in their lives. Apparently if one ran away from the facility, the most likely result was to die in the desert before any help could be reached. Not many ran away, and many apparently were helped.

This group was more like an Outward Bound trip, teens from the US who wanted an adventure away from the influence of parents. Of course, mastering hiking and summiting passes on the trail were incredible accomplishments for the young folks, and they were mighty proud of themselves. We all struggled up the highest pass on the trail, going slowly to gain the needed elevation. Once on top, the joy was obvious. Judy became a camera tree and I a photographer, meaning she held about twenty-five cameras on her arms and neck as I took many pictures of the group with each of their cameras for their everlasting record of the event. Then their leader took our obligatory picture with the cement marker showing we were now at the top of the pass, leaving France and entering Italy.

Note to self: You could be these kids' grandmother. Accept the admiration.

The day was perfect. Blue sky, warm sun, a magnificent panorama, and lots of people. We gasped when we saw bicycles. While we were lugging our packs and bodies up the French side of the trail, several young Italian men were bringing mountain bicycles up the trail on the Italian side of the pass, only to turn around and ride them back down while trying not to hit hikers. Then there was a Japanese crew who had pack animals bringing their supplies with them. Judy and I stared at them when we saw one of them in a full ski suit and large, bulky boots. He was sweating so much that it worried us.

I had on my meager layers of clothes: long nylon pants that zipped off should I get very hot, hiking boots and socks, then a shirt to keep off my sweat, and a long-sleeved nylon shirt to keep the sun off my arms. Once hiking, it was enough to wear just a layer or two, even at high altitudes, because of the work involved in hiking and carrying the damned pack. I learned to keep a lightweight fleece shirt and lightweight jacket close at hand should the weather turn colder, and never to keep them in the bottom of my pack. Dressed the way we were, at least we appeared as if we belonged here, whereas the Japanese hikers were dressed like they belonged on mountain ski slopes.

We hiked past farm buildings, small rock buildings with slate roofs, and fields of sheep, cows, and goats. The cows wore large metal bells that rang in the wind. Not every cow had a bell, but the larger animals had awesomely large bells so their location was easy to find. More than once, we would sit on a rock to rest and just listen to all the variations of the cowbells. One Sunday, it became our church, looking at the wildflowers, laughing with each other, and hearing the cowbells.

We hiked into the town of Courmayeur in Italy. Where the trail became a road near the town, we had an option to take a bus into town or to continue walking. We continued walking as a busload of teens waved to us as they passed us. We were the real troupers.

Walking on the pavement, especially the small winding roads, was different and not in a good way. The pavement was hot, cars sped past us, and it was harder on my feet than the dirt trail. We decided we didn't particularly like being on the pavement, but we still wanted to continue on foot rather than hitch a ride in a bus or car.

Making it into town was long and tedious, but necessary. We could see glaciers high on the mountains around town and even watched as a glacier created an avalanche, in the distance, high on the mountain. Usually we could hear a crack when an avalanche started, and then we'd try to locate it in the mountains. Sometimes we saw them as we were safely eating ice cream in a small town.

Courmayeur was surprisingly upscale. People were dressed up—well, certainly better dressed than we were. During the winter, this is the jet-set place to go for skiing. We found a café that had service outside, and we sat down at a little table with a black umbrella. It wasn't easy for us to maneuver our backpacks somewhere near us, and others in the restaurant gave us a stare I interpreted as, *What do you think you are doing, not dressing up, having these large packs, and appearing like you haven't bathed in days? I hope you don't sit too close to me.*

After lunch we wandered around town, and in front of the church, on a large table, were crafts from South America. Judy knew we were in trouble when she saw the display, knowing how much I like crafts. Kind soul that she is, after she made a small purchase, she sat down in a comfortable seat to people-watch and to enjoy the day.

I, on the other hand, was having a panic, anxiety, or craft attack. Apparently the church had partnered with a church in South America to sell handmade crafts in Europe, where the items would fetch a much higher price. To me, it wasn't that much of a higher price. Items such as plastic bag holders and glasses cases were displayed. Of course there were dozens of each type of item to choose from, each with a unique design. I was in craft heaven. As usual, I had to study each piece. Though it would seem like these were irreplaceable, expensive items, they were not really valuable objects—more like five-dollar things. I turned each one over and over. I couldn't decide which plastic bag holder to buy. Both items were made of burlap and designed with hand-stitched embroidery. You would think they were made of gold, the way I agonized. I couldn't discern if it was my quirky personality or menopause that caused my indecision.

"Should I get this one, or this one?" I asked Judy. She shook her head and shrugged, saying nonverbally, *I don't know and don't care.*

Then I started handling the glasses cases too. I fondled them, turning them over and over to see the craftsmanship on each one. These were typical South American work, and the craftsmanship, although wonderful, wasn't particularly spectacular. I found one that had a purple back (my favorite color) with two belt straps. On the front was a visual story that told so very much about the person who made the pouch. Mountains were in the background, with a turquoise sky and very yellow sun. Condors and a raven speckled the sky, with cactus, bushes, and a cow dotting the mountains and foreground. Most interesting, however, was the family portrayed. A man fed yellow ducks while a child was collecting eggs. To complete the picture, a woman was weaving, with her loom attached to a tree. All in all, it appeared to be an idyllic life, happy and sunny.

Why was I having trouble making a decision? Was I jealous of a happy, idyllic life? I finally came to the conclusion that no, that was too big an idea to wrap my head around. It wasn't my longing that was the problem, but my indecision. Judy can attest that I spent a solid hour making my ten-dollar purchase. The lessons learned here were blame it on menopause and relish a friend's patience.

We decided to hike longer that day so we could get to a small refuge in the hills above town where our smells and appearance wouldn't matter. We managed to get lost in the hills, and after our trail became more and more faint, we decided to retrace our steps. Tired as we were, having lost about forty-five minutes of precious time when we could have been resting, we found the main trail again and eventually made our way to our refuge. This time we were two of about twenty sleeping in a large dorm room. It wasn't exactly quiet, but it was a cheap bed. Fortunately the snoring wasn't too bad among the group. Besides, I had learned from my dog sledding adventure to bring earplugs.

We hiked into Switzerland soon, and the rates for everything rose. Still, we were in the mountains, so there were few choices and prices were not nearly what they would have been in a large Swiss city. As we passed more small homes that offered Coca-Cola and tea, we stopped more frequently. It was a good business practice for us to support the local economy, and it just plain gave us a much-needed break.

In one town I had to sit and drink a large liter bottle of Coca-Cola just to restore the liquid my body needed. I could no longer move my legs, and my body told me that. Judy and I rested for over an hour since we owned our schedule. A stop here and there for fresh mozzarella cheese balls and bread were more and more welcome the farther we got on our journey. As I was drinking my Coke, Judy started reading the guidebook to me. She read something like, "Go to the church, turn right, and proceed up the dirt trail about two thousand feet of elevation gain, and eventually you will see the hostel in the distance, a few kilometers across the French border. You cannot stop to camp on the trail because it is too rugged and overgrown." Then she added, "Oh, there's an interesting note here: The innkeeper of the refuge is a little rough around the edges after years of service there—beware."

Judy looked at me after reading the passage and asked, "Do you think you can make it?"

I didn't answer quickly. No longer was I the Energizer Bunny that Judy was. She knew how to coax me but was always respectful of my decisions. "Well, let's give it a try. I would rather stay in a hostel than here in town. And someone can step over me if I have to sleep on the trail." I slurped the last of my Coke. "I wonder what they mean about the innkeeper?"

We started up the "overgrown" hill, and I realized that there really was very little place to sleep except right on the trail. It was early evening, and there would probably be no other hikers that day, so I would be fine with sleeping on the trail if needed.

Eventually we made it to the top of the hill. I was really pooped and ready to stop for the night, but there was nothing to see there—no refuge, only darkness creeping in at about eight in the evening. Judy was in front, as always, and finally exclaimed, "I think I see it! Can you see it way up there at the top of the hill?"

Oh joy, what the heck is she staring at? I saw nothing and started squinting.

"But it's really up there—I can see it!" Judy said. "Can you make it?"

I turned my eyes uphill again, squinting more until I saw something that appeared to be a big rock in the distance. "Oh, sure I can make it. But I will be an hour behind you," I said, just to make sure she knew I wasn't happy about it.

We trudged for another hour, saw a sign that we were entering France, and finally, about nine o'clock, arrived at the remote refuge. We took off our heavy packs in front of several young German hikers who had stopped talking when we arrived. They were astonished to see us pull in that late. Soon, however, they broke into smiles to see us old ladies arrive. Quickly they offered to bring in our packs, but then they abruptly set them down when they realized how heavy they were. Their glances were full of *I can't believe you carry such heavy packs!* The packs were too heavy, especially for me. They contained tents, cooking gear, cold weather clothing—heck, everything to make sure we could survive any circumstance.

Walking into the front room, we encountered a tall, old reception desk. We only had to wait a minute before our questionable innkeeper came out. We had to remember that dinner was normally served at seven, and it was now nine. *No chance for dinner. Just beg for a bed.*

Note to self: Be nice.

I STARTED MY SIGN LANGUAGE ROUTINE. I POINTED TO JUDY AND THEN myself, put my hands together by my ear to indicate I wanted a bed for us for tonight. The innkeeper just shook her head quickly and looked stern. She seemed as if she had been born a hundred years ago in the refuge, and it was her domain—she owned it and made the rules. I started again with a sign for *please* and repeated the routine. She repeated her routine. Finally she asked one of the young German hikers to help us interpret, appearing annoyed that we could not communicate. I told the hiker that we just needed a bed for the night and would love breakfast in the morning.

The interpreter told the innkeeper in French what I wanted, and the innkeeper immediately started shaking her head. I lost hope. More French was exchanged between the innkeeper and the hiker. Then the hiker turned to me and said, "She said if you stay here, you must eat *dinner and* breakfast." Oh my! I was just trying to be kind and get a bed-and-breakfast. She was offering us dinner also, even though it was hours past dinnertime. I could have kissed her—and I would have if I'd thought I wouldn't be slapped. Maybe she was taking mercy on us older women. We smiled broadly and nodded to say *Yes!*, then gladly paid the twenty-five-dollar equivalent for the room and meals.

We sat at a small wooden table in the small dining room. Curtains on the wooden windows showed whimsical designs, welcoming everyone. The wooden-framed windows were beautiful next to the stone-and-cement building. First, the helper brought us a salad, which we devoured. It was so very good, fresh, and made with loving hands. The kind innkeeper came out to laugh at us, as if to say, *I thought you weren't hungry!* I replied silently to myself, *I didn't say we weren't hungry. I didn't want to trouble you since it was so late!*

We continued with an omelet, bread, and fruit for dessert. I could have cried, I was so happy to be eating after such a long, long day. We had been on the trail for over twelve hours, so any reason to stop, eat, and sleep was welcomed.

The bunk bed situation, however, was something else. Apparently this French refuge had not been upgraded for a long time. Judy and I had been taking turns for who had to sleep on the top bunk, dealing with the challenge of climbing up and down, and it was Judy's turn. But when she climbed up this time, I realized she was the lucky one instead of me. When I laid on the bottom bed, I could see deadly metal prongs protruding several inches from each of the ties in the spring of the upper bunk. If Judy got frisky and somehow dislodged the bedspring so it would fall, a dozen prongs would descend on me, and surely one of them would find a fatal spot to embed itself. I took a deep breath, looked at the bedspring, and imagined seeing the sky. Silently, I said,

Universe, if ever you need to look after me, make it be tonight. And don't let Judy toss too much in bed.

I awoke the next morning feeling grand that I was alive and not mutilated, and we enjoyed a hearty breakfast with the German hikers and others. We continued hiking on regular trails without difficulty until about six in the afternoon, when the trail suddenly got very, very steep, with larger rocks to navigate. It was then that we saw the cables.

We had chosen the shorter trail for this leg instead of the longer one, and now we knew why the longer one was suggested—it didn't involve a cliff. Nearby, we saw several young men rock climbing, practicing their skills. I yelled out to one of them, "Is this the Tour du Mont Blanc trail?"

He replied, "Yes, just follow the cables."

By this time at night, I was pooped, so I decided to use my old lady routine and said, "Would you mind spotting us?" Spotting someone means that you stand underneath someone and help them make decisions as they ascend, hoping no one makes a misstep and splats onto you. It made me feel more secure to have someone below me. He agreed, luckily, and came over to help.

He came below us and pointed out the way with the cables there to use for handholds on the route up, which included a few small wood-and-cable bridges. I felt it was a bit gnarly for me this late in the day, but there was little choice except to go up. We still had light for our journey, so after a few moments of protest, I started up with my pack. The footholds were only inches wide, and I prayed my feet stayed on the ground while I clung to the cables. I made it straight up one cliff, over a bridge to another, and held on for dear life at the last one, which took me to the top of the ridge. Judy navigated the whole thing just behind me.

As we rounded the ridge, a head popped up—not human, but an animal I hadn't expected. It had the curved horn of a bighorn sheep attached to a body of what looked like a domestic sheep. It peered at us for a long time and then ambled off. I researched the animal eventually and decided it must be a chamois, a goat-antelope type of animal found in European mountain ranges. It was helping us celebrate our accomplishment.

That night we pitched our tent along the trail, considering it a room with a view since it looked out on the mountains and Chamonix—spectacular. One more night in a hostel above Chamonix, followed by a wrong choice on trails that led to extra time, and we were back at our railroad station in Les Houches to return to Chamonix. We had completed the trip in nine and a half days.

In the Geneva airport, Judy slept on the floor as I nervously remained seated upright all night. True to the clerk's word, the airport was locked up after midnight and we found ourselves surrounded by other homeless souls. After several such adventures, I'd discovered that Judy could sleep anywhere, anytime. She had lost her mom instinct—the one that makes you a light sleeper in case anyone needs protecting—and would have been able to sleep through a fireworks display or bombs exploding, in my opinion.

About four in the morning, a Zamboni appeared. Because I had ice-skated as a kid, I recognized the machine as an ice groomer, important when kids who didn't know what they were doing roughed up the ice while skating. Quickly, I realized it was there to clean the floors, made of some conglomerate material, and it was headed for Judy. I didn't know whether to make a mad dash for her to wake her before she became polished with this machine or to let what was going to unfold just happen.

Selfishly, I waited to see what would happen. The young driver was used to all the people around, so he turned sharply just before he got to Judy and went around her, getting back on course after her five-foot detour. I started shaking my head. Judy had no idea what had just happened.

Other than that, we made it home safely and without incident.

Note to self: This was a lesson in self-sustainability. You self-sustained—and thrived to boot.

CHAPTER 9

Dolomites

AT HOME IN LOS ANGELES, I SPENT MY WEEKS IN MY COMFORTABLE-ENOUGH human resources job, hiked on the weekends, lived cheap to save money for travel, and persistently planned my next international adventure.

Italy's Dolomites were third on Judy's and my list, following the Alps and the French Pyrenees. It was almost as if I was on a quest to fit in all the amazing mountainous areas in the world before I kicked the bucket. I wanted to complete my bucket list first.

As we were landing in Venice on our way to the Dolomites, I giggled when I remembered landing during our trip to the French Pyrenees the previous year. "What do you think about over there?" I'd asked Judy. We'd had our faces plastered on the airplane windows, looking at the rural countryside near Pau, France, as we were landing. We kept our eyes on the ground to see if there was any place we could pitch a tent near the airport on the night before our departure. This was a rural area, and we saw no reason why we couldn't camp the night before leaving France. We were also being cheap. We spotted a cornfield adjacent to but just north of the airport where we could stealthily camp on our return to the area if we were brave enough.

At the end of the Pyrenees trip, when we hailed a cab in downtown Pau and asked the driver to take us to the airport, he said, "Well, what time are you leaving?"

I blurted out, without thinking, "Well, we're actually leaving in the morning."

"Then, which hotel shall I take you to for the night?"

I realized my mistake and said, "Well, just take us to the airport for now, please!"

"But there are no hotels close to the airport." He seemed puzzled and continued, "Well, I might as well take you where you are staying instead of you making several trips."

I thought for a minute and replied, "Well, for now, we're just going to the airport. We have to take care of some business," leaving him little room for more questions.

Apparently two attempts to make us see the light were all he needed. He dropped us at the small, quiet airport. We walked nonchalantly inside, set our packs down, and sat in chairs for a minute to look at each other, to laugh, and to figure out our next step. Shortly after our break, we put on our packs once again and headed outside to the cornfields we had spotted several weeks earlier. We'd scoped out the possibilities of camping for free and weren't going to let go of those possibilities.

We walked to the back of the airport buildings to see how far the cornfields were from the airport itself. We could see them easily, so that meant the possibilities were endless. Trying to be invisible with large packs on our backs wasn't going to be easy, though. We had to take the chance—either we would or would not be caught. Besides, it was kind of fun to bend the rules. We had enough life experience that we certainly had earned the right to try, or at least we had a good excuse for our boldness.

With our packs on, we walked down a dirt road that led into the field for a short distance. Judy found a perfect place in the middle of the dirt road, plopped her pack down, and said, "Well, this spot in the road seems good to me."

I thought about it for a minute. "Let's think about this. We are in the middle of a dirt road, in the middle of a cornfield, in the middle of a remote farm, on a Friday night. If I were a teenager with a boyfriend, this is just where I would come on a Friday night. What if kids come out here, they've been drinking and are driving, and they may not be able to identify the lumps on the road in sleeping bags as something alive? I mean, we could be flattened by a truck. Let's move off the road."

We found what was basically a cul-de-sac in the dirt road and set up our tent. I said, "Goodnight, Judy!" and fell asleep, eventually forgetting about my safety. We slept well, miraculously without incident or being squashed, and made it to the airport the next morning in plenty of time. No one was the wiser about two old women spending the night in the cornfield next to the airport in this small French town.

Note to self: Aunt Bertie would have approved.

NOW, WE WERE LANDING IN VENICE WITHOUT ANY OPPORTUNITY TO SLEEP in a cornfield, and as we'd soon find out, without our backpacks. I mean, we landed just fine, but our backpacks were nowhere to be found. After a few conversations that consisted mainly of us showing our luggage tags to some luckless fellow who happened to be forced to help us, we were told that the luggage was on its way in a few hours and the airline would be happy to bring it to our hotel. We had no hotel. We tried to explain the situation, but it all seemed puzzling to the fellow helping us. We finally were able to convey that we would simply wait at the airport for the luggage to come. The fellow just shrugged his shoulders behind the counter and we settled in for a nap.

After our luggage arrived about two a.m., we slept at the airport for the rest of the night and, as soon as daylight came, hopped on a train that took us to the Dolomites, the most northern mountain range in the country. We decided not to do the *via ferrata* (iron path) routes because they involved climbing gear, iron chains, and scariness. Apparently, the Italians had built fixed iron cables that men could hold on to while navigating routes over the Dolomite Mountains before and during World War I. The cables could carry men and supplies over the routes, but you wouldn't find me carrying anything awkward or heavy there.

Our first day on the GR route from Bolzano in Italy was hot and therefore hard for me, of course. It wasn't a tough route, but as usual, I had not taken the time or made the effort to get into great shape for the trip. Our overseas trips usually occurred each summer, and Judy and I both worked around what our companies would or wouldn't allow concerning time off. Although we often mountain climbed in the desert during the winter, it wasn't uncommon to not hike for a month or two at a time. The older I got, the harder it was to rebuild my fitness level, and the less likely I was to convince myself to hike before leaving.

Along our route were World War I historical viewpoints where men had been stationed to spot enemies. These were tiny stony barricades where men had spent the winter, probably freezing with little or no heat. We were able to go into them and really understand what a wretched spot it would be in the middle of winter.

At some point after World War I, tourists discovered the trails. The rest is history. The routes are very popular, whether climbing the fixed iron chains or trekking as we did. In general, we wanted to hike near the German and Austrian border to get a broad view of just what the Dolomites are.

As we talked with others on the trail, we learned about an area where Italy, Germany, and Austria meet and a unique language is spoken because of the remoteness of the high valleys. The language is a blend between Latin and languages in the area and is still spoken. According to the Lonely Planet guidebook we used for this trip, it is called Ladin. We were able to hike to one refuge in this area and sign up to stay in hopes of hearing some of the language. It really would not have mattered, however, because we couldn't speak French, German, or Italian, so we wouldn't have recognized it anyhow.

This particular refuge was cute, with friendly staff who welcomed us. Made primarily of wood, probably pine or fir, it appeared to be like a mountain chalet with flowers all around. The tables were set up individually for groups of two or four—groups of whoever showed up at the table for dinner. We laughed, passed the food, and got to know the others at the table. Not that Judy and I were sick of each other, but we welcomed company from other parts of the world to talk with and learn from.

Eventually Judy and I started talking about edelweiss. We had wanted to see some and talked about its shape, not that either of us had a clue. Not long after that, a young man leaned over the top of our booth and said, "You know, there is a ton of edelweiss right outside here, on the hillside in front of the refuge."

My mouth fell open, and I immediately started asking him questions: "What does it look like? Can you show us where it is? Can you take us to see it?" Ever since I'd heard *The Sound of Music*'s song about edelweiss, I had wanted to see it. Plus, I had heard that it was disappearing.

He answered, "White, low to the ground, and yes, yes."

After dinner the young man and his girlfriend followed us out of the refuge and pointed to a low-lying hill to the left of the cabin. Even though it was the middle of summer, I worried that the sun would go down before I saw edelweiss. The young man walked on the grass, which sank like a sponge under his weight. The hillside was lush, green, and dotted with many different flowers. I pointed to a white flower, and the young man shook his head. I spotted another one and pointed. No, again.

He stopped and pointed to a flower about the size of a quarter that appeared as if it grew right out of the ground. When I got closer, I could see that there were two white flowers with thick, velvety leaves of green. The flowers were fuzzy also, an off-white color, and very beautiful. I was told that these flowers were found only in special areas of the Alps, and it was a blessing to see them at all. These little plants only grow in areas between approximately 6,500 to 9,500 feet, and as the planet heats up, they may lose their cool mountain climate. Additionally, they are used in cosmetics and picked in the wild occasionally. They must have liked the environment there, because they were everywhere.

We continued our hike all over the mountains, on a loop route so we didn't have to repeat our steps, and eventually made our way to Cortina. We put our packs down and sat at a restaurant where we ordered homemade ravioli and lemon sorbet with seven different kinds of berries on it for dessert. After sharing both, we ordered a second dessert. This became our all-time favorite restaurant, and this dessert would be one that we would always order.

From Cortina, we caught a train to Venice. It would be a fitting end to our journey in the city of incredible charm and history.

The railroad car took us right to Venice, coming in next to several other trains on parallel tracks. We got off our train, still grubby from a fourteen-day backpacking trip. Although we'd had a good night's sleep, I'm sure our bodies, clothes, and backpacks smelled like all the dirt and grime that we'd come in contact with.

The first order of business was to find a place to stay overnight. Next order of business would be to find lemon gelato or sorbet to treat ourselves after our hiking journey. We looked at each other, silently saying, *What now? Where do you think we should go?* Understanding our silent body language, we looked around, to get oriented and to figure out our next step as best we could.

We spotted a big *I* on top of a small information stall. There was a line of probably thirty people waiting for whatever information was available. We reluctantly got in line and resigned ourselves to waiting.

Note to self: A lesson of patience here.

WE WERE TIRED AND READY FOR DECISIONS TO BE MADE FOR US. WHILE we talked about our options, I felt a presence. I glanced in front of me and saw a man approaching with a brochure in his hand. He appeared a bit scruffy, but not homeless. He had a smile on his face, a shirt on his back, and a friendly hand outstretched to me. I knew it was a setup but waited to make any judgment call until I could see what he wanted or offered. My red flag signal was at half-mast.

The middle-aged, potbellied man approached us and simply asked, "You ladies need a room tonight?"

My guard up, I gave Judy a quick glance to get her nonverbal take on the situation. She didn't give me any signal, which was fairly normal because she often left decisions such as this to me. I turned to the man and said very simply, "Yes."

He handed us a color brochure and said he had a room available for the night if we wanted it. It had a private bath and two twin beds, and it appeared clean in the picture.

My immediate question was "How much?"

He replied, "Forty dollars for two." That was a bargain in this tourist town where rooms normally ran $200 and up. Another trust-the-universe scenario was about to unfold.

With that decision made, he motioned for us to follow him. We did, after he tried to silently verify that we were going forward with the deal and following this person we didn't know. We really weren't sure about this one, but we were used to people approaching us to get us to stay at their places, so this should be no different. A short distance from the information booth, he turned around and said, "I'll need some money for the water taxi because it is a little distance away, and that is the shortest way there."

That should have been a signal that there might be a problem, but we had mentally decided that all would probably be just fine. Since it was the middle of the day, we could scream loudly if necessary, and we could probably claw like angry cats. Always trust two old women to be able to really scream when necessary and to put up a fight. Don't mess with us.

We handed him the equivalent of about five dollars for the water taxi and followed him on the crowded boat. He pulled out a map of Venice, showing us where we were and where we were going. One of our missions in Venice was to find the Jewish Ghetto, an almost five-hundred-year-old place famous in Venetian history and also in Shakespeare's *The Merchant of Venice*. We wanted to replace Judy's eighty-year-old friend's glass rabbi that had broken, and she had bought the original in Venice, in the Jewish neighborhood. Our guide pointed toward the back of the city on the map, locating a remote but accessible area in Venice. He said it was easy to walk to the area and that it was off the beaten tourist track. That was fine with us because we loved to explore areas where locals go. We would be in Venice for two nights, so we needed areas to explore. I was liking and trusting our guide more and more.

The three of us got off the water taxi and started walking, following our guide like ducklings. Tourists were everywhere on the main streets, so my intuition antenna didn't go up. We walked through the crowds and eventually started down an alley. Then my instinct antenna perked up a bit. The streets of Venice were tiny, with very tall buildings extending above the first-floor shops and upper-floor housing. Several of the second floors of the buildings protruded a few feet over the street, making the alleys even darker. We wandered through the alleys, following our guide. I looked up at the little sky I could see and reminded myself: *This will probably not be the day you will be raped and murdered.*

At the end of the dark alley, our guide turned to the right and rang a doorbell beside an unmarked large gray door. The stucco building entrance was stark, with no distinguishing markings, no signs like any hotel would have. There was a step or two going to the door, and the door was behind a screen door with a large lock on it. A buzzer sounded, and I could hear a sound of someone unlocking the door from somewhere in the building. Inside, my stomach was starting to turn circles. We followed our guide in and walked up a narrow flight of stairs to the second floor.

At the top of the landing, to our left, was a tiny desk with a man standing behind it. In Italian, he nodded and then said hello to our guide as he bowed his head to us and extended his hand to indicate for us to follow him down another small hallway. So far, there was nothing to worry about, although Judy and I stayed close to each other. He opened the door to our potential room, and, lo and behold, it was just as described in the brochure. It had two beds, a tiny, tiny bathroom with a tiny, tiny shower stall, and it was clean. It was forty dollars, as stated, per night. We paid for two nights with smiles. We weren't going to be a story in tomorrow's newspapers after all.

Judy and I both slept soundly, and safely, and then awoke to a new day full of discovery and a mission: the Jewish Ghetto. Apparently the area we were seeking was in the nontouristy area of Venice, and the way there first followed a river then the canals, not easy navigating. In reality, it was kind of like a treasure hunt. We looked at our map to get a clue about where we were going. We wound through narrow streets, probably along former ancient cow paths, and through walkways and doorways. We were walking farther and farther away from the tourist area, although the area we were traveling through was not really scary or run-down. It wasn't uncommon for us to point to the map and ask locals for directions. Without exception, they helped us even if they didn't speak English. I was good at pointing, and so were the locals. We hiked for over an hour and found streets along canals with few people on them. Those we did encounter seemed to be local folks, and the shops were not catering to tourists but to local needs.

Eventually we entered a low doorway that led to a large courtyard. We quickly realized that we had found our mission location: the Jewish Ghetto. We knelt to go through the doorway, saw a few other tourists at this famous location, wandered past several small local stores, and then turned to each other and grinned. There, in front of us, was the glassmaker, with several handmade rabbis in the store window. Of course, once inside there was another decision: which one to purchase for Judy's friend. I decided the best way to decide was to ask the owner, "Which is the most popular?" He brought one to us, and while Judy made her decision, I surveyed the store. Everything in the store was handblown glass and beautiful. I decided on a small necklace with a glass pendant. Judy and I smiled at each other and checked off that mission.

My mission was to buy a pair of good Italian scissors. I had made quilts for many years, did sewing as necessary, and for some reason wanted a good pair of small, pretty Italian scissors. I didn't really expect to find my special scissors, but we kept our eyes open as we left the Jewish Ghetto and walked near the waterway again, where local stores lined the meager street. Not having to dodge any cars or tourists was a gift we enjoyed. We passed hardware stores, small grocery stores, and eventually we came to my mission location: a fabric store. There in the window, a small box caught my eye. It contained two beautifully matched scissors, a pair, mostly gold with silver blades. I had to have them.

A young clerk took them from the window for me, and fortunately they were a reasonable price. I'm sure a store in the tourist area would have doubled or tripled the price. I prided myself for finding this in a local store, giving the merchant a fair but not inflated price. In Italy there is no bargaining for prices like there is in many other countries, so the no-haggle atmosphere made it easy to make (or not make) purchases. The only other purchase I made was at a kitchen store somewhere, where a knife and fork with pretty handles caught my attention.

After dipping our toes in the Mediterranean, eating lemon sorbet from about four different stands so we could make a comparison, and walking the tourist routes along the canals, Judy and I ate dinner. Being in Venice has a charm like no other place we had visited, so we decided to walk along the canals at night. We went on ancient stone bridges, tiny overpasses for the canals. We could stop on any of them and watch the gondolas below us taking lovers, friends, families, and who knows who else on boat rides. Each guide had a huge, long paddle to keep the boat going and to steer it around obstacles. Usually it was a man who was guiding the boat, pushing it along the canal while those above watched and the passengers settled into the boat's hull. The boat guide was also expected to sing to his passengers. It would have been fun to evaluate each one musically, but there was too much else to do.

While we were stopped on one bridge watching boats in the lazy canal below, we heard music. All over Venice we'd encountered signs for local concerts. There were small events with ensembles, quartets, and larger symphonies advertised everywhere. I glanced to a nearby open window and saw a small ensemble, about eight players, playing Mozart. From our vantage point, through the window that was open about twelve inches, I spotted a violinist, cellist, and viola player, all dressed in formal black and white, all playing and smiling, clearly loving the music they were playing.

They played the melodies perfectly and warmly sent them to everyone, even us interlopers outside. Judy and I sat on the stone wall as others gathered around us in the calm evening air to listen to the music. I made a mental note that snatches of incredible beauty such as this moment are to be savored and never forgotten. No photograph or video would do it justice.

The next day, we took a water taxi and train back to the airport. Our plan was to spend the night in the airport since we needed to catch a 6:00 a.m. flight. By this time, we were no longer asking permission but just assumed it would be all right for us to stay at the airport. If not, we would just plead ignorance and go to plan B, whatever that was.

We got to the airport in late afternoon, with plenty of time to eat dinner there that evening. We had no idea if there would be anything more than vending machines, but it was our choice. We always had granola bars of some kind, though our supply by this point in the trip was dwindling.

The first thing we usually did when we got to an airport was to find a cart to put our luggage on. In Europe, the carts are free, whereas in the US they usually are expensive to rent. After unloading our trusty backpacks onto a cart that we could push all night, we went on a mission to find food. We found a cafeteria, and it appeared just fine to us.

The next order of business was to review our funds. As was our practice, we were just about out of money by this time. Sometimes there is a fee to exit a country, but at this time there was no fee to exit Italy. I took out my remaining money, surveyed the menu, decided that I could afford a little food and a split (about half a bottle) of wine. Judy could do the same. We got our food and precious wine and sat down to eat.

Halfway through the meal, and all the way through our wine, I asked Judy, "How much money do you have left?"

She squinted and instead of asking why, she said, "About the equivalent of two dollars."

"Let's pool our money and get another full bottle of wine."

Judy reached into her pocket and gave me all the Italian money she had left. I bought another bottle of Italian wine, and we started on it while we finished our dinner.

We finished our meal and the next bottle of wine easily. As we were talking, a couple at the end of our long table caught my eye. They were getting ready to leave, and I spotted half a bottle of wine on the table where they had been sitting. This was Italy, land of cheap and plentiful wine, so it doesn't mean too much to leave wine on a table. I kept my eye on it while they got up to leave.

As the person bussing tables came over to that area, I got up and snatched the bottle, bringing it back to our table. We had nothing left to do that night except drink wine, so drink wine we did. We finished our two splits of wine, our full bottle, and the half bottle so generously donated by our wine patrons at the end of the table. We were totally soused and knew it. We also knew that we couldn't act drunk because the security officers might not be very kind to us. That led to our next dilemma.

We found a place to sleep, albeit not too comfortable. In most European airports, there are not a lot of good sleeping chairs. Sometimes there is a bar between the seats, or sometimes there are just chairs and nothing longer than the expanse of one chair. Judy is much shorter than I, so she finds more ideal sleeping situations than I do.

Judy was, again, sound asleep while I struggled a bit to get as comfortable as I could in an awkward set of three chairs. *At least I'm not on the floor*, I thought. I had just settled down and fallen into some kind of sleep when I felt a poke on my shoulder. I woke quickly and found a security officer staring at me. It was about one o'clock in the morning.

"I need to see your boarding pass," he said. I got up, fumbled a bit, and handed him my passport and ticket reservation. He handed it back to me and said nothing more than, "She with you?"

I looked at Judy, then back at him and said, "Uh-huh."

He said, "I need to see her boarding pass also."

"We are traveling together."

He did nothing more than stare at me. I scooted over to Judy, poked her, and said, "I need your passport and ticket information."

She was groggy but was able to find her passport and eventually her information folder showing her flight without saying a word. I was downright proud of her because our drunken state wasn't showing. Apparently the security officer was satisfied and let us stay in the airport because our flight would be leaving at 6:00 a.m. We were getting bolder with each trip.

We had two young neighbors sleeping in the same airport gate who weren't so lucky. Judy immediately went back to sleep, and I watched as the security officer asked our neighbors for their tickets. Their flight was leaving at one o'clock the next afternoon, and he told them they had to leave the airport. I imagined myself in their place and thought I would just spend the night outside the airport and pray that no one pounced on me in the middle of the night.

The next morning, Judy and I were in the check-in line at about four thirty. We checked our backpacks and had small daypacks with our stuff of importance to take on the plane. I had just gotten to the inside security line when an extremely nice fellow in charge of security said to me, "You know, the US doesn't like—probably won't let you bring in this kitchen knife and fork through security."

I said, "Oh, I didn't pay much for them. Just take them."

He continued, "Well, that would be okay, but I think your government would *really* not like you bringing in these two pairs of scissors."

Oh my goodness, I'd forgotten that I had my prized scissors with me and had not packed them in my backpack. It was normal for me to take any prized purchases on the plane with me. The only thing I really wanted to bring back with me was a good pair of Italian-made scissors.

I turned to him, thanking him so much for finding everything, and waved frantically to Judy, who had made it through the line. Our time to board the plane was getting closer.

"I have to check some more things," I tried to yell and make her understand. I was panicked and made my way back to the ticket counter where there were what seemed to be a thousand people in line. I was desperate to keep my scissors.

I made my way to the front of the line and pleaded with an unsympathetic agent to please, please check my scissors and knife/fork set.

He stared at me with the expression, *Here's yet another crazy American.* He said, "You don't have enough here to check in this plastic bag. There must be more in the bag."

I started unloading everything I could out of my daypack to satisfy him. I grabbed the plastic bag and held it up, half full. "Enough?" I asked, hopefully, knowing I would never see him again.

"Okay." The agent nodded and taped the bag shut.

I said, "Thank God," and hoped for the best. There was nothing more to do. I went back through the security line and was admitted past it, almost home free. Judy was there laughing and shaking her head at the story, and we rushed onto our flight home, boarding just in time. The scissors made it home, and I still use them.

Note to self: No one will ever see you again, so do what's important to you.

CHAPTER 10

Patagonia

BY THE MID 2000S, JUDY AND I WERE BECOMING MORE FAMILIAR WITH meeting each other in foreign countries, having half a dozen trips under our belts. Patagonia, the mountainous region shared by Argentina and Chile, would mean more wilderness, backpacking, hostels, and figuring it out as we went. We loosely planned the trip around backpacking so we had room to change plans if needed. In reality, all we did was agree on dates and get airline tickets. I was proud of us for getting to this point, a little more secure in our travel life.

About this time, I heard of Couchsurfing.com. I was intrigued and explored the website. Eventually I figured out that people all over the world were staying on strangers' couches for a night or two, and this website made the connection.

I typed in *Chile* and found that there were several couches available, even one in Puerto Natales, which was our destination. I read on: "Stay in Puerto Natales on a couch near the cat litter." The picture was of a single man, probably in his thirties, and he seemed okay to me. At least he had a picture posted—some of the other hosts didn't post pictures. I decided to call Judy.

Judy was a business coach who talked on the telephone all day long. At night and on weekends, she didn't answer the phone unless she knew the person. When the call went to the machine, I said, "Judy, answer the phone. It's me, as in friend Linda." Judy picked up the phone, and I could almost hear her smile on the telephone as she said hello. "Hey, wanna try something very unusual and fun?" I asked.

"I'm in," she replied without hesitation. "What are we doing?"

"Ever heard of couch surfing?"

"Oh, dear, what are we getting into? What's that?" she replied. I briefly told her, and she repeated, "I'm in." Then she added, "But I'm not going to tell Dave," knowing that her husband would worry about the two of us.

Dave was a real sport about our travels, but Judy sometimes used prudence to determine how much to tell him. I remember him asking her, "How can I get in touch with you?" one time as we were leaving. Judy turned to him, staring directly into his eyes, and said, "You can't." They both started laughing as she and I left for the airport. Hard not to smile at that one. He usually found out about our antics—like sleeping in the cornfield—after the trips.

After landing outside of Punta Arenas, our first challenge was to get to Puerto Natales. We had no idea how to do that. Luckily, between our primitive sign language and my broken but useful Spanish, we discovered that there was a bus that went from the city of Punta Arenas to Puerto Natales. It would make a stop at the airport if we called to request one. Then we began our quest to make the telephone call.

By then I'd found that making a call in a foreign country involves several steps. First, I had to find change—specifically, exact change for the use of the telephone. I found a telephone, put in the coins, and dialed. Miraculously, someone picked up on the other end. I explained our request in broken Spanish—I think I said, "I'm at the airport and want to take the bus to Puerto Natales." He answered, "*Sí*."

"*A que tiempo?*" I asked, hoping I was asking something like, "At what time?"

I think he replied something like, "*En una hora,*" which I took to mean in about an hour.

Marvelous. I hoped I had just arranged our ride.

Judy and I waited outside, watching for anything that looked like a bus with some kind of indication it was going to Puerto Natales. We waited. We waited longer, probably over an hour. Finally we went inside again to question anyone we could find who might confirm there was actually a bus coming. We were still on a California time frame, thinking an hour meant an hour, not having absorbed the sleepy South American time frame yet.

The bus eventually came, nonchalantly if nothing else, and picked us up. Trial number one of the trip was over. Of course when we got on the bus, we verified everything several times: "*Puerto Natales, verdad?*" Our take-things-as-they-come attitude was shining through. We were getting more courageous.

We made it to small Puerto Natales with no directions to our Couchsurfing.com host, just an address. We knew that appearing pathetic was a plus when asking for help, so we tried to seem both pathetic and old, which got us a double sympathy vote from the locals. I knew enough to write the address in large letters and show it to folks passing by on the street in front of the bus terminal. With enough pointing, we eventually found the way to the correct street. With a little more exploration, we found a high, old wooden gate, which we opened. There were several small houses behind the gate, and we found the one with the address we were seeking.

Judy and I glanced at each other as we approached the door. The area where the house was located seemed as safe as anywhere, but it seemed rustic. My definition of *rustic* includes descriptions like *cracking paint, door hanging unevenly, sketchy landscaping,* and *window panes knocked out with cardboard over them.* We knocked on the door.

After a few moments, it flew open and in front of us stood a young woman, her hair wrapped in a towel from a recent shower. She quickly said in perfect English, "Oh, Mark told me you might be coming tonight to stay on the couch. Come on in. I'm watching the rest of a Spanish soap opera so I can improve my Spanish, and I can't miss it!" We entered the small house with not much of an introduction.

As it turned out, Mark was away for a few weeks on vacation. We would be staying with Sarah, his girlfriend, who was teaching English to local teens. Apparently Mark was doing the same thing, and life was good for them in this small South American town. Both Mark and Sarah were from the States.

The house had one bedroom. It was tiny, with a couch almost blocking the front door. The listing had mentioned kitty litter nearby. Sure enough, there was a pan with litter in it near the couch. Apparently Sarah was prone to rescue some of the street animals, which revealed her big heart. Across from the couch was a tiny stove, complete with burners and an oven. There was a sink and not much else—no refrigerator. We found out that it was cold here, so refrigeration meant that things were kept outside if they needed to be kept cold. We'd brought spaghetti and a box mix of cheesecake, which was a hit since it was nonexistent in Puerto Natales.

After the soap opera, Sarah talked with us for a long time, describing life in the small town. She was teaching many young people to speak English because it led to better jobs for them. Eventually we found this to be true in many countries throughout the world. One of her students knocked, stopping by for conversation with his teacher and two other Americans, us. He was a young man, robust and jovial, with a huge appetite to learn about California, movie stars, and almost anything American.

Eventually Sarah asked the student and us if we'd like to go for a drink. Of course we wanted to go. It was an opportunity to go with a local to a local bar. We walked to a bar where Sarah ordered an appetizer and our drinks. Pisco was the name of the drink we ordered, on Sarah's advice. It was amazingly delicious, made with liquor called Pisco, lime or lemon juice, and egg white. It tasted like a lime whiskey sour to me, but better.

While we enjoyed several drinks, night descended, and our day should have been ending, though the young student's day was just starting. Judy and I talked, laughed, and soaked in the culture. Eventually the student asked if we'd like to come to his house for dinner. He had fresh fish and was ready to share it. Judy and I glanced at each other for permission. We both were considering it as a huge opportunity, though our fatigue was also showing. I looked back at the student and said, "Of course we would love to come!" It was only about ten at night and eating dinner at midnight was not uncommon in this area.

Sarah gave me a look that told me something was wrong. While we prepared to leave the bar, she leaned over to me and whispered, "There's a problem."

I gave her a questioning stare. "What's the problem?"

She answered, "His father runs a brothel."

I asked again, "What's the problem?"

"We have to walk through it to get to his house."

I laughed and said, "That's no problem! That's opportunity!"

Unfortunately, Judy didn't get the message, although I did try to communicate it to her.

We walked the old streets, made of dirt or cobblestone, to a small house. Houses in Puerto Natales are narrow, with a small front entrance to the street, yet are long inside. The house had the curtains drawn, and I could only see muted lights inside. The young student entered the house nonchalantly, with Sarah following him, then Judy and me. I was all eyes. Judy was still in the dark, although a sign in the window, *Mujeres Querían* (Women Wanted) gave a clue. The lights were red and low, giving a warm yet inviting ambience. There were deep-red brocade drapes across the walls, matching the gaudy red chairs.

I surveyed the room as long as I could as we passed through the brothel, since this was probably my only opportunity to experience one. Two stout women with smiles on their faces were in the room, with tights on their legs and not much else. Their clothes were skimpy, provocative, and in sync with their occupation. Two men were also in the room, drinking beer to add more dimensions to their big bellies. The dimly lit room was as large as a good-sized living room and had nothing but chairs, rugs, and a few scattered tables with beer bottles on them. The whole experience didn't last long enough for me, but I soaked in as much as I could. Later, Sarah would tell me, "You know, everyone has to make a living around here, and this is just a way of life." It made sense to me, and it brought home the lesson of being nonjudgmental.

Shortly, we entered a well-lit area of the house. It became a regular house again, filled with smells from the kitchen and rambunctious kids running around. We sat, talked, and eventually ate fresh fish at about midnight. The entire experience was magical because we were engulfed in the local culture.

About one in the morning, we left with Sarah and marched past three doors as we left the main house. The first door had a large *1* on it, the second door had a *2* on it, and the third door had a *3* on it. I think at this point, Judy had an epiphany. She turned and threw me a quizzical look. I smiled and said, "Yep, those are the doors for the brothel."

We walked home with Sarah, and then spent the night on her little couch and floor, with the kitty litter about a foot away. I was proud of us, jumping into new experiences without judgment and paying attention to serendipity and opportunity. Dave would never know—well, at least not right away.

THE NEXT DAY, WE HUGGED SARAH GOODBYE AND LEFT TO FIND ANOTHER place to stay. The street where Sarah lived was several blocks from downtown, high in the hills, so we were hoping to find a place closer to the bustle of town. We appeared to be old hippies as we walked down the street with our backpacks and became perfect targets for locals. Shortly, we were being pursued by an oversized lady who came out of a doorway of a corner house. "Need place to stay?" she asked us.

"No," I said but then thought for a moment. "How much?"

"Ten dollars."

I slowed down. I looked at Judy and said to the lady, "Ten dollars for one or two?"

"For two." She was getting hopeful that we'd stay.

"Breakfast?"

She said, "Yes. I show you room."

Five dollars for each of us, including breakfast, was a deal—my kind of deal. She showed us a room with two twin beds, which meant no roomful of other guests who snore in bunk beds. The room was clean. In fact, the entire place was clean and wonderful. There was an old computer we could use. Additionally, we could store extra bags there since we would be returning to Puerto Natales after a backpack in Argentina before we flew back to America. The innkeeper asked that we review her advertisement on the computer and correct any English spelling or grammatical errors so she'd appear more professional. It was a win-win situation.

I knew enough by this time not to go to dinner at the lacy-curtained restaurant with the *Mujeres Querían* sign across the street. My compulsion to find local crafts crept in. Judy went with me, and we stumbled onto a small craft market in a building courtyard with small shops around it. An older man, whom I assumed to be a local, was talking with one of the shopkeepers. My curiosity led me to ask him about the market. I discovered that he had developed the building to help the local craftspeople have a place to show and sell their wares. He was educating them in business and enhancing their skills such as displaying their wares and providing customer service. Basically, each person, sometimes with their relatives, had a stall and could develop it as they wished with his support and business skills to help the entire operation. He asked me for suggestions as a consumer, and the only thing I could say was that I would have wanted to know about the complex when I first got into town. We had just stumbled onto it, so better advertising was one suggestion.

I went slowly from stall to stall because each artist or salesperson was so interested and interesting. There were earrings and other jewelry on display, which they placed into small bags with the name of the artist or vendor on it when someone made a purchase. I bought a tiny wooden box with a penguin shape burned onto it, plus an unfinished penguin carving. I liked it just as it was. I bought my very own ostrich taker-downer: a set of three rocks, each covered with white leather, all combined with long braided leather strings. To take down an ostrich, a hunter twirled these rocks above her head and flung the contraption at the ostrich with the hopes of wrapping it around its neck. I was happy to pay the vendor the forty dollars he was asking for the unusual craft. I asked him to sign the concoction, and he beamed as he did so.

I talked for a long time with a weaver in her stall and bought a crocheted hat as well as two hanks of spun wool, one creamy colored and one dark brown. The wool was one of my prized possessions because it was hand spun with a drop spindle, which is a stick with a wide bottom. The spinner collects the wool from the sheep, washes and cards the wool (combs it to get out dung, leaves, and so on), and then wraps it around her arms to hand-feed onto the drop spindle, which twists it and stores it. It seemed to be an ancient method of making wool yarn. I was fascinated and watched her for a long time. Her big grin will stay with me forever.

Judy and I were about to go downtown to get bus tickets to Argentina for our hike, but the kind innkeeper insisted that she get them for us. We felt comfortable enough to give her money for our tickets and watched her waddle down the street. We would be going with the locals on a public bus from Chile to Argentina. We were getting more used to depending on the kindness of strangers for help and directions, becoming less afraid to ask. We usually looked like local homeless or penniless folks, with our crumpled T-shirts, frumpy long-sleeved shirts, well-worn backpacks, and always-dirty long pants, and people were kind to help us.

We bid her farewell the next day as we tramped out the door with our packs. Our adventure to Argentina was to the little town of El Calafate and then to the tinier town of El Chalten to start backpacking to see Mount Fitz Roy.

The bus took us through the pampas areas I had heard and dreamed about. I felt like we were on a tour bus, so I didn't hesitate to go to the driver to ask him to point out any animals he happened to see. I'm sure he was ever so tired of tourists asking, but this was my time and I wasn't going to miss my chance. Besides, he would never see us again. The plains spread ahead of us, everywhere, with tall grasses and few trees.

We saw flamingos, as in *pink flamingos*. They were at a distance, of course, but really there, at the ponds. Each had a long, graceful neck, those famous long legs, and pink feathers. They were grouped together, clinging to each other for safety if nothing else. My aunt Bertie would have loved to have seen them too. I knew she was with me in spirit.

Not long after, we saw our first wild ostrich. I wasn't ready to use my new weapon—I never would be—I just wanted to admire it. Regal, tall, with huge eyes, it was unlike any bird I had ever seen.

We got to El Calafate and, as is common, were approached by several people waiting at the bus station. These folks were all trying to get tourists to stay at their particular hotel, hostel, or pension, like the man in Venice had. Usually they have pictures of the places, and I've never been disappointed. This time, we decided on a fair-priced and nice-looking place and hopped in the car with the young fellow. The car should have been our clue. If we wanted a place in the middle of town, and the bus station is in town, we probably would not need a car ride. The place we chose turned out to be a bit of a hike to town but nothing we couldn't handle, so we took the deal.

By this time, I'd started a tradition of collecting fabric from all the countries I visited so I could incorporate them into a future quilt. So our quest was on to find a piece of fabric in this small place in Argentina. The primary problem was that I had no idea what the word for *fabric* was in Spanish. I pointed to my nylon pants, my T-shirt, and anything else I could think of to describe fabric. Finally, after being directed to several clothing stores, we wandered a bit outside of town and found the fabric store. By this time in our travels, I'd enticed Judy to also collect fabric pieces, so we bought a yard and had it cut in half.

The next day, we were off for our backpacking journey from El Chalten. At the trailhead, I tried to put on my backpack but realized the belt buckle was broken, probably from someone stepping on it. This wasn't the first time this had happened, so I knew enough to carry a spare and took the time to fix it. I fumbled with it a bit, got out my handy-dandy sewing kit, and it was ready for use again.

I slung the pack on and looked at Judy, who was chomping at the bit, ready to go. We started down the small, dusty road past a few last houses on the edge of town. As usual, my eyes were searching everywhere for clues for anything special or worth investigating down the road.

I spied a small sign: *Panadería*. I started waving my hands at Judy, who was ahead of me, as usual. I called out to her, "Hey, look—panadería!"

She stopped and gave me that signal of *We have to make time. Let's go!* By this time in our traveling relationship, we knew how to work with each other. I told her I had to stop and would be just a minute.

I walked off the dusty street to a small house about fifty feet off the main road. The small white house had a hand-painted sign outside, and it appeared to me as if the front of the house was the bakery, while the family lived in the other part. I walked into the bakery, which was painted white, was long and narrow, and had a few tables with bakery items on them. While I knew it would never pass FDA standards, I loved it and was welcomed by a beaming owner and the smell of calories. I started scouring the goods and finally decided on a pastry filled with a caramel-colored concoction I had not seen before.

When I asked about it, the owner said, "*Dulce de leche*." I bought one, walked out of the house, and took a big bite while Judy waited for me. I nearly had an out-of-body experience when I tasted the dulce de leche. With a full bite in my mouth, I said to Judy, "You *have* to try this." She tried it, and we immediately went in to buy three more to take with us. I have to remember at times that Judy travels with me because I see everything *between* point A and point B, whereas she is focused only on points A and B. Somehow, it all works beautifully.

We backpacked up a long hill for quite a while, and I did my usual stopping and resting and taking pictures. The trail was easy to follow, and we didn't worry too much about becoming lost. Coming around one corner in the forest, we spotted our goal: Mount Fitz Roy. It was a bit cloudy, with the top hidden by a few passing clouds. We got up to a place that obviously was a camping spot, although there was nothing other than a few flat spots that had been used for tents. No toilets, no drinking water other than a stream, and no tables. It was perfect.

We put up the tent. Having worked together for several years now, we were experts at putting it up quickly and needed little communication between us. The clouds were collecting, and the possibility of a storm loomed. We ate our meager dinner, including our pastries. Dinner on these trips was always cold because we didn't bring a stove with us. We had searched for peanut butter, one of our travel staples, but found that it didn't exist in this part of South America. I kept asking for *cacahuètes* but was greeted with blank stares and shrugs. I'm sure it was my pronunciation—surely someone had heard of, or tasted, peanut butter.

We settled into the tent as the temperature was dropping and it was starting to rain. In the past, I might have panicked because of the weather, but with all our backpacking experience, Judy and I now knew we had no control over the weather, so our motto was to relax and get a good night's sleep.

In the middle of the night, I awoke and pressed my handy-dandy Indiglo button on my watch to see what time it was. It was about two in the morning, and I couldn't see a thing above the tent. I put my hand on the roof of the tent, and it felt heavy. I punched the roof, and something slid off. When I opened the zipper on the tent and looked outside, I realized it was snow that had slid off—about three inches deep on the ground. Mental decision time: *Do I wake Judy up and we try to leave before we get snowed in more, or do I go back to sleep?* I decided to go back to sleep since there was absolutely nothing I could do about the weather.

Note to self: It was a great decision. Nothing you could do.

I MUST HAVE SLEPT INTERMITTENTLY BECAUSE I WOKE UP AGAIN AT ABOUT six o'clock, and again unzipped the tent to find the first light of the day surrounding the mountains and our little tent. I rubbed my eyes again and saw our mountain, Mount Fitz Roy, in full view, with the yellow and orange bands of first light shining on the rock and snow. For me, some peaks were to be simply viewed and savored, while others were to climb. This peak was beyond my climbing capabilities, and I was starting to define my limitations and learn to say no. The view this morning was like an orange-cream-and-lemon-sherbet swirl of light on our peak. I woke Judy so she could see what I was viewing, and we broke into large grins as we stared at the majesty of the peak we would never climb but would never forget.

Eventually we got up and out of the tent. We had no stove for hot water, and I longed for a nice cup of coffee or, better yet, hot cocoa with peppermint schnapps in it. No luck. However, I looked to the left of the tent to see a man, standing nearby but allowing an adequate amount of personal space. He was holding a gourd with a metal straw in it, probably filled with maté, which is the popular Argentinean tea. I waved to him, then wandered over to talk and smile in the universal nonverbal language that bonds people all over the world.

He spoke broken English, and I managed to communicate with my broken Spanish. He asked me if I would like some of the maté in his gourd cup, and I declined, thinking, *I don't know this fellow. He probably has some terrible disease that I can get by using the same metal straw. There are germs all over it.* Then the more adventurous and logical part of my brain stepped in: *You fool. This is the opportunity of a lifetime—go for it!*

Note to self: No more fish-fry stories. You're stronger! Have no regrets. Make Aunt Bertie proud.

I LOOKED AT THE MAN AGAIN AND SAID, "I CHANGED MY MIND—I'D LOVE some tea!" I expected him to offer me some of his drink, but instead he turned around and was gone. I had to assume that he was getting more tea or running away because I had spooked him. Either way was all right.

He returned about ten minutes later and extended his hands, offering me the same gourd cup, filled with hot liquid and tea leaves. I took the metal straw and started to stir the concoction. The man's eyes got big very quickly, and he started shaking his head and putting his right hand near the cup. "No, no," he said. "No stir maté!" All these rules were new to me, so I quickly stopped stirring. The tea was delicious. It was hot, fresh, and given in a gracious spirit, just the way I love it.

Judy and I packed out later that day, bussed back to Chile to our little inn in Puerto Natales, and then bussed back to Punta Arenas. We were feeling comfortable at this point. When we arrived in Punta Arenas, no one was offering a place to stay, so we were on our own. Maybe our bus was just too local to attract the messengers from the inns. We started walking, looking for signs.

I spotted a small building with a vertical sign in English on the corner saying *Room Available*. In this remote, foreign area, English was still used here and there. We stopped, and I knocked on the door. It was answered by a woman in her fifties with long dark hair and a full, round body. She had the typical Chilean broad smile, and she obviously was happy to see us. She invited us to a room at the very back of the house that had two beds in it, so we plopped our packs on the beds and left to see the rest of the town.

This was the last night of our trip, so we looked for restaurants that were unusual. We found one that advertised king crab legs at a very reasonable price, so we went inside and sat down. We ordered the king crab legs and were told to come back in an hour—they would not be available until then. Who knew if they had to buy them or catch them, but we were coming back. When we did, we were not disappointed.

After dinner, we went back to the room. Judy put some Vicks under her nose that night before going to sleep, I thought probably because she was getting a cold. She slept restlessly that night, but I slept soundly. The next morning she started talking about the bad smell. Mercifully, my nose doesn't work, so no smells bothered me.

We went into the small kitchen adjacent to our room and sat down for breakfast. We had cereal and toast, and of course, maté. Our hostess was serving us breakfast while her burly husband sat next to me. He had a mustache, was as round as he was tall, and had a very outgoing personality. Of course, his personality matched his desire to sell us some wares. He got out several bone items and asked eighty dollars for a simple carving. At this point my cash reserves were very low, so I couldn't buy much more than a carved hook. Then he started talking about all the taxidermy he did, including penguins.

I was interested, of course, so he wanted to show us his "gallery," which was outside and upstairs. We wouldn't miss an opportunity like that, so after breakfast we tromped out the back door—where we stopped in our tracks.

Picture this: Our little room was next door to the kitchen. We opened the back kitchen door and stepped outside to find, right in front of us, in front of the window where Judy slept, an old-fashioned, cast-iron, claw-footed bathtub half-filled with water—and a dead sheep. Its throat had been slit, and the blood was in the tub, but the sheep was intact with all the skin and dirty wool still on it. The sheep's small back feet were tilting out the top of the tub, and the front feet were submerged in water. The water in the tub was murky, a combination of yellow and red. It was hard not to react, and I had to tell myself, *This is not mine to judge.* Judy and I glanced at each other quickly, trying not to laugh or to make our host feel bad.

We silently climbed the stairs to the small loft where the taxidermy studio was. We were greeted with a penguin, an ostrich, and other smaller animals that had all once been alive and were now stuffed. I didn't have the heart to ask if he sold them or had some other purpose for the taxidermy.

We left on a late flight that night and arrived home filled with the graciousness of Chile and Argentina.

CHAPTER 11

Peru

"Machu Picchu?" Judy said on the telephone.

"Yep," I said. "Let's go. It's on the list. Peru will be inexpensive, exotic, and hopefully a lot of fun."

Machu Picchu is an incredible location in the Andes Mountains of Peru, built at the height of the Inca empire and probably used as a royal retreat or religious site. We would land in Lima and travel south to Cuzco, from which we'd backpack several days into the famous UNESCO (United Nations Educational, Scientific and Cultural Organization) site from the Inca Trail. That was the general idea, and now I had to hone the plan a bit.

Once in Lima, our guidebook warned of the taxis. It said to look for special credentials in the taxis to ensure they were legitimate and to pick up a taxi at an official stand, one that was located where there is a *Taxi* sign about the size and place of a parking meter. We were in territory that could potentially be dangerous for Americans—or anyone, for that matter. Everyone in the world must think every American is a millionaire and would have plenty of money for ransom. This issue would be one we would keep from Judy's husband, Dave, at least for a while. Catching a taxi at the airport was easy. We were able to go to the official stand to get a legitimate one.

After our jet lag, we stayed at a hostel that night and would head out the next day for our main destination: Cuzco and the Inca Trail. Our guide told us to catch the local bus from Lima to Cuzco on our own. It would be cheap, but it was an overnight bus ride. It wasn't until later that I realized traveling at night was a blessing; we couldn't see any of the drop-offs next to us or the high passes where we traveled. Luckily, I didn't know about the warnings of possible mudslides and bus robberies until after the trip. We hiked with all our stuff from the hostel in Lima to the bus station in town. It was a small station, and I asked, in my broken Spanish, if this was the correct station. Would the bus here take us from Lima to Cuzco? The answer was yes.

We had to wait a bit and then boarded the bus with a large *Cuzco* sign in the front left corner. Buses here had assigned seating. You would think we'd know that by now, but we didn't and had to move once the people assigned to our seats arrived. We sat still, enjoying the scenery in our whirlwind trip.

Leaving Lima was like leaving any large city. It took a while to get past the frenzy of the large town, and we were adjusting to the ride, the country, and our surrounding bus mates. Eventually we started to see environment changes. We descended to the coast, and as we did so, the barren landscape of the Atacama Desert began to appear. It didn't take long before the starkness of the land astounded me.

There was sand everywhere. There had to be classic places to visit in this barren land, but the bus had no intention of stopping. We were on a local bus that was taking passengers from one place to another, not on a sightseeing mission. We traveled near the ocean and saw high sand dunes and only a few bushes struggling to survive in the sandy terrain. I was glad to be in the bus and not seeking water in the Atacama area.

The trip took all night, over twenty hours. For me, the length of the journey simply added to the beauty of the trip. Eventually the old, dirty curtains were drawn past the windows so everyone could sleep. I usually am able to catch a few hours of sleep, and this was no exception. I didn't ask Judy about her experience. She always came out like a trouper, no matter what. She didn't put up with whining either—hers or mine.

Eventually we ended up in Cuzco and found a small, average hostel to stay in. We were tired and slept as soon as we were settled. The next day we had available to explore on our own a bit, so we took off to see the town of Cuzco.

The first thing I recall vividly was eating lunch. As usual, I was interested in finding the local mercado. A market in South America usually means not only food but also all kinds of services and products that the people of the region require for daily life. On the way to find the mercado, Judy and I both got hungry and started looking for a place to eat. I spied a clean, small, local restaurant with no English anywhere on the outside of the building and pointed to it. Judy nodded, so we went in.

As soon as we stepped in, we were greeted by a man and a woman who I assumed were the owners/cooks/servers all in one family. It made me happy to be able to find such a small, out-of-the-way place and give them our business.

The hostess seated us and seemed thrilled that we would come into her small restaurant. She insisted on serving us *sopa* (soup), and we nodded in agreement. We then asked for tamales, and she smiled broadly. After a very short time, the soup was served, and I had to admit that it was absolutely fantastic. Nice and hot, yet not too spicy for me. Judy was more hard-core and could take more spice than I.

The meal was followed by tamales and flan for dessert, even though we had not ordered it. We asked for the check, and the hostess started shaking her head. She brought us a book, like a guest book, and indicated she wanted us to sign it. When I looked at it, there were signatures from visitors all over the world. I could only interpret the book as an honor bestowed on us, and I treated it as such. I told the owner/hostess how grateful we were for the meal and to sign her book.

Shortly after signing the book, I asked for the check again. The owner/hostess shook her head vehemently. I protested and said, "Yes!"

She was offering us the meal for free, but I knew how dear the money would be to them, meaning very little to us in the big scheme of things. We insisted and gave her money for the meal, expressing our gratitude and appreciation.

We proceeded to find and explore the mercado. There were streets and streets of the market area, running both parallel and perpendicular. There was little room for any car, as most of the traffic was on foot. It didn't take us long to find that this local market was divided into areas. The largest area was of produce—all kinds, all colors, and all prices. The variety of foods was incredible compared with food I'd seen in other countries with colder climates.

Then there were hardware sections, clothing sections, utilitarian crafts and kitchenware sections, and a repair section including sewing machines and—my prize—the shoe repair place. I spent a long time there evaluating the samples of shoe soles and watching their methods. Two young men and one older man were doing the shoe repairs on the ground, under a tarp. I mean, the men were repairing the shoes *while the customers waited*. No waiting for two weeks for a repair. When someone needed a repair here, it was needed immediately. I saw an older, plump woman sit down, take off an old pair of flat black leather shoes, and hand them to the nearest man on the ground. She spoke quickly, in Spanish, and I didn't understand her request. Judy and I watched the cobbler take the soles of the shoes off, glue a new pair on, and then stitch them. He gave them back to her within fifteen minutes. I was hooked on the process.

I got the attention of the man who seemed to be in charge and asked in my broken Spanish and sign language if he could put the pair of lug soles that I pointed to on my boots. He totally understood and repeated my signs. I asked in Spanish the cost of the work, and he indicated with seven fingers that it would be seven dollars. In mountain-climbing terms, seven dollars would be a steal to put new soles on my hiking boots.

I sat down on the only folding chair available and took off my boots. I handed them to Fellow Number 1, who took the boots and somehow ripped off the soles. They were off within a minute. Judy viewed the process too, and we smiled at each other occasionally while the work was being performed.

I remembered how many peaks these boots had been up, sometimes in the Sierra Nevadas and sometimes in the Inyos of California. One time, I had taken my teenage son up Mount Tom in the Sierras. We backpacked in, and I watched as he caught one small fish after another in the lake where we camped. The next morning, we started hiking up the mountain and encountered two other men also climbing. Because I often deferred to men at the time, my son and I started following the two men. We made it close to the peak when the clouds, rain, and threat of a thunderstorm came in. I knew we were off-route a bit and on slippery boulders. I told my son that we needed to turn around, that the mountain was letting us know it wasn't a good day to climb. Reluctantly he turned around with me, and one of the other men also turned around with us after his leader went to the top of the peak and had not returned. When we encountered the leader again, he told us he had gone down another route. The fellow he left behind was ever so grateful to us for getting him back to camp safely.

A month later, when the weather was ideal, my son and I returned and spent an hour on top of Mount Tom. That Christmas, I gave my son two rocks. I told him, "This first rock is from our first climb of Mount Tom, and the other rock is from the second climb." I then asked him never to forget that the first rock is the most important one, for the lessons it could teach him.

My daughter and I also climbed regularly, from her childhood until she left for college. One of the most spectacular climbs we did was hiking Mount Whitney in a day when she was eleven years old. For *anyone* to climb Whitney in a day is a miracle, but to have a child of such an early age do it is incredible.

We started out about four in the morning after sleeping at the trailhead to become acclimatized to the over eight-thousand-foot elevation. We had to hike to the top and back—an altitude of about 14,500 feet and a distance of about twenty-two miles round-trip—in one day. She got down and back to the cars an hour before I did. It is something that makes us smile every time we think of it.

Note to self: The mountain doesn't care about you and will be there long after your short lives. Keep safe, your babies and you.

My boots were then handed to Fellow Number 2, who shaved the soles of the shoes to fit the boots, using a sharp, small knife. Once done, he glued the soles onto the bottom of my boots. The boots were then transferred to Fellow Number 3, who took an awl and hand-sewed the soles onto the boots. His job had to be the most difficult. Although it took them less than half an hour to do the repair work, I was astounded at the quality, the professionalism in the small outdoor shop with an awning and cobblestone floor, and the price.

The next day, we left on the several-day backpack trip, packing on the Inca Trail from near Cuzco to Machu Picchu. For some reason, I wasn't doing well. My body had been fine above Lima, but after the bus trip and traveling, I didn't feel well. Maybe it was the new boot soles, or just plain karma.

It was hot at the beginning of the trek, which was a handicap for me. I had my hiking poles and was using them. On this sacred, historical trail, we had to leave the rubber tips on the ends of the poles to ensure little, if any, damage to the trail. Judy was hiking well and, of course, was ahead of me. I was dragging, really dragging. There were two ten-thousand-foot passes ahead of me, and I had no idea at this point if I was capable of going over them.

As we approached the first one, I convinced myself that I couldn't do it, something rare for me. Judy was on top of the pass already, and I was below her but within hearing distance. She was up there yelling out to me, "Come on, Linda, I'm on top. You can do it! Let's go!" There was no way.

I sat down in the middle of the trail and glanced up at Judy. My head wanted to be up there where she was, but my body quit on me. It had never happened to me before, and I didn't really understand what was going on.

Looking back with perspective, maybe I was sick from the soup in the restaurant where we'd been treated like we were famous. Or maybe I'd swallowed some little drop of water and that drop was full of microscopic bugs I couldn't see. Anyhow, my body wasn't willing to go.

Finally two of the porters came back from where the others were camped and literally picked me up by my shoulders and arms and helped me walk the last several hundred feet. It was embarrassing, but I knew I needed the help and had the graciousness to accept it. Judy stayed with me to be sure I was all right once I got to the top of the pass.

The rest of the hike that day took hours because not only was the first pass hard but then we also went down the other side and up another ten-thousand-foot pass. Once I got over the first pass, I felt better and was able to go down by myself. I have little recollection of the second pass, but I know that I did it under my own power—probably because I am stubborn—with the porters' watchful eyes on me.

The following day, the terrain was becoming more lush and green. With the height of the passes and the cooler weather, I was doing better. We eventually rounded a corner, and there below us were the famed ruins of Machu Picchu. Aging rock foundations showed rooms and larger gathering areas on several terraces. There must have been many people living there in centuries past, but only memories and haunts of former times now.

Comparing the backpacking to seeing the ruins, the backpacking took the prize. While we wandered around the ruins with several hundred other tourists for several hours, it all seemed more like Disneyland than a remote adventure. At the end we were guided to the entrance where we would board one of many large, clean buses to take us back to Cuzco and eventually Lima.

Once back in Lima, Judy and I wandered the streets a bit. On a side street, we passed a local bar and took a peek inside, considering getting a beer. Inside was a plump young woman, dancing by herself, who motioned for us to come in, almost begging us to come in.

We did enter the bar and sat at a table by ourselves even though the young girl motioned several times for us to join her. A friendly young thing, she came right over to us and started a conversation. I noticed the young woman tending bar briefly shook her head at me while she tried to catch my eye, but I couldn't interpret her message.

As expected, the first question the dancing woman asked was "Where are you from?"

I answered, "From the States."

She continued, "What are you doing in Peru?"

"Having fun." I kept my answers short, feeling like we shouldn't engage too much.

"Have you been to the big Inca market here?"

I told her we hadn't been there yet but would check it out. She asked if we were taking pictures and pointed to Judy's camera on the front of her waistband. The girl started dancing by herself again and invited us to join her. She was so jovial and friendly that we decided she had to be drunk or very near it.

I stood my ground, trying to make her leave us alone. She implored Judy to join her, and Judy finally caved in. She went on the dance floor with the woman and started dancing, the only two people on the dance floor. It was a mistake, and my gut told me so. I was starting to understand the gesture I'd gotten from the barmaid.

It didn't take long before it happened. Judy's hands were in the air as she danced around her partner, and sometime when she did a turn, her partner stole her decorated leather pouch from her front shirt. I didn't see it, even though my antenna was up. Judy noticed it right away.

The girl disappeared into the bathroom. Judy told me what happened, that the precious leather case was missing and that she had moved her camera from the case to a more secure place before dancing. She had not lost the camera, mercifully, but she was extremely upset to lose the case.

As soon as the girl came out of the bathroom, I confronted her. As I stood right in front of her, lots of thoughts went through my head: *Can I frisk her? If I frisk her, can she call the cops and I'll end up in jail? Can I beg her to give back the case? Can I go into the bathroom and see if it's there?*

I decided I didn't want to go to jail so forgot about frisking her. I doubted that the police would care a whit about me, but I wasn't willing to take the risk. I asked the girl, who immediately didn't seem drunk at all, to *please* give us back the case. I told her it was a special case, from a special place. The girl shook her head violently, as if saying she had done nothing and didn't know what we were talking about. It quickly became obvious to me that she was a pro—a pro at pickpocketing.

I did go into the bathroom to search, finding nothing. I forgot, however, to open the lid of the toilet. Then, back out in the bar, I implored her again to please, *please* give back the case because it was of no value except to my friend. The begging fell on uncaring ears, probably because she was furious that she had not come up with the camera that she was after. It was a lesson learned, and there was nothing we could do about it. Judy let it go a lot easier than I did. The only good thing that came out of the encounter, besides the lesson learned, was the suggestion about the Inca market.

At the hostel where we were staying, I asked about it. The front desk person said, "Oh, you haven't seen it yet?"

I replied, "No. Is it worth it?"

The receptionist told me that visiting the market was a must, but it was a long walk to get there. After what we had just done, I figured it couldn't be any worse than walking on the Inca Trail. We were given some directions—something like, turn right outside the building, turn right at the store, go on a road winding to the right, and go straight for a long time—and tried to imprint them on our brains.

We left the hostel the next morning and started walking. Neither map nor GPS at hand, we trusted the information we'd been given plus our own instincts. At one intersection, I wanted to go straight and Judy said we should take a closer look at where we were. We bantered for a minute, discussing our crossroads. We decided to take the road to the right and hiked on the sidewalk for some time. It was normal to start questioning our decision as we kept walking with no results: no Inca market. When the market didn't appear, being female, we decided to take matters into our own hands and ask people where it was. I was willing to stop in a store or ask any passerby.

In my terrible Spanish, I would ask, "*Donde está el mercado?*" I knew that much Spanish. But I wouldn't ask just anyone. If someone appeared like he or she was either not going to be helpful or, worse, would possibly harm unsuspecting tourists, I didn't ask them for directions. I let my natural instincts guide me in my decision-making. The thought that Americans were frequently taken hostage in Peru at that time kept nagging at me and helped in my decision-making. I also had to tell myself that most of the people in the world are genuinely good and will be helpful if asked. *Trust your instincts*, I kept telling myself.

Eventually, after asking about ten different people, we were guided to the Inca market. We entered a large space, like an empty warehouse with makeshift walls that defined different stores. Many stores had some of their goods outside their door to draw customers in, whereas others had everything inside the store. To my delight, there were hundreds of stores and thousands of things to purchase. This fact dismayed Judy, because she knew me too well. My artistic nature meant that I wanted to spend a lot of time there.

We had to catch a taxi later in the day to get to the airport for our flight out of Peru that night. Here we were in the market, probably a mile or two from downtown Lima, and I was acting as if I had an early Christmas because of all the handicrafts.

I found a small alpaca rug and didn't have enough money to buy it. Judy looked at me, and I looked at her. Then I asked the store owner, "Is there a bank machine near?" The lady nodded and pointed, first to the right and then the left. Silent hand signals had to work. Judy gave me the *I can't believe you're going to an ATM a few hours before we have to leave* signal. I brushed it off and headed to the right with Judy at my heels.

Sure enough, about six stores and a right turn and left turn, and there was the prize: the ATM. I put my card in, and it worked—yet another miracle. I had figured it might be my luck that the machine would eat my card and give me nothing, a worst-case-scenario deal. I ran back to the lady and handed her the money for the rug, then rushed off with Judy.

About half a minute later, I saw another prize: small mirrors in hand-painted frames. I walked into the tiny shop and talked with the owner. Each mirror's unique frame had a specific meaning. Judy rolled her eyes once in a while, as I found out that one of the mirrors had a theme of women working. While I was making a decision about the mirrors, Judy was saying, "Come on. We must go!" as often as she could without causing a scene or making me feel too guilty. I finally bought one mirror, and Judy started pulling me out of the maze of stores. I didn't want to go, but my friend was keeping us on track. She never worried that I couldn't get all the stuff back home. Somehow, I always managed.

We got out to the sunshine once again, and I started laughing. It was all really too funny. I had my prizes, and Judy had me on the long trail to the hostel then to the taxi stand. We were able to share a ride with another tourist going to the airport, and we made it in plenty of time to catch our plane.

CHAPTER 12

Antarctica I

THE SAYING ON THE ICE IS "YOU GO TO WORK IN ANTARCTICA THE FIRST time for the adventure, the second time for the money, and the third time because you don't fit in anywhere else."

"Why on earth do you want to go to Antarctica?" my mom asked.

"Because it's there?" I answered, more a question than a statement. "Because I want to, and I can," I continued.

Who would have ever thought I would work in Antarctica? Had you told me I would work there when I was in high school, I would have shaken my head, scoffed at the idea, and said emphatically, "Never!" It hadn't been on my radar at that time. It became more intriguing, however, through my mountain-climbing escapades. Antarctica represented the ultimate adventure, the apex of life experiences, and the crowning achievement.

The idea of working in Antarctica had been born when I went to New Zealand in the 1980s and saw a grizzly-looking man coming off an airplane with a duffel bag tagged *Antarctica*. Define *grizzly-looking*:

he had a scruffy beard and dirty hands, looked haggard and tired, and seemed to be on his way home from a work assignment he loved, or at least tolerated. I wanted the same experience, except maybe without the dirty hands and beard.

Life happened between the 1980s—when I'd started to travel—and 2004, but as I was starting to cry every day on my way to work, that tag on the duffel bag crept from my memory bank into my present. I had worked for one company for twenty years, and I was a great deal more burned out than I would admit. The crying should have been a sign, but at the time, I figured it was my destiny to work several more years. While the appeal of the unknown was nudging me to branch out from my dull routine, I was comfortable and scared to venture into an abyss of unknowns. By this time my two beautiful children had fledged, had used their wings magnificently to fly away. My slate was empty, and I could finally fill it with travel beyond the one or two big trips I had been taking per year, as long as I made enough money to fund it. I knew there were jobs that paid people to travel or work overseas. There was no reason *not* to go.

Note to self: Your time on the planet is becoming shorter, and you're going to die one way or another. No one gets out alive. Both Helen and Aunt Bertie would have said, "Go. Have no regrets."

I FINALLY WENT ONLINE AND SEARCHED *WORKING IN ANTARCTICA* TO SEE what I could find. Magically, the United States Antarctic Program (USAP) appeared, so I started looking into this strange, whimsical world of white called Antarctica. The history of the area appealed to my adventurous side, knowing that Antarctica was truly one of the last Age of Exploration areas: the race to the South Pole had been an epic adventure in 1911 to 1912, and Sir Ernest Henry Shackleton's adventures are still known for their ultimate heroism.

Although I was a complete idiot on the computer, I was able to read about working in Antarctica and meandered through the mysterious listing of jobs available. I learned that Raytheon held the current contract from the National Science Foundation (NSF) during the summer, providing janitorial services, transportation and fuel needs, cooks, information tech support and so on. Just about any job it takes to run a small town. I wanted to be part of that village. It was up to me to make it happen.

There were several ways to apply for a job on the Ice: filling out an application online, sending in a résumé, or attending one of their job fairs. I figured going to Raytheon's headquarters in Centennial, Colorado, for their major job fair would be the ticket for me. I spruced up my résumé, booked an airline ticket and car in Denver, and headed out the door one day for the airport. There, serendipity hit me once again.

When I got to the Los Angeles airport, I took off my shoes at the security checkpoint, put all my items in the white plastic bins, and waited my turn. On the other side, after having no problem with security, I rushed to pick up my things from the bins and noticed a few coins in one of them. I stuffed them in my pocket, not thinking anything of it.

The day of the job fair, I dressed up, drove to a large building out of town, and walked in with my résumé in hand. Several greeters welcomed applicants into a room with various tables labeled by department, such as *Housing*, *Food Service*, *Recreation*, and *Supply*.

When I got to the trim lady at the *Human Resources* sign, she asked me which department I wanted to apply to work in. I said, "Human Resources." She asked me again which department, and I again said, "Human Resources."

The lady stopped to think for a minute then said, "You want to work *in* human resources?"

"That's where my background is."

She took my résumé and looked up incredulously, then asked if I really wanted to go to the Ice.

I shrugged. "Of course!"

Apparently not many people apply for the human resources jobs in Antarctica. She said, "It's very cold there!"

I replied, "I wouldn't expect less." I was confident that I would be headed to the Ice at that point.

When I returned home, I was ready to wash my clothes and felt in my pants pockets for the typical Kleenex or two that normally ruin my wash. I felt the few coins from the beginning of the trip and looked at them. I smiled broadly when I realized they were coins from New Zealand—the stopping point to get to Antarctica. It was another sign that I was going, and I knew it.

Note to self: Serendipity strikes again.

THE ONE HICCUP WAS THE PHYSICAL. ALTHOUGH I WAS IN EXCELLENT SHAPE from all the mountain climbing I was doing at the time, a stringent physical was required by Raytheon and the NSF, and everyone stepping onto the Ice had to pass. Past experiences with emergency evacuations had led to more and more requirements—and more and more procedures—for the physical. I lived in Los Angeles, and getting all the procedures performed at my local HMO medical facility would be another hurdle. In an HMO system, there are no easy ways to get a routine mammogram or stress test done quickly. I arranged for the physical and waited in a tiny room until my doctor appeared to complete the paperwork. The hospital had a short time allotment for each medical visit, and when the doctor realized I would need more than that time to fit in all the line items of my physical, he balked. But he was also intrigued that I was going to Antarctica. I smiled a lot, begged with my eyes, and used all my skills as a human being to get him to complete the form and order the multitude of other tests I needed.

That's when I started running into roadblocks. Luckily, the mammogram was scheduled—check. The blood work was done—check. The first drug test was in Pasadena, another long drive before work, and was done—check. The second drug test, again in Pasadena, was done—check. The stress test for my heart would take several months to get—uncheck. Then the mammogram results were lost or somehow didn't get to me—uncheck.

One day in the summer, with my time limit running out, I sat down and started crying. It was too hard, too complicated, too whatever. I was letting the chatter in my head and all the *I'm a poor thing* thoughts get in the way. I had to get over it and tell myself, *I am not a victim. I am in charge. Act like it.* I had to rise to the occasion.

I worked for a medical facility, so I finally asked our medical director for a referral for a stress test. He liked and respected me, so I was hoping that would work. Ah—doors opened! I was scheduled that same afternoon for a stress test from a doctor he knew. I scheduled myself for another mammogram at a local facility. Lo and behold, that appointment happened also and the results were sent off to Centennial to complete my records.

Doors opened when I took charge, despite my history that had dictated that I wait for good things to come my way. My current life experience was telling me not to follow but to lead. I led and doors opened. My one remaining hurdle might be my own trepidation right before leaving on the plane to New Zealand.

As the time to leave drew nearer, my uncertainty about the whole outlandish idea started to grow. All around, people were asking me questions and showing their own concern about my safety, and it rubbed off on me. My mother, who avoided computers, even got a very simple email account so she could be sure I didn't slip off the end of the earth without her knowing it.

I told Judy about my decision once I started the physical. She was happy for me, though maybe a little jealous. She decided to climb Kilimanjaro that year without me since I had indicated I didn't want to climb it. That would prove untrue shortly.

I kept turning my mind back to the thought that I was doing something amazing, something very few other people would choose to do. Plus, I was choosing to take charge of my unhappiness related to my current job as well as to feed my large travel appetite. I decided to update and renew my will, just in case of, well, anything tragic. Although I was terrified as the days before leaving grew fewer, I also held in the back of my mind that I was darned proud of myself for making the entire thing happen. For once in my life, I was truly taking charge and leading rather than following. Maybe I was crazy, but it was all coming together.

I headed to the Ice in early October 2004, with my New Zealand coins in my pocket. The other new recruits and I convened in Christchurch, New Zealand, and boarded one of the last C-141s that would land on the Ice, and everyone was talking about it. It was a large military aircraft, and it reminded me of a huge bug with wings outside and an empty belly. The cargo was in the middle of the plane, and we were positioned around it on each side. I had my back to the outside of the plane, and the people four feet across from me faced me. We wore bulky clothes and boots, so I usually had a white boot on either side of me or on my lap, as did the person across from me. We each had coats supplied by the NSF, at large costs because of the quality of the Canada goose down coats. The one I had was bright red with fur trim, and it would have kept Santa Claus warm and toasty at the North Pole.

We'd been flying for about four hours when the plane started to turn abruptly. Shortly after, an announcement was made that our flight was going to boomerang, which meant we had to return to New Zealand because the Antarctica ice runway had been damaged by the prior flight and would not be repaired in time for our landing. I, for one, was particularly relieved that at least we weren't going to try to land, since landing on the Ross Sea ice was tricky to begin with and damaged sea ice didn't sound good. We returned to Christchurch and had to be ready for a very early flight the next morning. When we didn't take off that morning, we had to be ready early the next—and the next after that. Once the flight was canceled each morning, we were able to do whatever we wanted with the rest of the day. I was in a boardinghouse with many beds in each room and a bathroom down the hall, so I was able to be comfortable even though I really wanted to be on the Ice. The bigger issue with the delay was that the person who would be training me on the Ice was going to have less and less time to train me.

After a few days, we took off again to fly to Antarctica. We passed the point of no return—meaning, we'd run out of fuel if we turned around—and had to forge ahead and land. All I could see when the plane neared McMurdo Station was ice. Lots of ice. I was actually in view of Antarctica, going to land on Antarctica, and I was paid to be there. The trip there was paid, my physical was paid, my time in Christchurch was paid, and I was going to get paid to work in Antarctica. Considering I had no living expenses, it worked out well.

The plane hit the sea ice roughly, and we came to a stop near several buildings, if you can call them that. They looked more like huge boxes on skis. Most of the buildings, I assumed, could be disassembled and carted somewhere else when the ice thawed in the Ross Sea. Not a good idea to have a building sink to the bottom of the ocean. I had heard that the ice at the early part of spring in Antarctica was about fifteen feet thick, and somehow it held this huge military aircraft. I had no control over the universe, so I had to trust it again, especially as we made the bumpy landing.

I waddled off the plane in all my clothes, taking a lot of time to clomp down the stairs with the heavy bunny boots and gear. Then I stepped onto the ice, which felt like stepping onto the moon to me. I'd made it to my moon: Antarctica, the Ice, the Ultimate Adventure, and I was there.

A large piece of equipment was there to greet us. It looked like a huge bus on very expensive tires, each the size of a small car. I read the side of the bus: *Ivan the Terror*. I climbed into this vehicle as I wondered how soon I could take off all that gear that made me feel like a much overloaded, unstable Santa Claus.

Once in the village called McMurdo Station (*station*, not *base*, which implies something military), we unloaded from Ivan the Terror. I was met by the HR person who was holding down the fort from the main headquarters office until I got there. She was obviously glad I was there, and glad to be leaving in a day or two. She had not been there long, landing at the station as soon as the winter season ended in August, when planes could land on the ice safely. The period from mid-August until the first of October was called winfly (Winter Fly). It was the time when several flights brought in new personnel to help during the transition of personnel and equipment from winter to summer.

I was there for the mainbody session, which basically is Antarctica's summer when the majority of scientists come to complete studies. It got up to a balmy thirty-two degrees occasionally in December and January, but most of the time, the temperatures were much lower.

McMurdo Station is the largest of three current stations that the US has on Antarctica. In 2004, it held about 1,100 folks including those of us running the village and scientists, pilots, and management. The elusive South Pole held over 200 people, and its facilities were on top of ice two miles thick, therefore always on the move. The actual South Pole marker is moved about thirty feet every year because of the drift. Palmer is the third station and is on a peninsula below Chile. We learned to call it the banana belt station because a few plants actually grow in the area. Nothing was growing at McMurdo except the streams of water running beside the muddy main street of town. It truly looked like an old mining town, with Quonset-type buildings and dirt everywhere. I loved it.

I learned that no one owns Antarctica. In 1959, many countries ratified an international treaty, developed so that no one country could own the continent; there can be no military presence, and no mining for minerals or other commercial business. It is to be a stable, peaceful continent with a focus only on research. Many countries now have stations on Antarctica, although no one has a station at the South Pole except the US. It became my obsession to go to the South Pole.

I lugged my large duffel as my counterpart told me about life on Antarctica, though I wasn't listening. It was hard to comprehend all I was seeing, much less hearing. We headed to my new office for the next five months to drop my duffel off. I walked in, and it looked like an anywhere-in-the-US office. It was large and had a couch, large desk, computer, and a few storage areas crammed with miscellaneous items. Eventually I took my duffel to my new off-duty home. It was a three-story building, and my room was on the top level. No elevator. I was still dressed warmly and carrying my duffel. I schlepped everything upstairs, found my room, and fell onto one of the beds. There was a pillow and comforter on the bed and nothing else because we'd been told to bring our own bedding.

My room was the size of a large motel room, was very basic, and had a sink in one corner. I learned that the sink was coveted because most of the workers were on bunk beds with a bathroom down the hall. My room shared a bathroom with a shower with the adjacent room, so only four people were sharing it. There were two twin beds in my room, with back-to-back wardrobes dividing the room. Sue, my roommate, had occupied the room for several weeks before my arrival. Apparently much of the furniture in the rooms is gathered from unoccupied rooms as the seasonal staff changes, and she'd picked up our wardrobes that way. As I'd learn later, furniture was piled in the common room during the break, and people schlepped their prize pieces down hallways. It wasn't long before I found Skua, a free thrift shop. As the winter folks left, the amount of free, really good, brand stuff was amazing. No one staffed the shop, and it truly was a free-for-all. The name Skua fit well because a Skua is a bird of opportunity, appropriately related to the seagull family. Not only will it kill and eat young penguins, but it has also learned to dive-bomb and steal from any food tray carried outside by an unsuspecting worker.

I went to eat in the cafeteria called the Galley, washing my hands first in a large sink with foot pedals meant to keep germs at bay. A massive attack of the flu or some unknown disease could be disastrous on such a small station, even though the station had a medical department. The Galley was able to house over a thousand people as groups came and went. There were several stations with main courses, veggies, desserts, and even salads when "freshies"—real fresh fruits and vegetables—were available. Day one in Antarctica was coming to a close, and I sat on my bed, trying to evaluate my feelings. I was totally out of my element and pretty scared. I put on familiar pajamas and slippers, trying to be comfortable as I reminded myself why I'd wanted to come to Antarctica. All of a sudden, everything was scary. Would I be able to rise to the task, to meet the company's expectations? Did I have the skills I needed? Self-doubt crept in. I had not given credit to how totally burned out I was from my other job. And now I was on the Ice. I had worked for one company for over twenty years, resigned from it, and taken one week off to rent out my house before jumping to the Ice opportunity.

I had nothing to return to after this short assignment. True, I'd had over a week of training in Centennial to help prepare me for the job, but even that was all clumped together in my pages of notes. The hard-core job was one thing; my personal feelings were quite another. I had to integrate them so I wouldn't fall apart along the way. No one could see my tears that night, but I needed to stop overthinking everything.

I survived day two also. My HR counterpart was obviously ready to go, and I had arrived a few days later than expected, so she was extra-ready to go. I had one day of real training from her, and she was on her way. A HR coworker was to come shortly, so I'd be fending for myself for a few days. Now I was really scared. For the workers who came annually, this was like high school homecoming week. I could easily spot them as they greeted other longtimers who were arriving at the station.

I could tell already that life in Antarctica is tough, really tough. The people who had wintered over seemed like zombies, pasty colored and emotionless. They'd had no sunlight all winter. They sometimes cracked a smile as they left to catch planes to return home.

The season did progress, my coworker arrived and became my best friend, and I lived to tell it all. I had tried to have no expectations going to Antarctica, but in reality I was amassing more expectations as the job and time progressed.

WORK WAS WORK. HR SEEMS TO HAVE THE SAME ELEMENTS IN IT NO matter where the company is, even in Antarctica. I was in my little office day in and day out, working six days a week for ten to twelve hours a day with Darlene. Hours were longest at the beginning and end of the season, and I had a little break back to normal forty-hour workweeks in December.

Play was play, and it was incredible. We were able to walk the two miles to Scott Base, the facility run by the Kiwis from New Zealand. While on the base, the Kiwis sponsored additional activities such as the Polar Plunge. I had heard rumors about the Polar Plunge and, of course, asked to learn more.

"What's the Polar Plunge?" I asked someone who brought up the subject at McMurdo.

"It's where you jump in the ocean through a hole in the ice."

"How can that happen?"

"To do it the *right* way, you have to be nude. The Kiwis have a large hole they cut in the ice, they put a rope on you, and you jump in. To be counted, you have to do it nude."

It became an obsession with me. I had to do the Polar Plunge, the *right* way.

The opportunity came just after Christmas. The rumor mill at McMurdo was as sound as any workplace, and I started hearing that the Kiwis were going to "man the hole" on a weekend when I was off duty, just after the Christmas holiday. I questioned everyone I could about the timing of the event to ensure I made it there when the hole was open.

Not everyone will talk with the HR person, because usually we're the people no one wants to run into. Among other duties, we're expected to correct bad behavior, to solve problems with employees and management, and to fire someone when behavior is not corrected. Because I was the rule keeper, I was sometimes dreaded and people didn't want to talk around me. But I had a group of people who weren't afraid of me and would keep me in their loop. These people were usually more my age, seasoned travelers themselves. I befriended David, who had left a professional career to drive a forklift in Antarctica, and Naomi, who had three master's degrees and worked here as a janitor.

Eventually I convinced my roommate, Sue to go with me for the plunge, and we headed to Scott Base on a Sunday.

The walk to the base was beautiful, as long as the sun was out. This particular day was stunning. We traveled the dirt road talking and laughing all the way, as we were both nervous and excited at the same time. We walked up the long, uphill road then descended to the base quickly. We caught the attention of a local there, and he pointed us to the direction of the ice hole. We walked down and saw a bunch of commotion near a hut—another of the small mobile buildings. As usual, I first observed what was happening so I'd have a good idea of what I was in for.

There was a hole in the ice, about six feet or so in diameter. A man dressed in full Antarctica gear was above the hole. He was holding a rope that had a rock-climbing-type harness on the end of it. The water reached the top of the ice where the hole had been made. In the hole was a wooden ladder (thankfully not metal) reaching into the water. The ice was very thick around the hole, so there was no danger of the fellow, or me, falling through the ice. The nearby hut apparently was a warming hut and had a stove or electrical warming of some kind to help people recover from the plunge. At least I didn't have to be number one in line.

People were coming out of the warming hut with their parkas and boots on, and that was all. They were huddled over, trying to keep warm as they walked on rubber mats to the hole so their feet wouldn't freeze to the ice. Many peered into the hole and tried to hide their excited yet frightened reactions. The gatekeeper put the harness on the next hole jumper and snapped the carabiner shut. He apparently asked the participant something, and then almost immediately, the fellow jumped into the water in the hole. He was underwater only a few seconds, and he came up screaming, "Oh crap, holy crap, this is *cold!*"

Hmm. Could I do it? The fellow very quickly found the ladder and scrambled up it, found his coat and boots, then ran for the warming hut. He had lived, and I decided I would too. I knew I would be sorry if I didn't do it. I couldn't doubt myself. Sue, on the other hand, wasn't talking much, so I couldn't tell what she was thinking.

Sue and I went over to the warming hut and went inside. The recent participant/victim/fool was talking loudly and quickly, telling everyone how very cold it was and what an experience it was. I started undressing with my ear glued to his story. Sue put on her bathing suit. She apparently was going to do a pseudo plunge. Try as hard as I could, I couldn't convince her to go nude. Meanwhile, I was totally undressing. I put my bunny boots on my feet and my huge parka on my nude body.

I reticently opened the door outside to a group of faces peering at us, encouraging us. Many of them were my friends who had just plunged, and they were all saying, "You *have* to do it. Go in!" I slowly walked up to the plunge gatekeeper, and he put the harness on my nude body and clipped in the carabineer to the rope.

Then I made my mistake. I said to him, in my nervousness, "I hope I don't have a heart attack."

It couldn't have been more than a second before he raised his eyes to meet mine and I knew I had made a mistake. He was probably going to tell me I couldn't make the jump due to medical liability. In the next second, I jumped in—no opportunity was going to be missed here.

Just like the other victim, I came up screaming and yelling just to ensure my lungs were still working. I took a stroke over to the ladder and scrambled up it, my face lit and eyes smiling.

The gatekeeper immediately asked me, "Are you okay?"

I answered, "You bet!" In thinking about it after the jump, I don't even recall the cold. It all happened so fast, and I got out in a blink, put on my boots and parka so I wouldn't stick to the ice or get frostbite, and ran to the warming hut. I became the fellow I had just watched come from the plunge, with animated facial expressions and very graphic words describing the event.

Darlene and I worked long hours daily. But life in the small office wasn't always calculated. We paid particular attention to events around the station, like the chili cook-off, the Turkey Trot at Thanksgiving, the holiday choir, music events—a myriad of activities to keep us more or less happy and less homesick. The people in the community became our family. There was even a recreation department that ran events like taking a monstrous busload of folks to Robert Falcon Scott's historical cabin near McMurdo Station. With the constant low temperatures, everything in the early explorer's hut was preserved.

Whenever people started running past our office, my sense of curiosity rose. This didn't happen very often, but the few times it did, Darlene and I immediately closed the office and followed the crowds. Usually, it was because of PIT (penguins in town). The first time there were four very lost Adélie penguins that had wandered by the power plant and were playing on the ice, jumping into the pools of water on the ice near the shore. Our mandate was not to change the behavior of the penguins, so we could line up along the road, then sit and watch them, but we could do nothing to disturb them. They played for hours. They'd line up and waddle in a row for a few feet, then plop on their stomachs, turn, and paddle on the snow. They started up the small hill to the power plant and then returned to the ice.

Another time we followed the crowds and watched as a lone Adélie penguin waddled down Main Street (so we called it) on the station. He had no trouble with the dirt road and waddled as if his arms were starched and ironed straight. Photographers were lying on the road taking pictures, and the little Adélie just marched past, as if on a mission. We couldn't help but wonder if he would be all right, but it wasn't our job to change his determination or direction.

The Emperor penguins would sometimes stand behind a snowbank, taking protection from the wind. I never saw one come into town, but they were near the Sea Ice Runway buildings and road, like statues waiting for something—or nothing—to happen.

As the season grew to a close, someone suggested taking a collection of pictures of the *Amazing Women of Antarctica*. I wanted to be in the collection. I deserved to be in the collection. Turned out, many of my friends wanted to be in the collection also.

Darlene and I started talking about our vision for our pictures. She wanted a long dress that would accent her beautiful figure and eyes. She somehow came up with the dress. I asked her next where she would like the picture taken. Immediately she said, "In a Pickle." A Pickle, it turned out, was her favorite vehicle on the Ice. We had no idea how it got its name. It was a small but powerful vehicle, like a small golf cart, used for transportation, just as all the vehicles are on the Ice. Darlene thought it was cute. We happened to see one parked near the building where we worked—this was our chance. She put on her dress at lunchtime and posed in the driver's seat. It was where she belonged, that strong, wonderful personality. *Snap!* I took the picture.

My opportunity came a few days later. Imagine a soccer game on the Ice. Many fans from both Scott Base (the Kiwis from New Zealand) and McMurdo Station (all the US folks) lined the sidelines to cheer. The Kiwis brought a truck with a couch, clever folks that they are.

We were able to get a ride to the game in one of the largest people-hauling vehicles. Imagine a large orange crate, like the ones on a freight ship, on a truck chassis with huge tires. Once there, I changed into a thin, black, long-sleeved V-neck top and a long black skirt with buttons. I then gave the camera to one of my friends below, stood where the wind would open the skirt a bit, and told him to fire away. The *Amazing Women of Antarctica* series was in the Coffee House, our own little coffee shop, last time I saw it. And I am still friends with several of the women in the pictures, decades after they were taken.

When I recall the season, although it began wobbly, it became one of the most remarkable times of my life. I was proud of myself for making it all happen, for rising to the occasion. Without my perseverance, the physical would not have been completed, I would not have gotten on the airplane with my New Zealand coins, and I never would have had one of the most remarkable transitions in my life. I came out stronger than ever.

Note to self: You're alive to tell about it.

CHAPTER 13

Fiji

I WAS NOT DOING WELL AFTER WORKING AT McMURDO. I WAS REALLY whipped after the long hours and huge amount of work, particularly at the end of my contract when everyone was leaving the Ice and it was my responsibility to tie up loose ends. My thoughts were bouncing around everywhere in my head. Thoughts like *Can I survive without a job? Can I really retire? What am I coming home to after life on the Ice? What about my friendships? How is my family?* I had vowed to move to a small town upon return to the States so I could get a glimpse of my small-town roots once again, and I was going to make it happen. It all sounded overwhelming, but I was developing the confidence to make most anything in my life happen.

Before that, though, I needed a break. After surviving five months at McMurdo, nothing sounded better than a trip to Fiji. My friend David and I both were glad to be leaving the starkness of McMurdo. Its luster had worn off, and it reminded me of a weathered, dirty town in the middle of nowhere. Weather was starting to come in, and the dreariness of the scene was becoming all too familiar. Everyone had been working very hard, including many twelve-hour days with little time off to ensure the winter crew had all their supplies. We were all ready to leave.

I was one of the last summer people to leave on a flight that took me from McMurdo back to New Zealand's green grass, flowers, and smells. McMurdo had none of that. All of a sudden, life was alive again. I had to choose to enjoy it, even though it forced its way on me whether I wanted it or not. David brought me a rose so it would be one of the first things I would smell. He had left earlier than I had.

We took off for Nadi, Fiji, after a few days in New Zealand. Nadi is the capital of Fiji and has the only airport in the area. The rest of the hundreds of islands are reached by boat. After a night in Nadi, we caught a small old motorboat, carrying probably ten passengers, to a small island where our resort was located. We had booked something online because it sounded quaint and off the grid.

The boat pulled onto a beach in front of a palm-frond building that had several long wooden tables under the roof. It was very humid, and I was already sweating. It became obvious that only a roof was necessary over the dining hall because if there had been walls, tourists would melt with the heat. We would have roasted like turkeys in an enclosure, with our sunscreen being the basting oil.

David and I were taken to one of several small bungalows. Ours consisted of partial walls, a bed with mosquito netting, and a raised toilet and shower to make up the bathroom. We didn't need much else. The ocean was about twenty feet away, and a large string hammock hung out the front door.

After a day of doing very little, I finally put on a snorkel mask and fins. To describe the color of the coral is like describing the color in a Disney movie. Every color of the rainbow was there, and each coral had a greenish tip on it, showing that it was alive and growing. There were thousands of pieces of coral there, one on top of the other, each one competing for space and food. It was hard not to just look from side to side as each coral came into view. I was in my own private aquarium and magic kingdom, in awe of the sight.

After McMurdo, this was heaven. I was not able to do much of anything for a day or two as I recovered from the huge amount of pressure I'd endured at McMurdo. I was able to read the book I had taken to McMurdo and never opened, and to swing for an hour or two in the hammock with nothing but the warm, gentle breezes surrounding me. But after that, it is my nature to get bored, so I looked for things to do. Wandering the beach was always available, and it was easy to get lost for a few hours following the coastline while looking for shells.

Note to self: This is paradise—take pictures in your mind.

THE RESORT OFFERED ACTIVITIES DAILY. I SIGNED UP FOR A FISHING TRIP, Fijian style, which meant that I was given a string with a hook on the end and a little piece of wood to roll the line up and down. I had no luck, but the guide on the boat caught a barracuda, which was not happy. It was going to be dinner for the guide, but it fought valiantly with its sharp teeth.

The resort was owned and operated by the local village over a small hill, and I could only assume that it was typical on the islands for the villages to make money from tourism. One of the village leaders came to greet us at the resort regularly and offered us grog one morning. Grog is made from the root of the kava plant, which is known to have a sedating power that relaxes you without affecting your mental capabilities. He made the grog by putting the ground-up kava root in a piece of cloth like cotton, adding water, and using his very dirty hands to squeeze the cloth as the liquid seeped through it into a large wooden bowl. He offered us a small coconut dish full of the drink, and although I hesitated at first, I drank the liquid as I looked to the skies to silently ask for protection from all the germs I was drinking. I considered that the experience was adding to my immune system. I also had brought some Cipro, a prescription drug that could cure diarrhea in a heartbeat. I could take some, should all else fail, if I got extra unwelcome bugs in my stomach.

Having been in rough, cold weather for so long, the totally different temperature and humidity of Fiji caught me off guard. I was always covered with sweat, and I repeatedly headed to the ocean for a quick rinse. I had been out snorkeling for half an hour when I saw my first shark. It was large, swimming fast, and coming my way. I had to think fast without panicking. I knew from the electrifying movie *Jaws* that I shouldn't scream or make a lot of splashing noise. My instinct was to be calm and to slowly swim away from its path. Now, this was not like a great white shark—it turned out to be a harmless reef shark that really didn't care if I was there or not. I cared, but it didn't. It swam gracefully toward me and passed me on the right, as if I were just another large obstacle in its path. Later I learned that sharks regularly came into the cove in front of the bungalow. It wasn't newsworthy in that remote region of the world.

Sunday was a big deal in Fiji. All the resort guests were invited to go to the village to attend church. David and I decided to attend, and I wrapped myself in a large cloth that draped over my bathing suit, put on my Teva sandals, and got in line to traipse to the village. The village was over a hill that was no more than two hundred feet high, but with the humidity, it seemed like a few thousand feet high. It took me an incredible amount of energy to do this short hike. We followed a dirt path that the people of the island used daily to come to the resort to work and serve meals. With all the rain, it was slippery and had many obstacles ready to break our ankles. There were no roads, and hence no cars at all on the tiny island.

As we hiked over the hill, I started sweating. I had not brought water with me, which turned out to be a problem. We were the guests of the village, and I had to act gracious even though I was sweating what felt like gallons of moisture from my body.

We saw several vendors in the village once we survived the half-hour hike. They sat on the ground, on a piece of cloth or on a braided palm mat, with things like tapa cloth—a craft using bark with designs that can be used as place mats, pictures, and other things—for sale. Some vendors had woven fans from palm leaves, and others had made jewelry from local materials. It was hard not to buy something, knowing the vendors would be happy, but we needed to get to the church. I should have bought a fan.

The local chief showed us into the church, and we sat on a large wooden bench with a back. Mercifully, I was near a window, but it didn't help much with the stillness of the air and the humidity. I was swimming in my own water. It was hard for me to pay attention to the sermon without being preoccupied with my predicament. Heck, I had just come from friggin' Antarctica where it was eternally cold, never above freezing temperatures.

Note to self: Your body is in shock—or begging to go back to the Ice.

I SAT, MISERABLE, ON THE BENCH LOOKING FOR A SCRAP OF PAPER OR ANY-thing I could use as a fan. It wasn't until a large lady sitting in front of me turned around that I had any hope of surviving. She had been using a handmade fan for a long time, and I tried in vain to catch some of the wisps of cool air from it. Somehow she sensed my predicament and offered me her fan. Normally I would have turned it down, appreciating the help but wanting to wallow in my sad situation alone. This time I lit up like a Christmas tree and almost grabbed it out of her hands. I sat there and just tried to survive with my newfound tool. The tiny, regularly occurring breaths of fresh air helped immensely. Actually it was probably the idea that I had a fan more than the fan itself that made me feel good.

The service did end, and I gave the fan back to my savior. I thanked her profusely, and David and I walked out the door to see about the next event. I was up for serendipity at this point. I immediately went over to the craft area and bought a handwoven fan. Then we were invited into the chief's house for the main meal of the day. I think the leader of the town scouted out those he thought might have money to contribute, and David and I looked the part even though I was in a sarong and sandals.

Including the family, David, and me, there were probably eight people who sat on the dirt floor on mats, and I watched everyone around me because I had no idea of protocol. A large pot was boiling over the small indoor fire, and the chief's wife told us she was cooking fish. Well, this tiny island was surrounded by water, so it made sense that fish was a mainstay. The chief's wife handed us small pieces of fish, offered us kava, and served unusual foods to round out the meal. I was to the point where I wasn't asking what I was eating. Like a good little girl, I was tasting everything. Eventually we left, and fortunately I'd had enough water and kava to make it back over the hill, past the pig pens and squealing animals, to our bungalow without dehydrating too badly.

The next night David and I ate a lobster dinner by the sea. We had to place the order the day before so the local fishermen would have time to catch the lobsters. We weren't able to see them actually catch the valuable meal like I had seen in Costa Rica, but we knew it was happening.

As night approached, we walked toward the regular dining hut, where we expected to eat. As we rounded the corner, there on the sand was a table for two, complete with place settings and wine glasses. It was incredible to see it there, in the middle of nowhere, right beside the beautiful sea and on a sandy beach. Our host guided us to the table, and we sat as he served our special lobster dinner, one course at a time.

I so deserved this dinner after surviving the humidity of the day at the village. Plus, it was a terrific way to complete our much-deserved vacation after working so diligently and hard at the coldest place on earth. I ate every bite with gusto.

CHAPTER 14

Nepal I

For me, 2006 was a hard year. I spent about eight months going back and forth between my home in California to my parents' home in Virginia on Chesapeake Bay. My friend Helen—the one who'd inspired me to have no regrets—had died recently, Aunt Bertie had committed suicide because she was undergoing dialysis every day, and my dad was dying of cancer. It was my job to help my mother and father through that process while also trying to keep my sanity and watching for depression.

My father was diagnosed in April of 2006, and I had a trip planned to Nepal in October that same year. As the departure time grew closer, I was torn between staying to help and doing the traveling I loved. My mother gave me her support, saying, "You know your father would encourage you to go. Just go." The trip was for about a month, and I let my mom give me permission to go.

Note to self: Your mother is a wise woman.

Trekking to Everest Base Camp is to mountain climbers as visiting Nirvana is to spiritual souls. It is a spiritual journey in an amazing place, and it includes a lot of hard work to get there. Since it was near the top of Judy's and my bucket lists, as soon as we started to map out our journeys to foreign places, especially third-world countries, it was right up there near the top. I never considered climbing Mount Everest because it is so dangerous, and just being able to trek to see it was enough of a goal—so we set our sights on the base camp.

By that point, I had become interested in Buddhism, the religion of northern Nepal and Tibet, and I would be in those areas on this climb, so I wanted to learn more. I had to simplify the premise of the religion so I could understand it, but the core beliefs that resonated with me were that nothing is permanent, and that suffering is caused by attachments to things, including beliefs or people. I still scoffed at religions after my Midwestern upbringing, but sometimes I referred to non-Western religions to give me something to hold on to.

Note to self: This seems like something that can bring you peace.

Because we would be trekking in a third-world country, and because I didn't fully trust my navigation skills, I decided to investigate having a guide and, even more welcome, a porter who would haul our gear. I contacted an old friend who had led trips from the States in Nepal and asked him about guide services. It was important to me to use local people not only because they knew the land and its physical requirements but also so we could help the local economy.

I contacted the recommended owner in Nepal, and he seemed exceptionally helpful and had good English skills. We corresponded by email and set up a trip arriving at the Kathmandu international airport.

While Judy and I were on the plane, our eyes were glued to the ground as we were about to land in Nepal. It had been an extremely long flight, with a change of planes in Bangkok and a day lost and regained on the International Date Line. The mountains were shrouded in clouds and fog, so we were disappointed in the view. Shortly, however, the greenness of the valleys below became visible, and we couldn't say a word. We could see huge valleys with terraces like I'd imagined when I'd seen the terraces in the Sierra Nevada mountains in Spain. The terraces were cultivated lands with tiny houses here and there. There were no roads. The valleys eventually gave way to roads and more people until we could only see buildings and the airport.

We made it off the airplane and into the airport with hopes of finding our large and heavy backpacks intact and available. By some stroke of luck, they appeared and we hauled them on our backs as we made our way for the doors to the capital of Nepal, the huge city of Kathmandu. All was quiet and somewhat orderly as we walked the halls to the outside. Then we walked past the guards, who provided a little sense of security, and saw the real Kathmandu. Hundreds of people clamored on fences, trying to get our attention as we exited the airport. They were climbing as high up as they could. We obviously were tourists, we had backpacks, and everyone wanted to carry them for us anywhere we wanted them taken. We were astounded by the scene, and I had to check my emotions as we surveyed the mobs of people. I wanted to help all of them. At the same time, I was wary because of the political unrest and reports of a few recent murders here and there. I had to remember there are murders in the States also.

Luckily, before I attempted to pass through the mob on the street, I quickly scanned the crowd on the fence and happened to see a sign about ten feet up that said *Linda and Judy*. I pointed to the sign for Judy, and we looked at each other with huge smiles. We were going to live. Someone in Nepal knew that we existed!

We jostled through the crowd, trying to ignore people's pleas. Our two fellows met us, gave us each a traditional white welcome scarf, and led us to a small, old passenger car. We were happy to pile in while the two men talked excitedly. It quickly became apparent that they were the owner of the outfit and a helper and that they were taking us to a hotel that the owner hoped to buy (he did eventually). At this time in Nepal, the government was unstable, Maoists were trying to take power from the monarchy, and tourism was suffering somewhat. In reality all the small shops and guides wanted our tourist dollars. Financially, it was a good time to visit Nepal, especially for people like me who love indigenous crafts.

Although we were very tired from our trip, our eyes were glued on the scenery that was passing quickly. Kathmandu was exciting, very busy, colorful, and new to us. The streets were uneven, some unpaved, and I figured we were on a back road. Most of the buildings outside the main area of town were only two or three stories high, and some only one story. Space was at a premium as we got closer to downtown, and the buildings were taller, casting shadows across the streets. In the darkness, it was hard to absorb all the things we were seeing. We arrived at the hotel, which was tucked away from the main streets of the Thamal tourist area on a dark street just wide enough for one car at a time. The gray-and-white hotel was decorated with massive stone columns and marigolds floating in dishes all over the large front porch. Later we were told that the flowers were in celebration of Dashain, one of the most important celebrations in Nepal. The ten-day holiday symbolizes the victory of good over evil.

The hotel had a large entry hall, and several desk clerks were around even though it was late at night. Several men tried to help us with our luggage, so we let them as we were led to our spacious room. The beds were double-size and adequate, though a bit hard. I looked for a few more blankets for sleeping and put them on the bed because it was cold and the room wasn't heated well. We were grateful to have successfully flown to such an unusual destination and to have found the owner and hotel without being beaten or mauled. It was all new to us.

The next day, the owner of the outfit asked for our passports so he could get the permits required for our journey to Base Camp. It was a little disconcerting to hand over our passports in the middle of such an unknown place, but it was required. This was another trust-the-universe moment. We were told that we would meet our hiking guide that night and that another guide would be taking us on an introductory tour of Kathmandu in the afternoon.

Later in the day, a young man took us to all the most important shrines and holy places, where he explained the mandalas and figures of the gods and goddesses of Nepal. Apparently most of Nepal is Hindu, but the primary religion of the Himalayas is Buddhism. We were tired after our long journey to Nepal, but we weren't about to miss this introduction.

Kathmandu is worthy of a trip unto itself. Aside from visiting places like Mexico and South America, I had not been in many third-world countries. This was definitely third world. Streets were bustling with small cars, a few dilapidated trucks, motorcycles, rickshaws, and foot traffic. Stores were open all day and into the night. They had narrow storefronts yet were quite long. When closed, they had roll-down partitions with locks, like storage sheds. Everyone bargained for everything. In other words, every price was negotiable. In addition, there was no sales tax, and I had no idea where the government got its money without it. I was in full buying mode yet knew my pack would need to be carried and was worried about accumulating items. Luckily, there was space at the hotel to store things while we were on our trek.

After the several-hour tour, Judy and I struck out on our own with a hotel business card in hopes that a taxi or rickshaw could find it again. We wandered the streets in Thamal even though they were a bit confusing because they weren't straight. I started noticing details about the area, such as the electrical fixtures that were outside. As I looked up at something appearing to be a telephone pole, I could see probably over forty electrical wires connected to heaven knows what at the top of the pole. I could only think of all our regulations in the States and how dangerous this probably was.

Next we came around a corner and saw beaders. Nepal, known for its vibrant colors, could be described by its beads. I had to step back and absorb what I was seeing. It was a sea of colors, the popular reds and greens, yellow, white, blue—every color of the rainbow. Thirty strands of beads would be in one lot, and hundreds of the shiny beads were hanging from each vendor's stall. Young men sat on the ground on mats with strands of strings on their feet, around their toes. When I realized what was happening, I was amazed. These young men were stringing the minute beads on the strands by using their feet and toes for support. One bead at a time, the young men created each strand quickly and skillfully. I didn't know if this was a task that they would do forever, or if only youngsters did it until it took its toll, as I imagined the repetitive task encouraged arthritis or other debilitating problems. I could only absorb the scene.

Later that evening we met the man who would guide our trek to Base Camp, and he told us a bit about the trip and the porter who would help during the journey. We would just have one guide and one porter, who would handle both our packs. To be fair to him, each pack was weighed to ensure he wasn't carrying more than the amount allowed by the Nepalese government.

From Kathmandu we flew to Lukla, which I later found out is one of the most dangerous airports in the world. *In the world?* Judy and I both got seats on the left side of the plane so we could see Everest if it decided to poke itself out of the clouds. As we left the ground in the eight-passenger plane, I said a Hail Mary even though I'm not religious. We weren't able to see Everest that day, but the mountain range loomed largely within sight. I was seeing the Himalayas, one of the largest ranges in the world that contained the highest peak on earth. I felt I was almost in my Nirvana.

The flight to Lukla was less than an hour. This plane was going very slowly compared to the larger planes I was used to, so I had to trust that the plane would make the flight. It wasn't long before I could see land coming closer to us. It was the Lukla airport, or more like the Lukla landing site. We were over a deep valley, heading toward a mountain. Instead of veering up, away from the mountain, we headed right for it. We got closer and closer, and I looked more intently on what was going to happen. The plane was going right for a landing strip that had a huge cliff going up at the end of it.

The mountain zoomed closer, and my fear threatened to set in. I had absolutely no control over what was going to happen, so there was no reason to get nutty about the situation. The plane stayed over the valley until the landing strip was directly underneath it. Then it touched ground quickly and began braking so hard that we all were thrust forward in our seats. Miraculously, the plane came to a stop a hundred feet or so before the mountain wall. I was reminded of stories about crashes at this airport, planes *not* stopping before the wall, but our flight was perfect.

We left later that afternoon, with Judy and me carrying daypacks with water and snacks on our backs while the porter took both our larger packs, with sleeping bags, warm clothing, emergency gear, and other items we thought we couldn't live without. The porter carried one pack on top of the other, with no help from animals or the guide. Luckily, we were starting out at an elevation of ten thousand feet, and it wasn't as hot as it had been in Kathmandu.

Also, there were no cars. We were in an area where there were absolutely no roads and no cars. The stones of the buildings in Lukla were so perfectly cut that I thought the stonecutters were incredible. But there was no electricity and no electric tools. I saw a building being constructed and looked inside. There sitting on the ground was a man with a chisel making blocks. I realized that this was the primitive way the buildings in the area were made, and I was honored to be witnessing it. We were turning back centuries, entering a country where everything I was used to—cars, electronics, watches—was unknown. Also, everything was handmade, and usually made out of necessity, not commodity.

The guide taught us a few trekking tips, mainly to relax as we crossed the footbridges over the raging rivers so the bridge would sway. Also, he told us, always let the yaks have the right of way on the bridges. If they started from the other end and we were on the bridge, we were to *turn around quickly*. There is no room to squeeze past a yak on a bridge.

On the first day, I stopped after a few hours and threw up. The change in altitude had taken its toll on me, even though it was only an additional thousand feet from where we'd started. I exchanged looks with the guide. His nonverbal stare said, *You aren't going to make this trip!* My stare back said, *You don't know me.*

We reached a tiny town in the mountains en route to Everest. Namche Bazaar had a charm all its own. I had heard about its flavor from a friend who frequently climbed in the area. He said wistfully, "Oh my, I wish I were going with you to Namche Bazaar." I saw what he was talking about immediately. Sir Edmund Hillary came there, the Tibetans fleeing the Chinese takeover came there, and the Maoists were there trying to recruit new members into their political party. Our guide told us to steer clear of the whole mess. I decided not to rock the boat, even though we were approached by someone who started reciting Maoist lines to us.

At one point on the trail, before Namche Bazaar, we had come to a bend in the trail that was totally blocked by Nepalese people. Our guide had told us very quietly, "Walk on past me and keep walking with the porter. Don't say anything to anyone. I will deal with this." I didn't know what "this" was. Eventually, even though our guide said very little, we understood that Maoists were interfering with tourists trying to trek to Everest. Since this was the most popular trek in Nepal, it made sense for them to try to extort money for tourists to pass. We followed our guide's instructions and kept moving forward, without incident.

We stayed in Namche Bazaar for two nights. We were tired the first night and so did little exploring. The next day, however, Judy and I explored all over town to try to understand the town and its people. We avoided a large Maoist event, complete with a loudspeaker, even though it seemed to attract many locals. We stumbled onto an open-air Saturday market a short distance from the main tourist area and watched with fascination. People from all over the local valleys had brought their goods to the market. Those from above Namche Bazaar brought potatoes, which could grow at amazingly high altitudes, and those who lived lower than the town brought rice because the rice would only grow at lower elevations. There were other hearty vegetables in the mix, but there were not nearly the choices we'd seen in Kathmandu.

The next morning we started up the trail again, working our way toward Tengboche Monastery, famous for its monk population and daily services. On our way up the valley, we were stunned to see a middle-aged trekker being helped down with a friend on each arm. He was white as a sheet and obviously very sick from the altitude. He was stumbling and having a very difficult descent, step by step, even with the help. It was a solemn reminder that we were at the mercy of the mountain and to pay attention to our self-knowledge from all our hiking experience. He probably had no prior experience or was trying to impress someone and had pushed too hard too fast. We had mountain-climbing experience, but only to the altitude of Mount Whitney in California, which was about 14,500 feet. We had no idea how we would do once we got to 18,000 feet.

Along the way were toilets—well, more like holes in the ground. Any toilet was available to anyone. At one checkpoint several tourists, including me, stopped to use one. It was just a hole in wood, with a tiny, square wooden building around the hole. At this stop, and most of the others, we would open the door, turn around and lock it—if a piece of wood that turned to lock it existed—and then stand with legs spread over the sacred hole. Obviously, it was harder for a woman to use than for a man. At this particular stop, I recall a young woman coming out of the bathroom with a mixture of emotions. She was trying not to laugh, but she also obviously had something on her mind. It turned out, she had dropped her only pair of sunglasses in the hole and, wisely, decided not to go after them.

At another bathroom stop, I recall approaching the box with a hole and taking a second look at the box before entering. Basically it was a box for privacy, and a hole for outside access, but there was no pit below the hole. Instead it opened directly into the stream that ran under the hole a few feet below. I had to remind myself that this was not my country or my standards, and I wasn't allowed to judge anything. I was just allowed to observe.

As we entered what could be considered the town area, the monastery's presence took over. I couldn't see much other than a tiny store, several small houses with their individual gardens, and the famous monastery.

The guide told us that we were allowed to go into the monastery as long as we didn't bother the monks or the ceremony. I got the message and obeyed, but a middle-aged trekker did not. As visitors, we had to take off our shoes, leave them in the front area, come into the prayer room, and remain at the back of the room. The tourist either didn't get the message or didn't care. He had a fancy camera with fancy lenses and was fascinated by the monks. Apparently he had been granted permission to take pictures of the monks' prayers and practices, and he took advantage of it, in my opinion.

I watched what was happening and realized that the photographer was coming in close, taking what seemed like a thousand pictures just inches from a monk's face. The monk didn't flinch. If I read him right, he was trying to maintain his composure during the tourist's incredibly inconsiderate actions. I'm sure it must have tried the monk's patience and forced him to internalize his unhappiness about the whole thing. After ten minutes or so, the pictures stopped and the ceremony continued as if nothing unusual had happened. The monk seemed relieved—but maybe that was just me.

It snowed in Tengboche that afternoon. I tried hard not to take it as a forewarning about the days to come, especially since Judy got extremely cold during our visit to the monastery and I was worried she would get sick in the next few days.

As we resumed our trek, at one point I heard yelling from somewhere in front of me. As I rounded a corner, I saw a huge animal on the trail. It had the shape of the musk ox of the Arctic—old, fierce, intimidating animals with super-long hair. In Lukla, I'd seen cows that lived at lower elevations, much like the ones ranchers raised in the States. This animal in front of me could have taken me out if it chose to. It resembled a prehistoric creature.

Our guide quickly came back to me—I was always in the back—and told me to immediately get off the trail and get somewhere safe. Well, that got my attention, especially since I wasn't sure what a safe distance was. I turned around and quickly climbed a muddy embankment to get about four feet off the trail and watch from above. The guide gave me a thumbs-up, which I took to mean that I was a safe distance from trouble.

Apparently these amazing animals were the yaks we had been forewarned about, domesticated cattle owned by the people in the area and used to haul supplies up and down the mountain valleys. Because the trails are so steep and narrow, there is no room for an argument about right-of-way when encountering these creatures. You move off the trail, quickly. The yaks don't necessarily follow each other all the time, so one yak may be on the trail while the one right behind it is trying to pass it on its right or left. In other words, there were few safe places at all on the trail. I recalled the guide's early advice about the swinging cable bridges, filling in the blanks with the imagery of a raging river five hundred feet below, and realized that encountering a yak there would be another story altogether.

From my seemingly safe spot above the trail, I watched the first yak pass by. It had a huge metal bell attached to its neck with a handmade wool strap. The bell had a low ring to it, kind of like a hammer in a sock hitting a metal bowl. After a few more encounters, I learned that the first yak always had a bell, and sometimes others in the line did also. I could only guess that the first yak was probably somewhat more well behaved than the others and was chosen to be an example of what a good yak was supposed to do.

First Yak ambled on the trail as I stayed my safe distance from it. From then on, however, it was a crapshoot. Second Yak darted alongside First Yak, and then Third Yak decided to start uphill to avoid the mess that First Yak and Second Yak had created. Third Yak was getting close to me, and I didn't like it, so I scrambled to higher ground. These beasts easily could have taken me out, not even knowing what they were doing.

The swinging suspension bridges were incredible, and I was very grateful they'd been upgraded from the wooden ones from prior years. We still came across wooden bridges from time to time, but most of the major bridges had been replaced with steel cables and metal steps. Still, as one person started across a bridge, the weight and motion caused the bridge to swing and groan from yet one more passenger. Now, imagine starting to cross the bridge, being halfway across the two-hundred-foot bridge, and seeing a herd of yaks coming at you. They had no idea that their load could knock us over the cables of the bridge, but we knew it. More than once, we started across a bridge, saw a herd of yaks on the other side, and immediately turned around to run back into the safe zone, if we could find it.

We trekked, ever upward, and stayed in the teahouses the porter found for us. He continuously traveled ahead to ensure we had a place to stay each night. Considering he carried our two packs and still went twice as fast as we did, I felt fairly small in the hiking world, or at least on this trek.

The thing about how Judy and I travel together is, we really, really care about each other and will watch the other's back. On this trip, we had asked for a guide who wouldn't mind two older women who were slow. Actually, it was in our best interest to go slowly. We knew that going slowly gave us a much better chance of not contracting altitude sickness. At these altitudes, we could die if we didn't respect the mountains and their effect on our bodies. Meanwhile, porters carrying huge packs with heavy loads were passing us, wearing only flip-flops. In wet weather, it made sense to wear flip-flops in the occasional streams we crossed, but as the porters got higher on the mountain, the weather was much colder with the chance of snow at any point. I worried about frostbite without shoes and socks.

One man had carried four pieces of full-sized plywood from Lukla to help with new buildings. The man, small but with muscles most men would die for, was bent over with his load, carrying the wood pieces strapped together on his back. I had to believe that he had been carrying the wood for three to four days to be at this point from Lukla. Apparently the people of the region had decided collectively that they did not want a road, cars, and everything that accompanies modernization, so the transportation of goods remains as it has for centuries. The middle-aged man carrying the plywood was rewarded for his efforts because wages are paid by the weight of the load.

We made it to Gorak Shep, the last little town before Everest Base Camp, our goal. The porter had gone ahead to book a place for us since there were few accommodations. When we got there, I realized the sleeping arrangements were like cold prison cells, uninviting. Yet we welcomed them just because they existed and they were our only choice. We dumped our gear there.

By this time Judy was coughing terribly, but there was no holding her back. We were going to make it and started for Base Camp that afternoon.

We had passed several piles of rocks, cairns made for people whose lives had been claimed on the mountain. Monuments for Scott Fischer, Rob Hall, and Doug Hansen, to name a few from the 1996 Everest disaster, were there outside Gorak Shep too. There were more and more cairns the more we looked. I silently thanked the stars that I wasn't gung ho to summit the big one. Never was a fan and never would be.

We had been hiking all afternoon, getting higher and higher toward our eighteen-thousand-foot goal of Everest Base Camp. It was exhausting, and I was getting slower and slower with the altitude, whining about being tired, this was too hard, maybe I couldn't do it—things like that. Despite my complaining, of course I was determined to get to Base Camp, even if the avalanches were going to wipe me out on the way, as the warning signs said might happen. Judy, on the other hand, made no fuss even though every other breath was a sneeze. She was fairly miserable, but she kept it to herself, whereas I wore my pain on my sleeve, shoulder, or any other body part that could get attention.

Then I fell on the wet rock steps and twisted my ankle. It didn't hurt much and seemed to be just a twist, but I couldn't help thinking about the time I had broken my ankle on a mountain climb a few years earlier. Two friends and I had been coming down from the mountaintop when I slipped in mud above a lake on a trail-less area in northern Nevada. All three of us heard the ankle break, like small pebbles washing ashore together in the ocean. I managed to break both the tibia and fibula, so my foot was hanging off the leg, with the boot still on. Miraculously, my girlfriend was carrying a cell phone—one of the early, heavy ones—for the first time, so we were able to arrange a helicopter rescue from the Naval Air Station in Fallon. During the communications, they asked me my weight and told me to angle my legs uphill to prevent shock and to put snow in baggies on the ankle so it wouldn't swell.

When I realized that the trail was too rugged for the helicopter to land, and I was going to be lifted into the helicopter in a litter with a young man standing on top of me, I said to the young man, "I lied."

He looked at me and asked, "What do you mean you lied? About what?"

"With you and me on this litter and the tiny cable going up to the helicopter, you should know I lied about my weight. Add fifteen pounds to the number I gave you."

He cracked a smile, and I was hauled up successfully then taken to Elko, Nevada, for care.

It was the aftermath of that trauma that changed my life. After the immediate trauma was taken care of, I was home for several weeks by myself. I never asked anyone for help because, heck, I didn't need anyone and could do everything for myself. For the most part, I did do everything for myself, but I couldn't drive since the injury was in my right leg. I couldn't get to the grocery store, and I was as stubborn as ever. I ate what I had in the house, which didn't include any fats or sugars. I wasn't really hungry, but I wasn't eating all I was used to either. My supplies, and my weight, dwindled. Ultimately, I lost forty pounds in two months and looked incredible. I remembered the familiarity of being thin and having a great appearance. Once my ability to drive and eat became normal again, I wanted to keep my weight down, and bulimia raised its ugly head again. By this time, however, I was becoming more confident with myself and wasn't totally depending on my looks to buy compliments. My relapse lasted awhile before I was able to get it under control again.

Note to self: Your self-reliance pendulum swung too far. Give yourself permission to ask for help, and accept it graciously.

FORTUNATELY THE FALL ON EVEREST DIDN'T HAVE SUCH AN AFTERMATH. After hiking hours that day, the pain of another four to five hours to get to Base Camp the same afternoon was setting in on what would be the hardest day of our trek. Judy and I both trudged along slowly, ascending step by step to our destination at almost eighteen thousand feet, the highest I had ever been at that point in my life. We made it by midafternoon, hooted and hollered, made several dedications, and shared the limelight of pictures with several dozen other people who'd made it to the same place.

I'd brought two things with me for this milestone. I gently got out the snow pants of my girlfriend Patty, who had recently died in the mountains I loved so much, the Sierras in California. She had been on a mountain climb with a friend when she fell to her death in the prime of her life. I also pulled out the University of Southern California (USC) T-shirt I had purchased in the airport to surprise my friend David, who was a diehard USC fan. I posed for pictures with each item to commemorate Patty and make a keepsake for David. Later, Pete Carroll, the USC coach, signed the picture for David with, *To a true Trojan, Pete Carroll.* No one told him I'd graduated from UCLA and was a true-blue Bruin. No need to set the record straight.

I also picked up three small granite rocks and put them on the Everest Base Camp rock shrine and said a silent prayer for my father, Aunt Bertie, and Helen. Each of them, in their own ways, had helped me reach the camp.

The next morning we started out early and very slowly. We'd made it to Base Camp, but we still hadn't accomplished our goal to get a really good view of Everest. The goal that morning was to hike to the top of the highest peak in the area, Kala Pattar, which was almost 18,500 feet. Ideally hikers get to the top of the peak as the sun is rising and hitting Everest. "Roly-poly," our guide kept saying, meaning go very slowly and take our time. Of course we were going slowly, whether he said so or not. We passed kids, twenty-year-olds, who were giving up on the climb and others who were just a tad weaker. There were a few who were better than us, but not many. We made it to the top of Kala Pattar for the sunrise, just as we'd planned. The air was still at this time in the morning, and, except for human voices here and there, it was extremely quiet. The sun came up slowly as we sat to soak it in. I got goose bumps as I realized that Everest was in full view, with the pink and then yellow light hitting the world's tallest mountain. It was a sight few people ever see, and we had earned it.

CHAPTER 15

Nepal I, Continued

ONCE WE RETURNED TO THE KATHMANDU HOTEL, I TOOK A WELL-DESERVED shower, and it was like watering a flower. Judy did the same, and we were refreshed and ready to go on another adventure for our final week. Not knowing if we would ever be back to the region, I wanted to go to Chitwan National Park in southern Nepal, just above India, to see the elephants there.

The plan was for Judy and me to continue on to Chitwan National Park on our own, so the company owner left us with a driver and gave him instructions, of sorts. We were in a small sedan with a driver who spoke no English. What we didn't know, and quickly found out, was that he had no idea where he was going. It all was scary and exciting at the same time.

The young man just kept staring straight as he drove. We watched the countryside, which didn't change very much, for hours. Eventually we started seeing a refugee camp with people milling around. It was a large camp, with hundreds of tents, and I was sorry that we couldn't find out more about what we were seeing. Shortly after the refugee camp, we saw a small wooden shack with several men dressed in military clothing and carrying large rifles. We were stopped briefly before proceeding ahead. It seemed a little odd to me, but what did I know?

We went forward, through the military post, for another few miles until our driver stopped in a local town to ask for directions. When he returned to the car, he turned the car around and went past the military post and the refugee camp once again, until he stopped at a local house and asked for directions, again. I figured we had driven to India by mistake and now had returned to Nepal. It occurred to me that we were totally at his mercy.

Judy and I waited in the car again, nervously glancing at each other from time to time. It must have been less than five minutes that our driver was asking directions, but it seemed like half an hour. An older woman was helping him, pointing to the dirt road we were heading down, waving her finger as she talked. Her four children clung to her skirt.

The driver opened the car door and got in, wearing an expression of *I know where I'm going now*. We bumped up and down on the narrow dirt road, passing water buffalos and herders with sticks to make the large animals go faster than their always-slow speed. We passed houses along the way. Houses in southern Nepal are shacks in the States. Whereas the houses along our treks had been made of wood or stone with corrugated metal roofs for the owners who were lucky, the houses to the south were more stable, most likely because of the greater availability of natural materials and the more arid land where we were at the moment.

We drove probably five or six miles, continuing on our journey to Chitwan National Park. Our expressions to each other changed from anxious to excited as we thought we were nearing our destination. We tried to see the visitor center or some kind of structure announcing we were truly at the right place.

The car rounded a bend, and we noticed a large river to our left. There were people, probably a dozen, around a spot in the river where a small fire was burning. Our car stopped for a minute, and Judy and I studied what we were seeing. As we looked closer, we could see that people were crying and some even held others up in the small crowd. It finally dawned on me that we were watching a funeral. The body of the relative had been placed on a wooden raft, with a fire built near the bottom of the raft underneath him or her. We were watching their common way of dealing with death. The body was cremated on the raft and then sent down the water to become part of the river. We watched as they pushed the raft off, smoke still rising. I secretly asked the universe to take care of the soul being released to its care and thought of my dad, Aunt Bertie, and Helen.

Not much farther down the road, the car stopped. All we saw was a large wooden sign with two layers of wood saying *Welcome to Chitwan National Park*. That was it. That was all we saw, just the sign. The driver seemed confused. The sign was about eight feet high, had signs of deterioration from the jungle it was protecting, and simply announced that we had arrived—somewhere. After our nervousness, to see this, all Judy and I could do was burst out laughing at the difference in this national park from those we were familiar with in the States and other countries we'd visited so far.

We waited with the driver as each of us surveyed the area to see what to do next. After probably ten minutes, the driver honked the horn. That seemed like a logical thing to do in my view. We waited. After probably another ten minutes, we saw something moving in the river near where we were parked. Shortly, a long wooden dugout canoe appeared with a boatman standing at the back of it with a long wooden stick to guide the boat. He yelled out to us, probably saying something about being right over. The boat must have been twelve feet long, with seats for passengers in the middle. Crocodiles in the river crossed my mind for an instant.

When the boat arrived near where we were parked, our driver indicated to us that he was staying locally and would be back in two days to get us. At least, that's what I thought he told us. The boatman motioned for us to get into the canoe, and we followed his directions. We waved goodbye to the driver and trusted ourselves to the boatman, who shoved the boat off the shore quickly.

We went down a tributary to the larger river. Once in the river, the current was still very slow and no problem for our boatman to navigate as he was standing with the paddle. The temperature of the water and the humidity in the air were equal. It was dripping-wet humid weather, but we were more excited about the two-night stay at the resort than the weather, which we couldn't change.

After a fifteen-minute trip on the river in the boat, we landed at a mud bank on the river. The boatman helped us out with our backpacks and motioned for us to go up the embankment. Again, we could only follow directions. We saw a marked trail and followed it to a set of individual cabins to our left and some kind of larger building in front of us. An erasable board listed activities, such as *Bird Walk*, *Botany Exploration*, and *Elephant Walk* with specific times. I knew we could get on the elephant walk—heck, it was what we'd come for. The one listing that really caught my eye was *Elephant Washing*. I had no idea what it was, but it was that afternoon, and I wanted to be a part of it.

Meanwhile, we found something of a reception person. An older man with a beard seemed to have been connected with the compound for a long time. He verified our names and then pointed to one of the few bungalows down a stone walkway. We assumed that was our home for the next two nights. He told us that the only lighting at night was with kerosene lamps and showed us how to light them. Then he gave a cautionary lecture about being sure to leave the windows open a crack to avoid dying from the fumes. No problem.

I asked about the elephant washing. He told me, "Just show up at the river at the time on the board." That, I could do.

We entered the small bungalow and each settled on one of the twin beds in the room. The room was small and had native bugs and other unmentionable critters, but it was more than adequate. We relaxed for a few minutes and then headed to the river for the elephant washing, taking no expectations with us.

Judy and I found a muddy area in the river where a few large elephants were lounging with their trainers. I imagined trying to wash these huge animals with a garden hose as they towered above me. Each trainer was responsible for one elephant, and one by one, they told each elephant to lie down on its side in the river. One trainer then motioned to us to get in the river and use our hands to splash water on the male elephant he was working with. We waded into the water and started splashing water on the mammoth animal while he raised his trunk up and down in what I hoped was appreciation. We were able to rub the weathered skin and the occasional coarse hair, and feel the joy of the animal to be in the warm, muddy-colored water. If there were any leeches, barracudas, crocodiles, or anything else in the water, the mud hid them.

After a few minutes, the trainer had the animal get up. He then looked at me and, using hand signals, asked if I wanted to get on the elephant. I didn't hesitate. I handed Judy the camera, promising to hold it for her next.

Then the trainer said, "Swim?"

I nodded my head.

Then he motioned a few more times, pointing to the left of the elephant and shaking his head no. I understood him to say, *Don't get off on the left side of the elephant into the main part of the river*. He motioned to the right of the elephant and said, "Okay." The instructions I was getting were, after the ride, get off on the side of the elephant toward the shore. Unsure why this was so important, I looked quizzically at him as he snapped his hands together. He pointed to the left side, saying only, "Crocodiles." I understood immediately.

My elephant got down on his knees in the river water, and I was motioned to crawl on. Forgetting any crocodiles, I crawled on the back of the massive animal, hugging him and looking into his huge, beautiful eyes. His eyelashes were incredible. I held on to whatever I could, mainly his skin, as the trainer ordered him to stand up. Get this picture: Here I am on a huge elephant, in the middle of a crocodile-infested river, and he is going to get up from his kneeling position, meaning that I must hold on for dear life so I won't fall off and get eaten.

He rose slowly, shifting from right to left as he stood from the kneeling position. It wasn't just a gentle shift, more like leaning ninety degrees as he rose. I made it up, staying on and embracing the situation. Once we were up, the trainer gave some kind of signal, and I saw my elephant's trunk go in the water. About ten seconds later, he raised his trunk and splashed all that water from his trunk directly on me. I am eternally grateful for Judy getting a perfect picture of me, with my hands in the air, as the elephant tossed all the water on me. It was one of those moments that will live in my memory forever—perfect joy. I got off the elephant on the right side and swam to shore.

The next day Judy and I rode the elephants in the jungle. We climbed up large wooden platforms to get on the elephants, four to a small seat on top of the elephant, with the trainer riding just behind the ears. In countries such as Nepal, there are few rules and precautions. As the elephant took off, searching for the rare white rhino in the area so we could view it, we very quickly learned that there was no trail. The elephant made his own trail, and his own way. Another quick lesson was to duck if we saw any branches, vines, or even tree trunks coming our way. The elephant didn't care about them, and we had to care to prevent personal decapitation.

Someone on another elephant started whistling, and apparently it was the signal that the poor critter, the white rhino, had been spotted. I was sure it was quite tired of having tourists interrupt its afternoon, every afternoon. Our trainer directed our elephant toward the whistling until we stopped and he started poking both feet at the back of the elephant's ears. We waited to see what the animal was going to do. So far, we'd seen the trainer poke at the back of the left or right ear, and the animal would go that direction. I didn't know what poking with both feet meant.

The elephant wrapped its trunk around the trunk of a tree about two feet in diameter, spiraling around it like the red on a white peppermint stick. With another verbal command, the elephant pulled the tree out—with the roots intact—so we could proceed forward. Forget rules in US national parks and ecology preservation.

Eventually we came to a clearing where we met three other elephants with riders on them. Our trainer pointed into the jungle, so we looked closely. As my eyes tried to adjust to the shadows, I saw movement. It was eerie to see the white rhino in the dark area. I'm sure it was thinking, *Darn, they found me again.* This incredible creature was huge and a light gray color, with its horn totally intact. We were able to ride for hours after seeing the rhino, and every moment of it was etched indelibly in my mind.

My father died in December, after my return. I spent a few weeks with him, and because the trip had revived me, I was able to be more present during his final days. Watching him sleep one day, I silently thanked him for allowing me to go on the trip, even though he had not given official permission. Honoring him, Helen, and Aunt Bertie's memories on the trip had been a deeply spiritual event for me.

Note to self: Surely, they each gave you their blessings to go.

CHAPTER 16

Bali

EACH OF MY BIRTHDAYS IN MY SIXTIES WAS GOING TO BE HARD. THE NUMber sixty was scary enough, and it seemed as if I was passing into yet another era. I decided to go to Bali for my birthday. Warm weather seemed appealing in February, even if I was living in California, and Bali was definitely on my list, mainly because of its beaches and crafts. This time, I didn't allow much time between making plans and actually going, though. It was too late to find someone to go with me, so I decided on the spur of the moment to go alone. As soon as I told a few friends, I got a common reaction: "You're going where? You're not going with someone? Why would you go to a country that doesn't like Americans?"

Winters are a hard time for me, especially after the holidays. Sweeping feelings of loneliness were taking hold that year, so I was looking forward to the trip—until my sweet brother's first response to the news of the trip was "Why aren't you sharing this with someone? And what about safety?"

Cue old feelings: *Oh my God, I'm going alone again* and *I will grow old alone, to boot*. I checked myself again. *I'm not going to Bali to prove anything, but just to do it. I'm okay. I'm content. It would be nice to share this with someone, but I hope to share it with the world.*

Note to self: It would be a shame to die without finding a way for all these experiences to help, teach, or inspire someone. Celebrate that you have developed the skills and courage to go alone.

BALI—JUST THE NAME SOUNDED EXOTIC AND MYSTERIOUS. I'D HEARD ABOUT amazing crafts on the Indonesian island, and I'd been told that the people were incredibly nice, plus staying there was cheap. It fit my requirements.

Now that I had my ticket, I looked on the globe to see specifically where Bali was. I found it just next to Java in the Pacific Ocean. It's a small, long island that has one major airport on the southern part. I started doing a little research and decided to stay away from the very popular tourist area, where tourists had recently been bombed and killed. My mother would be proud of me for that.

I was fortunate that the library had a copy of Lonely Planet's *Southeast Asia on a Shoestring*. Usually I ordered used guidebooks from the internet, but I had no time to do so this time. I thumbed through the pages to find the list of hostels and cheap hotels in Bali and took a look. I wanted to stay by the beach the first day or two, so I decided on Sanur. Sanur sounded enchanting. There had been no bombings there recently—always a plus. I emailed a local hostel to ask about availability.

The hostel manager turned out to be an expat from Australia. He emailed in perfect English that there was one very small room available for ten dollars a night, but there was no air-conditioning. He wrote that the hostel was about two blocks from the beach. Perfect! I booked it for two nights and asked for someone to meet me at the airport. I made no other reservations, which some would find astounding and plain scary, especially since I was going alone.

On the plane to Singapore, the first thing I did was engage in a conversation with a geophysicist, a professor from Texas who was meeting his son near Singapore. I was sitting in a row with French, Dutch, Chinese, and

English travelers. The Chinese girl was nervous because she was going by herself after her girlfriends had backed out for a tour they had scheduled. It's always fun for me to find out why people are traveling.

The next thing I did was order a Singapore sling because the drinks were free on Singapore Airlines. Next I ordered Baileys for my coffee and then a Bloody Mary. I *love* Singapore Airlines—all this was free in my economy coach seat.

Once I arrived at Denpasar International Airport, I understood once again the importance of having someone with a small sheet of paper with my name on it appear when I wearily got off a plane in a completely foreign country. There was my name. The fellow holding it was short and chunky, with a smile that was nice but also depicted a burned-out *Oh, here comes the next tourist* nonverbal language. He spoke little English, but I was able to ask him a few questions as he drove me across town from the recently bombed tourist area to my quiet little hostel.

We pulled past small shops, large apartment buildings, some new construction, and some very poor sections of town. As we pulled into the cobblestone courtyard of a mosque, I realized that this was home. The hostel shared its space with a mosque but was set back from the common courtyard. A few dogs followed me into the courtyard. They were thin and probably starved, and it was hard for me to ignore them, though I had no food to give them.

My driver drove away as I walked into the front area of the hostel and met two people from Norway. I imagined I would probably want to escape Norway in February also. Wife spoke broken English, and Husband spoke none. Later in the day, Wife would apologize for Husband's lack of conversation, telling me that he felt silly sitting nearby as we jabbered. I smiled and nodded with complete understanding. Wife told me that the Australian owner was away at the moment, so I should just put my bag down and enjoy the two outdoor tables, couches, and shade in the small but welcoming front area of the hostel.

As I sat down, I could see there were two very small buildings connected with an outdoor hallway. The smaller building had three doors, and I could see the white curtains blowing against the open window frames from the fans inside. These were the rooms with no air-conditioning. Actually, at the end of the trip, I would discover there was only one room that had air-conditioning.

The other building had another set of three rooms and a long hallway leading to the kitchen where Wife told me breakfast was prepared daily. She said I was probably going to stay in the smallest bedroom, the one in the dark hallway. I looked down the hallway to catch a glimpse of my new room for the night, but it was hard to decipher any information about it.

We talked for a long time, as I decompressed the stress from the long journey getting to Bali. I needed to rest anyhow, so spreading out on the couch and talking was fine with me. Meanwhile, I began sweating from the humidity. I mean *really* sweating. Coming from very dry California, I was not used to the humidity ranking of 100 percent.

A young woman worker brought me a juice drink. I had no hesitation drinking it, though it would have given me pause in the past. Aside from the trust I placed in any business that relied on tourism, no one else appeared to be sick in the complex. I could have had five drinks right then—I was so thirsty—and I made a mental note to drink fluids regularly to replace those lost in my sweating.

I had worn long pants on my flights because the airplanes could be cold, so I'd arrived overdressed. After talking with Wife for about half an hour, I was drenched with sweat, something I would become very used to. I reached for anything that could become a fan, and vowed to get as undressed as possible and to wear appropriate but lightweight clothes as soon as possible. It would take several days to learn to chill during midday, the hottest part of the day.

After an hour or so, the Australian owner walked into the courtyard and sat at our table. A large, middle-aged, handsome man, he apologized for not being there to meet me when I'd arrived, and I dismissed it quickly. He showed me to the very small room, which had a ceiling fan and its own bathroom. Having my own bathroom was a real plus in a hostel because usually bathrooms are shared. The room had one large window that opened from the bottom, a small dresser and bedside table, plus a twin bed in the middle. It was perfect for one person.

It was evening, so I bought a banana at the nearby produce stand and headed for bed since I had not slept much during the two-day flight. I could hear many people roaming the streets at night, and because anyone could walk into the courtyard and potentially sneak into my room, I closed the windows, turned on the fan, and hoped for the best.

It wasn't long before I had to strip off all my clothes and lie on top of the bed to survive the sweltering heat in the small room. I reminded myself that I was saving money, but the thought wasn't very helpful. I finally decided I would survive the night and could scream loudly for help if someone were to sneak in, so I opened the window. A blast of hot—but circulating—air rushed in, and I felt better. Eventually I drifted off to sleep, hoping to awaken with a renewed spirit and curiosity.

It was wonderful to have a hostel with breakfast included. As the few people staying at the hostel wandered from their rooms in the morning, the young cook would come with coffee for the two tables. There was a short menu to pick from: three variations on the same things: bread, eggs, and fruit.

Next I walked to the beach, past many shops with their owners trying to convince me to part with my tourist dollars. There was a shop where the fellow would make a pair of leather sandals for me for twenty-five dollars, one where I could get a five-dollar massage, one to get pills from a doctor for an upset stomach, and dress shops galore. By the beach, the shops were piled with all sorts of different items, from plastic rings for floating in the ocean to buckets and toy shovels. There were even tiny new sea turtles from a preserve, who were to be released once they were large enough to survive predators in the ocean or in the sky. I bought a brightly colored plastic ring for bobbing in the ocean.

I kept walking toward the beach and didn't stop until I had immersed my feet in the beautiful white sand and water. It felt delicious, even if there were two hundred other people around. Restaurants with outdoor seating lined the oceanfront, with a sidewalk that must have been miles long. I figured I could secure a beach chair and stay as long as I wanted if I kept a bar or restaurant tab going. Soon I realized that no one really cared whether you kept a tab or just nabbed a chair. It was so hot that taking it easy was the order of the day, every day.

I had taken a beach towel with me, so I sat on the beach for a while. It's normal for me to sit in one place and soak in the sun and, more importantly, the culture. I saw a large area where large ladies sat talking. I mean *very* large ladies, with very friendly smiles. They clumped together catching up on the latest gossip until they could nab a tourist to sell a massage. Eventually one of them came over to me to ask if I wanted a massage. She explained to me, in English that I could easily understand, that she offered several different types of massages. She had a special talent, she said, to give massages that were directed toward specific muscle problems. She had enormous hands, and I knew she could do a great job. I eventually let her talk me into the hour-and-a-half massage for fifteen dollars. It felt wonderful, as I told her about this or that pain and her hands relieved my sore muscles. I'd read in the guidebook that good massages in Bali were normally about the equivalent of five dollars, but I was happy to have the more expensive one, right on the ocean sand, looking at the ocean as my muscle pains were relieved. It really was paradise, this Bali, and I was excited to explore more of it.

I made my way back to the hostel and bought a sleeveless dress on the way. All the shopkeepers were begging me to stop. The shop had colorful dresses hanging outside, mimicking the colorful country. I picked out a bright-pink one. I had to get over all the years of comments about my arms being big. I certainly was self-conscious about them but decided no one would really care one way or the other in Bali. Most of the women there had big arms.

Once back in the hostel, I changed into the one-size-fits-all dress, and darn it, it was cute on me. It was sleeveless, tie-dyed, and knee length. From the side view, I appeared to be pregnant—a look I'd always avoided—but I didn't care at this point. I wanted to let go of the time when I'd cared dearly and to instead choose comfort and acceptance.

Note to self: You are lucky to be alive at this age, so rejoice and let go of old thought patterns. Eat more chocolate.

I STARTED TALKING WITH A VERY YOUNG COUPLE FROM ARGENTINA who were staying at a nearby hostel. They were headed to Ubud, the tourist capital of Bali, the next day. I listened with a smile, thinking, *I need to go to Ubud also.* There had been no bombings or unrest there, and most likely it had amazing crafts. I was more comfortable in Bali than I'd originally anticipated. Eventually we agreed to catch a cab together the next morning. My next challenge was to find a place to stay there. I sat on the couch outside and used the hostel's computer to email a few, but the rates were sixty dollars or more per night, which I didn't want to pay. I was just about to splurge to book a place when I relaxed for a minute.

It was then that I met a Canadian couple from Saskatchewan who told me where they'd stayed in Ubud and highly suggested I try it also. They'd sold everything they owned, including their house, cars, and all belongings, and were traveling around the world for two years. They had checked out all kinds of places with the following criteria: not too far from town; quiet, clean, nice people; and most importantly, a pool. Mindful of their money, for the place in Ubud, they'd paid thirty-five dollars a night for the two of them and said I could probably get the room cheaper as a single person. I decided to wing it and make no reservations. The Canadians gave me general directions to the place: Once you get to the soccer field on your right, go to the end of it and get out of the taxi. Go to your left down a *gang* (an alley too narrow for a car but wide enough for a motorcycle), and you'll find it on your right.

The next morning, the taxi driver arrived at the agreed 10:00 a.m., but no Argentineans came. I started fretting, common to my nature, then had a flashback about South American time. I relaxed a bit. Just as the driver and I were ready to go, at 10:05 a.m., the Argentineans rounded the corner into the hostel parking area. The three of us piled into the car, and we took off on our adventure to an unknown place on an island foreign to us. There was something about the multinational nature of the people I had met so far that really made me smile. And I took note: everyone from all these amazingly different countries was able to get along and play nice. Isn't that what we learned as children—play fair and be nice to others?

We stopped at a few displays of huge wooden art pieces, wood doors, and other ornate carvings. On the very winding streets, we passed artisan shops, houses with gated front entrances, and villages with small grocery stores. I later discovered that each family usually lives in a larger family complex. Grandparents, newlyweds, and everyone in between live in the same complex but in different buildings. Instead of having something like a social security system for the state to take care of the elderly, each family does it. I thought about how the United States had been like this, sometime in the early twentieth century, when each family took care of its elderly instead of grandparents, parents, and grandchildren living so far apart. In Bali, it's a matter of necessity and certainly tradition. I admired the tradition and felt a little guilty being far from my mother. Somewhere along the line, long before me, my family had broken the chain of living together.

At my new place, I quickly learned that I could go to the local internet café, spend half an hour on the computer for fifty cents, walk the many streets of Ubud, and then return to my room before noon. Often, I would get the little plastic swim ring I bought, take it downstairs, and fall into the pool where the water took care of my dripping sweat. I learned to relax there, to bob up and down in the water, and to understand the true meaning of taking a break.

I loved that pool of water. During the day, the manager would turn on the waterfall, which was a large, eight-foot wall of water that trickled into the pool. It had never been easy for me to be in the moment, even with my Buddhist studies, but I forced myself to listen to the waterfall and the birds, to see the clarity of the water and surrounding jungle, to touch the water and feel its healing power, to feel what little wind there was on my cheeks, and to absorb the healing power of the moment. It had taken most of my life to get to this point of relaxing. My usual mode had been to scurry forward, to break through, and to accomplish four things in one time frame. In that pool something shifted, and I let some of that old mode go. To this day, whenever I have my blood pressure read, I think of bobbing gently in that pool.

I also learned to relax the rest of the day. I would read in the morning when I woke. I'd brought one or two books, and when I finished them, I found a library at another hotel where I "borrowed" several books—until I read a really uninteresting one and gave up. I would sleep late and then read, and when I stirred at all, a thermos of coffee and cream arrived on my porch table. When I went out to enjoy the coffee, breakfast seemed to automatically appear. It was heaven.

Note to self: You so deserve this.

RAIN, OFTEN MONSOON-STYLE SHEETS OF WATER, IN UBUD WAS ALWAYS expected. It reminded me to feel the moment, be present, and be *here*. Often I was in the pool when the rains came, and they felt magical in the water. When I was caught in rain during the day, it was normal to just jump under an awning or under a house eave. Umbrellas were uncommon. I was usually not the only one under a shelter, and sometimes I shared a small space amid laughter with the locals also there. It was a microcosm of wildly different people huddling together until the rain stopped, and then everyone separated and went on their way.

I walked to the monkey forest, where monkeys eagerly waited for new customers to go through the gates into the tropical setting so they could steal from unwitting tourists. At times, a monkey would become courageous and steal a few of the tiny bananas from a local store. The store owner would chase the brazen monkey down the street, where the monkey quickly retreated to the tall trees with its prize. I could tell this was a scene that played out daily because the store owner's frustration showed.

I'd heard about the danger of monkey bites, but I observed for a long time and decided all they really wanted were the bananas. I handed one to a monkey who sat on my lap. Then he started to get into my sack, and I had to shoo him away. I learned that they don't go easily. Their long fingers shot into my bag with hopes of finding delightful snacks, and their humanlike faces, begging for goods, were awe-inspiring but brazen. I was reminded of a friend who'd had to get a series of rabies shots after a monkey bite in Nepal. This was Bali. I hoped for the best and tried not to be bitten.

A stone's throw from the place where I was staying was a spa. I didn't indulge myself in spas or massages in the States because of their cost, but I wanted to immerse myself in the culture. The spa was on a terrace with inviting doors and friendly smiles. I walked in to find out the scoop. Massages were five dollars, milk baths five dollars, pedicures five dollars, and so on. On my first trip there, I decided to do a full three-hour job, starting with a massage. The hour-long massage was wonderful, with the sound of a small waterfall and the smell of flower fragrance surrounding me. During the last few minutes of the massage, I could hear the masseuse filling the large bathtub in the room. At the end of the massage, she covered me in turmeric and then yogurt. I wasn't quite sure what I was doing, but I followed my intuition and took a shower. Then she guided me to the tub containing milk-looking water covered with flower petals, saying, "Relax, enjoy, smell! Use your senses since they are usually so dull with all your activity. Soak in the experience and be inactive!" The first thought that came to me was *I deserve this*. I got in the tub, and a tray of tea and fried bananas appeared at some point. Lastly, I got the pedicure, and I felt that all was right with the world.

On my way to a Bali dance show, a tall young man stopped me on the street and very graciously asked if I would speak some English with his "sister." He must have had many, many sisters because about six young women approached me and giggled as they asked me in very broken English, "How are you?" and "What is your name?" It was endearing, so I spent a long time conversing and shaking hands with the young women.

It was easy to hire people in Bali. I hired a guide for a day to take me to several of the places that people would describe with "Oh, you must see this temple and that royal spot." I found myself hiking up and down stairs, buying a craft or two here and there, and of course, sweating constantly.

The most interesting part of the daylong excursion was when I asked for a coconut with a large amount of "meat" in it. I'd noticed that often coconuts are simply discarded after the "milk" is finished. I was trying to find the older coconut with little milk and a lot of white meat. My driver understood and took me on rural dirt roads until he stopped in front of a gate. Then we went inside, to the compound where his family lived.

He asked his nephew to get a coconut and take off the husk for me, and the young fellow scurried off. Meanwhile, my driver introduced me to his brothers, sisters, mother, father, grandchildren—heck, the whole compound. It gave me a huge sense of family and understanding of how family units survive in such a poor country. The family truly takes care of its own. Having children must be very important.

Each day I would walk to the local market area, purchasing fruit and other interesting-looking foods that I could wash with bottled water before eating them. I continued getting daily massages, treating myself well.

When I had to leave Ubud, I took a public shuttle back to my little hostel by the beach and shared a room with another lovely expat from Australia who was now living in Bali. The hostel owner had double-booked rooms and asked if I would mind sharing the large room with air-conditioning with this complete stranger. I would have a bed to myself; we'd just share the space. I was proud of myself to be so open to a situation like this.

I decided to eat well on my last night in Bali, so I went into a restaurant that displayed a large sign with pictures outside: *Seafood Platter with Beer, $20*. I was going to splurge and get the platter dinner. The restaurant had no doors or windows, which was normal on this tiny island. The dinner arrived with large prawns, fish, calamari, and other ocean products I didn't recognize. I felt a little odd, sitting there by myself enjoying this dinner. Usually I would eat quickly and leave when loneliness set in, but this time I felt comfortable in the moment and relaxed.

My wait wasn't too long before my flight, and I had some money left. I had choices with this currency—there was a bin for extra money for the children of Bali, there was ice cream for me, and there were probably other choices. I decided on the *me* choice and bought ice cream.

Guilt set in, however. *You should be doing something for others in this poor country,* my inner voice told me. I remembered two young ladies I'd seen cleaning the toilets in the airport bathroom—they probably cleaned the entire facility. I remembered that I had five dollars from the US hidden somewhere in my gear, found it, and went back to find the girls. I found one of them, who was thin and tall with her hair pulled back. She held a mop, and her expression said that she was resigned to her task. After I'd traveled through airports throughout the world, the people cleaning the toilets and floors had become anonymous. As I thought about it, I realized they'd disappear into the walls as I walked by, as if they didn't exist.

I walked up to the young girl and handed her five dollars. She looked up, shocked. She didn't speak English, but anyone could have interpreted her thoughts. She got very excited, as if I had handed her a million dollars. She didn't know what to say, was speechless. Eventually she motioned to me to follow her, and she unlocked the toilet for disabled folks for me, but I shook my head. I wanted her to understand that my gift came with no strings attached, with no needs or requests. I gave her another dollar I had found, folding it into her hand, and left, smiling.

Note to self: Happy birthday, Linda.

CHAPTER 17

Antarctica II

IT TOOK SEVERAL YEARS TO RECUPERATE FROM WORK BURNOUT, BOTH FROM my previous job and from working at McMurdo Station. After five years of rest, I was able to consider working again in 2010. In the interim years, I had been the alternate, which meant that should something happen to the primary person doing my job in Antarctica, I would have been dispatched to the Ice.

After that five-year rest, I applied again to be the primary in Antarctica. When asked my preference between working at McMurdo and the South Pole, I told my contact that I only wanted to go to the South Pole. I had missed out on getting to the South Pole when I worked at McMurdo, and I wasn't going to pass up the chance to go there now. Besides, most of the employees at the pole had worked there for years, so maybe there would be fewer HR problems. I had heard that the cream of the crop go to the pole, so I was certainly hoping everyone could get along for the few months that I would be there.

Somehow, the magic worked and I was dispatched to the South Pole in October 2010 for their summer season.

Once again, I traveled to Christchurch, New Zealand. Once again, my aging mother protested. However, she knew that her concerns would not stop me from going and that our main means of communication would be telephone and letters.

I was able to face the five-month job with enthusiasm. As a matter of fact, I was downright excited to go even if I would miss the holidays with my children. That was always the biggest downside.

The C-141s were no longer flying, and I was grateful to have had the experience on one of them. Somehow, having flown in one pushed me up into the *that's really cool* level with engineers and pilots. This time we flew to McMurdo on a C-17. Once at McMurdo, I carted my stuff off the plane, onto a transfer bus, and grabbed a bunk at McMurdo for a day before my flight on a C-130 military plane with propellers and skis for travel to the pole. For once at McMurdo, I was the guest and not the employee, so I could do what I wanted while waiting for my ride.

It all seemed familiar. This time I was not required to gather mental information as I wandered through town. I knew the town and its different buildings. I could immediately identify those who were coming from the winter-over season. Going to the South Pole was like hitting the jackpot. The majority of folks who go there want to do their stint, do a good job, and go home for several months before repeating the journey. There was only a handful of new folks who landed on this sea of ice and didn't have a clue what working on the Ice entailed. It would be my job to keep an eye on them and help them adjust.

My job, once again, was as the human resources specialist, but because there were only a fraction of folks at the pole compared to McMurdo, I had an additional job: banker (financial specialist). Traditionally, human resources deals with people, and banker-type folks deal with numbers. In other words, these are not two professions that naturally go hand in hand. I was not a numbers person, but the job intrigued me and I knew I had the brains to do it, if only my emotions would let me. During the training I'd taken in Denver, it all kind of made sense. Once on the Ice, however, it would *have* to make sense very quickly. I would have a one-day turnover time frame before the winter-over HR person left. I'd been told in Denver that it was almost impossible to train a banker-type quickly in the HR field, with its land mines of legal information and communication skills, so for this position they consistently focused on getting an HR person and training them in the banker/financial field. They wished me luck.

The military C-130 landed on the huge expanse of the Antarctic ice cap at the South Pole. As it landed, it opened its bottom flaps at the rear of the plane to let pallets of gear, food, and other supplies slide out the back as the plane was coasting to a stop. The process looked like a large bug depositing its young from its rear end. Workers with forklifts would pick up the pallets quickly from the ice, getting them out of the way and to a safe place in the warehouse.

I got off the plane, lugging my gear, and then just stood there. I had made it to the South Pole. I was standing on top of two miles of ice and seeing a large, strange metal building and many temporary Quonset-type buildings, a few larger buildings, and other small structures on skis. Looking toward the horizon, everything was ice—just ice—and very white. Turning totally around, I could see only ice. There were no mountains or any landmarks on the horizon. If anything, the horizon and the sky just melted together somewhere out there. I was truly about as far away from suburbia as anyone can be. This time, however, I was mentally ready for the job and the challenge. It had only taken five years to get ready again.

I walked into the building by climbing a set of metal stairs to the second story. My large bunny boots clunked with every step, and the metal rang out like a muted bell. I walked into the main management area with offices, two conference rooms, and Mylar palm trees. The trees made me smile because it meant there was, or had to be, humor in this desolate place. Where else in the world would fake palm trees exist and make someone smile? My new coworker escorted me to my future office and then to my room.

My room was in a hallway off the main floor. At this time, the Amundsen-Scott South Pole Station was an almost-new structure with two long, large halls, one on top of the other, for offices and then perpendicular hallways for sleep areas. My bedroom was in one of these hallways, about halfway to the end, in a tiny room with no windows. Having no windows sounded scary until I remembered that there would be sunlight twenty-four hours a day.

When I opened the door, the first thing I saw was my super-high bunk bed—only a top bunk—with a large, open storage area underneath. There was a tall closet for all my clothes, two drawers, a tiny desk with a chair, and that was it. It wasn't hard to understand that I would have to stand on the chair to get on the bed since there was no ladder. The bigger issue was that, because there was no window, night was instant when the light was turned off. The only problem was that the light switch was on the wall beside the door, which meant unless there was a flashlight somewhere, the maneuver to get on the chair and into the bunk bed would be an act done in darkness. I found my flashlight.

My office was a typical space, about the same size that my office in McMurdo had been, and once again, it could have been an Anywhere, USA, office. This would be home for the next five months. In my HR role, I would encounter homesick folks, upset folks, and people from the general population who had questions about their benefits or jobs; I never knew what issue would walk into the office. In the HR role, I was sometimes not very popular. However, in my banker role, I was very popular. Everyone loved to take money from their paycheck to use at the store. Paychecks were issued once every two weeks, and employees could request money in advance. I doled it out.

The station store was the size of a large walk-in closet. Once in the front door, there were cashiers on the right and shelves with clothing, souvenirs, and alcohol around the other walls. In the middle were shelves of DVDs and movies for loan. Many employees had their own DVD players. Over the course of the summer, this tiny store was the only outlet for those like me who love to shop. I bought souvenir clothes for people I didn't even really know.

Volunteers ran the store, and I ran the finances. I would collect the cash at the end of the day and have to balance it with my cash drawer. It all seemed simple enough, and for the most part, it was. I didn't cry once during my tenure at the South Pole, much unlike my time at McMurdo. Regrouping after my McMurdo tenure and regaining my sanity after burnout had made me whole again.

I met Chuck somewhere early during my stay. Chuck wasn't his real name, but his chosen name. He was a lot of fun, and we conducted two experiments.

"Hey, Linda, my son wants me to do an experiment here," Chuck said to me one day. He explained further, "He wants to see what happens if someone pees off the second floor onto the ice."

Hmm. That didn't sound like something we could ethically do, and I wasn't willing to risk my job to do it.

"No, no, I don't mean that we'd really do that. We can use water and a syringe from medical—I've already asked Doc if he has a superlarge syringe," Chuck explained.

Hmm. Now, that sounded plausible.

We arranged a day and time during our off hours, and Chuck was assigned to get the syringe. We could get a cup of hot water easily.

When the time came, we went out on the balcony, filled the syringe with hot water, and let it rip over the edge. More precisely, I did the filling and distributing while Chuck recorded the event for his son. The results? As I sprayed the warm water from the syringe, the water/steam/substance that came out looked like fog, like a very tiny cloud that disappeared before ever getting to the ice on the ground. The recording went to Chuck's son for verification of results.

The second experiment was more modest. Chuck ran across a bubble machine. I have no idea where he found it, but it intrigued both of us. He wanted to see what would happen to the bubbles as they came into different weather temperatures. We first tried out the machine in the normal inside environment. Result: normal bubbles, as expected. We then took it outside, temperature probably zero degrees. Result: no bubbles at all. Lastly, we decided to see what would happen in the two-story spiral staircase area, where the two long hallways are connected by a covered outdoor staircase. Magically, the bubbles appeared and then froze. They froze all over the steps, staircase, and anyplace else they landed. Result: many of the people coming up or down the staircase had puzzled expressions as they encountered bubbles stuck on the cold stairs and railings.

The pole's doctor and I had a mission in us just before we were to leave the station. We found folding chairs that we could bury in the snow to look like beach chairs, towels, bottles of beer, a Hawaiian shirt and shorts for Doc, a bathing suit and straw hat for me, and a photographer. We thought about taking out some of the Mylar palm trees, but as soon as we got to the front door, we realized the wind would carry the fake palm fronds away and litter the Ice, so we had to scratch that idea.

The temperature was brutal. It had to be about zero degrees, if not negative ten degrees, in early February, and we were leaving no later than mid-February. We layered our bunny boots, red parkas, and anything we could find to keep us warm over our outfits, and then our little team headed out, trying not to attract attention.

I looked at Doc, and the photographer and said, "You'd better be ready when I am!" Then I added, "Let's do it on the count of three." I counted down quickly, glanced at Doc and the photographer, and then stripped to my bathing suit. The camera started taking pictures as soon as we were on the chairs—somewhat, that is, on the chairs. The snow drifted across our towels as if it were a sandstorm, not a snowstorm. We were freezing and smiling as we lifted our beer bottles to toast the skies and our good fortune. Photos were snapped quickly, we put on our gear again, and ran back to the building, laughing all the way. The entire photo shoot lasted only about a minute at most. At these temperatures, with little on, frostbite in unusual areas was a certain threat.

I LOVE PEOPLE—AND WHAT MAKES THEM TICK. HUMAN RESOURCES IS A terrific field for me to be in, even if I had backed into it. When I was younger, I often would work for a temp agency, where I would be sent to different locations to work for different companies. I worked for a company that I really liked, and the job was in the personnel office (former name for human resources). When they offered me a full-time position there, I took it and then worked my way up in the field.

Being at the South Pole and working in HR gave me a real bird's-eye view of people at their best. Most everyone was very happy to be there, appreciated the unique opportunity being given to them, and greeted me with a smile. The people at the station seemed to understand that I was doing a job, and they treated me well.

The food at the South Pole is the most expensive in the world. It has to be brought in by plane. No problem with freezers—just put food outside. There are only human critters around, so no raccoons or bears. It was not uncommon to have soup full of mussels and seafood. One of the very best things about being in Antarctica was the head chef at the pole. He was an amazing fellow who cooked delicious food for us. The staff served filet mignon and lobster for Christmas dinner. We were all away from our families, and this was something that helped make up for that loss. Chuck played his guitar, and we sang at the galley entrance before our special dinner. When my mom sent cookies for me, I put up a sign on the corner leading to my office: *My Mom's Cookies Are This Way* with an arrow to my office. The cookies disappeared quickly.

Another coworker, Thomas, came up with the idea of the Polympics, to be performed on a Sunday. His vision was to invent competitive games that might be a challenge in our environment. Envision this: Try to ride a bicycle (yes, there was a bicycle at the South Pole) on the powdered sastruga (powder snow on top of grooves or ridges of hard snow). Or try to strip out of all the required layers of outer gear the fastest (indoors), or, better yet, see which of the firemen can put on their required equipment the most quickly (indoors, again). There was even a triathlon that included riding a bicycle for a mile on a track, followed by running for a mile, and then cross-country skiing a mile.

I volunteered to track some of the times of those who signed up for this event and then realized that there were no women signed up. I decided I could get a gold medal, so I signed up at the last minute. I would have won the gold medal if another contestant hadn't wandered by mistake into the shed where we were conducting the event. She didn't know how to cross-country ski very well, so I almost won the event in spite of myself. I won the silver.

All too suddenly, it was time to get ready to go home. People started scurrying around, packing, and sending off boxes at the post office. We were all ready to be off this place of ice.

I had grown accustomed to work, including the financial aspect. I had taken care of a few large problems, keeping the place running smoothly from the HR perspective. My mom and my children survived my absence, and looking back, it seems like my job at the South Pole was just an instant in my life. I was honored when someone anonymously gave me a ball cap that said *Antarctica Women Rock*.

Note to self: You *do* rock!

CHAPTER 18

Australia Alone

While working on the Ice for several months, I decided to travel to one of the continents I had not visited: Australia. It would be a hop and skip from New Zealand, where I would land when my job in Antarctica ended. I discovered that New Zealand was not part of the Australian continent, but instead was part of Indonesia and kind of a non-continent. There must be a more technical explanation, but the bottom line is that I had not been on the Australian continent.

I landed in Melbourne, picked up a rental car, and headed for my hostel. Having not driven for five months, I became nervous when I had to drive on the left side of the road, not my familiar right side, feeling the pressure to be instantly good at it. I told my brain that after surviving the South Pole, I didn't want to die on a road in Australia. In addition, I was in a city and not on a lonely country road, so more diligence was required.

With no navigator to help me get to the hostel, I had to recall turns and streets as best I could and pull over when necessary to relook at the small map I had ripped from a book. Eventually I pulled up to an address, hopefully the correct one, and looked at the front of the building. It had a large door that was kind of inviting, and the building itself was mostly brick. It was several stories high, and I could see into a large room with comfortable couches and chairs. I had chosen this hostel because, according to its description, at one time it had been an old convent where nuns had lived and most likely died. I walked into the large entryway and admired the old wooden floors. To my right was a huge room where several people were quietly reading or relaxing on the comfortable furniture. I felt comforted at this hostel because I could feel the calmness of the place once inhabited by nuns. I needed the calmness after Antarctica. I made my way to registration and signed in for my two-day stay. My room was upstairs, about three floors up a huge staircase with stained-glass windows at every landing and a banister that would have been a lot of fun to slide on. I walked into the small room that would be my home for the night and quickly located the community bathroom down the hall. I lay on the bed and congratulated myself for getting here.

Note to self: Thank the universe for allowing you such a wonderful life.

I STAYED IN THAT NIGHT, SLEEPING OFF THE ICE EXPERIENCE AND WELcoming in the new experience with smells and green lawns. Sometimes it takes a day or two to shake off whatever might bring me down, all that negative stuff, and I recognize that I have to shed it because I want to embrace the new experience. Sleeping that night worked.

The next day I walked everywhere. To me, walking is like opening doors to new experiences because I never know what will be around the next corner. About two streets over from the hostel on a parallel street, I found hippie-town. It was wonderful, charming. Old homes and small storefronts were everywhere, with coffee shops and unique shops in abundance. I walked probably a mile along this street, popping in here and there. It all seemed a little upscale, expensive, and just plain fun. I stopped to get a mocha because I thought I deserved it. I did.

Dinner was simple, yogurt and a banana I'd purchased from a convenience store. I was ready to embrace the next day and start traveling.

The first order of business the next day, after checking out of the hostel, was to find a used sleeping bag. I had a tiny car that could be my home for the next few weeks, but I needed a sleeping bag to cuddle up in. The back seats of the car adjusted to lie somewhat flat, so I could crawl into the hatchback and sleep—well, somewhat sleep.

It wasn't long before I found a thrift shop in a small town. Somehow, signs for thrift shops kind of jump out at me, and I find them everywhere. I walked into the shop and focused my thrift-store-trained eyes on the items in the store. It didn't take long to find the camping section, and in it were several sleeping bags. Some of the bags were torn, others fairly dirty, and some in decent shape. I picked out a bag for the equivalent of five dollars and checked out, my prize in hand.

The Great Ocean Road starts not far from Melbourne along the southern shore of Australia in the state of Victoria. When I'd picked my destinations in Australia, my criteria included mountains, critters, and ocean with beaches. After my icy stay at the South Pole with nothing but white at any distance, the criteria sounded right. The Great Ocean Road seemed enticing; besides, the book said it was fun, so I started out. Other than my limited criteria, my motto was just to explore and have fun.

I made my way along the magnificent road until I saw a few cars stopped. Years ago I'd learned that when I saw cars parked in an odd spot on the road, there's generally a worthy explanation. One time, people were parked to watch a buffalo herd in Yellowstone, and another, to watch the tule elk in a pasture in the California Sierras area. My sense of curiosity had kicked in each time.

I walked to the spot where several people had gathered. Then I happened to look up. In the trees, not in an aviary or zoo, were the most magnificent birds I had ever seen. They were Australian king parrots, and they were eating seeds from a stranger's hand. They were everywhere, landing on shoulders and outstretched arms. Most of us just stood in awe as the birds flew past us, near us, and onto our body parts. A sneaky, guilt-ridden part of me said, *You shouldn't be feeding the birds. Let them live naturally.* But my sense of wonder won the battle, and I stretched out my arm too.

Later in the trip, I stopped to see hundreds of cockatiels in an Aussie park. No one else was parked nearby, so I had the birds to myself. Plus, I had no birdseed, so I left guilt-free because technically I hadn't fed them.

On that trip, and others since, the freedom of traveling by car and by myself lends itself to amazing adventures as long as I'm open to them. I can turn around if I miss something, or pull into a parking lot to see a natural wonder.

The first night, I saw a sign to a beach, missed it, and had to turn around to find it. I followed the dirt road, and there, not too far from the main road, was a campground just over a sand dune from the beach. I was home for the night.

There were only a few other campers there, so it wasn't crowded at all. This was in February, and although the seasons there are opposite from North America's seasons, it was obviously not high season. Besides being a little cold, the wind would kick up at times during the day. A small family group wandered the shore looking for tide pools. I did the same and relished the windy coastline.

Dinner for me consisted of bread and cheese. You'd think I wouldn't gain any weight, but unfortunately the opposite is true. It was all a little bare bones, and my neighbors at the campsite took note of my plight. I struck up a conversation with this amazing middle-aged couple, and true to the Aussie sense of hospitality, they quickly invited me to have dinner with them. Both were jovial, and they adopted me like a daughter for the night.

It was hard to even think of turning down the invitation for dinner since they were housed in a large motor home. It must have been at least twenty-four feet, if not longer, and looked like a mansion compared to my economic compact car. My new best friends and I laughed over glasses of wine and a great dinner of pork chops and veggies—just the most wonderful food ever. They were leaving the next day and gave me their phone number. When I traveled back through Melbourne, I was to contact them and be a guest in their house. My first thoughts were of murder and mayhem: they could be mass murderers or want a three-way sex game. Then my rational instincts took over, fortunately, and told me to trust them and my judgment.

My instincts were unwavering. I trust that. If there was a question in my thoughts, I would pay attention. In this case, I was sure all would be just fine. I called them and stayed with them just before leaving Melbourne. Once again, I was treated very graciously at a beautiful home. No more visions of missed Michigan fish-fry opportunities.

Sleeping in my little car was a contortion act. After dinner I surveyed my situation and jury-rigged the car a bit. The back seat would fold down, and I could maneuver myself into the trunk with my legs on the folded seat, or the other way around, whichever was most comfortable. Nothing was really comfortable, and eventually I decided to sleep in the back seats, putting the hatchback of the car in its original position, to spread out as best I could. All this in the name of austerity. It was a bumpy night, but eventually I did fall asleep and get a good night's sleep. I couldn't help thinking that no one else in their sixties would do this, but I'm sure I'm wrong.

I awoke the next morning and was ready for the next adventure, whatever it happened to be. Down the road was a boardwalk in a jungle-type area. I stopped and hiked above one of the Aussie landmarks: the Twelve Apostles in Port Campbell National Park. Once again it was cold and windy, therefore a brisk and brief visit. Later in the day, it was the mystery of parked cars that grabbed my attention.

I parked my car with the others and wandered over to the two or three other people standing in the area. I had been driving on a dirt road and was surprised to find any cars along this route. I asked the first stranger, "What are you looking at?"

He gestured. "Over there—the koalas are all over this area, eating."

"Koalas? You mean those cute bear-type critters I've seen on television?" I asked, almost incredulously. Almost before I could finish my sentence, I saw a koala bear almost directly across from my face. Sitting on a limb, it was peering at me with a piece of eucalyptus leaf in its tiny hand. It looked to me like a very old man with white hair sticking out in tufts, or a cute, chubby baby with little baby hands holding a branch of leaves. I couldn't believe it. These little nocturnal creatures were awake and active during the day.

It was all very surrealistic and darned cute. There was a small group of them. Unlike the other wildlife I'd seen so far, these guys had no intention of coming to your arm for food. They were doing just fine, thank you very much, munching from a distance. I watched them for a long time, even after my stranger-friends left. Feeling I'd gotten only a taste of the Australian experience, I vowed to find kangaroos and wallabies before I left too.

In my curiosity-seeking mode, as I encountered other people on the trip, I started asking about kangaroos. As a woman, independent as I am, I ask for directions and I ask for things I want to see. It wasn't unfamiliar for me to put on the nice-girl-question face and approach a gas station attendant with a can-do attitude. I've found over the years that people all over the world respond to a happy, nonintimidating face. It also helps to be a woman, and I regularly played that card.

With my best nice-girl face, I approached the attendant behind the cash register in a gas station along the road. For some reason, I don't feel compelled each time to actually buy gas or a candy bar when asking for directions. Typically, the person behind the cash register feels sorry enough for me because I always appear like I slept in my car the night before. My hair is combed but escaping from the stretchy round purple thing that ties my hair up in a ponytail, and I have on jeans and a nondescript top. Nonthreatening is my motto, and it always works.

"Sure, there are kangaroos around here. They are *everywhere*, and are a real nuisance," he emphasized. "Just go up the road about two miles, and there is a park on your right. Stop there to park your car and take a walk in the park," he continued in his down-under voice. He was a sweetheart.

I left for the short drive and turned into a parking lot near a building. There in front of me was a creature that was as curious about me as I was about it. Sure enough, it was a kangaroo. And there were many of them, similar to when our deer congregate in the forests of California.

If anyone doubted Darwin's theory of evolution, well, darn it, you'd be hard-pressed to deny it after looking at this creature. My kangaroo had huge, developed hind legs to jump long distances and yet pathetically tiny hands and arms. They almost seemed like human-sized arms, and they hung at his side like a human's hands would. I tried to see if a joey was around, but there was no baby in the pouch. I tried to study the kangaroo with scientific eyes, but I changed to fascinated eyes because I'm not a scientist. The head seemed like that of a deer, with long ears to hear sounds at a distance. Sometimes one ear changed from facing me to twisting as it heard another sound from another direction. The other one remained on me to ensure it was not missing a threat from me. Its enormous tail was like a furry rat tail, except enlarged as if radiation had caused a rat to mutate a thousand times its normal size. Its fur reminded me of that of a deer, with its white belly and gray coloring everywhere else. Overall, the kangaroo reminded me of a welded junk car made up of a deer's head and fur, a rat's tail, a human bodybuilding champ's legs, and a monkey's front arms, but proportionately shorter.

I watched the kangaroos in the park for an hour, taking pictures as they would let me, and studying them as they individually determined when I was invading their space. When they would leave my area, it was interesting to see their hind legs at work, instantly increasing the distance between themselves and me. All in all, they reminded me of the deer in the States, considered a nuisance as they clean out a flower garden but also admired when a young one with spots appears.

That night I pulled into a dirt pullout along the road where another large camper had also stopped. I went up to the middle-aged couple enjoying glasses of wine and made my usual request: "I'm traveling alone and would so appreciate it if you would let me stay near you." My nice-girl look was included. As I expected, they allowed me to stay and invited me to have a glass of wine with them as they pulled out a third folding chair.

The next day I decided to make a loop of my journey and head north to the outback, toward Grampians National Park. My trip on the Great Ocean Road was ending, and I wanted to understand the outback as much as I could—by experiencing it, of course. I journeyed up a road that was narrow and paved for the most part. There were very few other cars, so it wasn't a problem. When I got near the park, I saw a sign for aboriginal rock art—rocks painted with pigments—just a short hike from the road. As I hiked, it occurred to me that I was truly experiencing the outback. It looked the way I'd envisioned, felt like it, and smelled like it—dry, rocky, with bushes but few trees.

That afternoon I headed to another campground, where I encountered someone who made my instincts bristle. He seemed like a survivalist, or at least someone I couldn't trust. He drove an old, rusted car and was leaning against it and smoking when I drove by. Smoking a cigarette didn't bother me, but the fact that he had long matted hair, he was dirty, and he narrowed his eyes as he sneered at me *did* bother me. I interpreted his body language as telling me, *I don't want you in here, and I can cause you problems if you challenge me.* It didn't feel right here. I drove as far away as I could get from him in the campground, but it was too lonely for my taste. I decided to stay for a while to rest and then leave before it became too dark.

It wasn't long before another car pulled into the campground. I waited to see about these new campers, but my fears were already falling away. Shortly after parking, two women in their thirties emerged and came over to say hello. They told me they were taking vacation time to see this part of Australia before going back to their jobs in Sydney. We collected another couple, from Michigan, and a single fellow from Europe. Eventually we were able to gather a little wood for a campfire and laughed, told stories, and learned different histories from the eclectic group. The odd fellow out kept to himself and was never a problem.

I ended my Aussie adventure by completing the circle from Melbourne, to the coast, to the outback, and back to Melbourne. Just before returning, I deposited the five-dollar sleeping bag at the same thrift store where I had purchased it. It would allow someone else to enjoy its new energy and to embrace the people and environment of the Aussie world.

CHAPTER 19

Alaska—Driving the ALCAN

I HAD SEEN ALASKA MANY TIMES BUT HAD NEVER DRIVEN THERE FROM THE lower forty-eight. It was definitely on my bucket list, and I had the winter in Antarctica to think about the trip. In order to drive to Alaska from Northern California, I had to get an RV for my critters and myself. I had two forty-pound rescue dogs and a cat. Finding an RV would be hurdle number one. Then I would have to do a little research, not so much that it would take the serendipity out of the trip, but enough to estimate the time it would take, understand the route, and form a general idea of whether I would survive or not. Before this trip, as I had with other trips, I worried about issues like being eaten by a bear, suffering an attack by a deranged person, getting stranded in a desolate place, and not being able to fix the RV.

In 2010 I was renting out rooms in my house in Northern California, and I mentioned to one of my roommates that I was looking for an RV. He told me that his wife's father was selling an old Toyota Sunrader, an eighteen-foot RV that was twenty-six years old. In Toyota terms, she had very low original miles: 88,000. I was assured that she was sound and that the owner had kept her maintained and covered. I was also assured that I would love her. Well, she turned out to be more of a hippie van than a luxury RV, and I was sure she would creak and moan during our future trip since she had a huge load on a small, four-cylinder pickup-truck chassis. I fell in love with her as soon as I saw her. On top of everything else, she was a steal at $6,000. I named her SusiQ.

I bought her and drove her up the canyon to my home, my hands on the large steering wheel that kept bobbing from side to side. The steering wheel was fine, but the RV drove like a ship. I was terrified most of the way up the canyon, going about twenty-five miles per hour on a road that had dropped into a canyon varying from a few feet to death-defying hundreds of feet deep. It probably was most frightening because she was twenty-six years old and I knew nothing else about her. Of course, she made it just fine, like the sturdy old girl I envisioned.

I took SusiQ immediately to my mechanic. I told him, "Keep the RV for a month and look her over. Repair or replace anything that is unsafe or that won't help me drive to Alaska." In mechanical terms, working on SusiQ's Toyota 22R engine was like working on a prized '56 Chevy. Well, almost like that. SusiQ's belts were checked, shocks replaced, engine tuned, lights and brakes inspected, new tires put on where needed—the works for an old engine and vehicle. It took less than a month for the mechanic to fix her up, and I felt fairly confident about the RV when it was done. It was a matter of trusting the universe once again.

In the meantime I explored the internet for information on Alaska and the ALCAN (Alaska-Canadian Highway), bought an Alaska atlas plus maps of Canada, renewed my AAA membership—not realizing that I probably would not have been covered in case of emergency because I didn't have the additional RV coverage—and tried to get used to driving with SusiQ's large steering wheel, which seemed loose to me. As much as I tried, there was little more I could do to get ready for the trip except make sure the RV was equipped with everything for the critters and me. The good news is that the ALCAN, a highway that had been quickly completed during WWII to provide a road between the contiguous United

States and Alaska for military supplies, was now paved and there was a chance that my windshield would make it without damage.

My plan was not to pay for campgrounds unless I had an emergency. This would keep my costs down and allow me to afford the trip. Most of my expense would be gasoline, which I could handle. Food—well, I had to eat whether I was in an RV or at home.

To seal the deal, I started telling my friends about my upcoming adventure. That disclosure would ensure I would really have to go. As it turned out, my brother decided to celebrate his sixtieth birthday by meeting me in Anchorage, even though his birthday is in March and I would be in Anchorage about early July. Additionally, two of my best friends asked if I would join them in Skagway, Alaska, to backpack the famous Chilkoot Trail. I loved the idea—the only issue with this was the critters, and timing.

Note to self: You have always worked all the details out. This time will be no exception.

THE FIRST WEEK OF JUNE CAME, AND I HAD TO LEAVE. I DELAYED A DAY OR two and then decided that I was procrastinating and we had to go. "We" included my two dogs (Pepper and Kami), The Cat, and me. I never name my cats until my grandson makes me. I guess I thought if one died, I might not be as attached so it wouldn't hurt so much. That was a lie. I am always attached to my critters. Since my mother objected to pets, and I had very few growing up, I love to rescue as many as I can handle at one time. They are ever-entertaining and make me feel comforted and safe. I was glad not to have to put them in the kennel for this trip.

I laughed when my friends started making bets on who would come back with me when I returned. I had people saying the two dogs would return but not The Cat. Others said, no, this dog would disappear but the other dog would return with The Cat. SusiQ pulled out of my driveway with the entourage. I said a quick prayer to the universe to give me luck.

The Cat started wailing immediately. She came to the area behind the driver and passenger seats and clung to the mesh netting I had placed there to prevent the critters from getting in my way while I was driving the vehicle. She hung there like a panicked prisoner fighting a jail cell. The cell would always win, and so did my mesh net. She clung to the netting for about fifteen minutes, wailing at the top of her little kitty lungs, and then stopped, got into her bed that I'd made from an old rug-type toilet seat cover, and never said another word on the three-month trip.

The two dogs, however, were content to be with me, whether we were in a jail cell, a closet, or this vehicle that had room for them to each have a couch in the back. They quickly learned that being in the RV meant that they were headed for daily adventures. In their own way, they were excited, and they let me know it each time I opened the RV door. It meant *Adventure* with a capital *A*.

I whisked through Oregon prairies, past small towns, and eventually into Idaho, where I visited a friend I hadn't seen for over thirty years. I crossed into Canada and, wanting to avoid the crowds and not pay for expensive park campgrounds if I got stuck, I decided to skip Banff and Jasper and go to Canada's Glacier National Park instead.

Along the way I would pull off onto dirt roads, on lakeshores, in Walmart parking lots, on side streets, and in miscellaneous parking lots to spend the night. The reason? I stopped at one RV park along the ALCAN, and the fees were forty dollars for a site with no electricity. I gave them five dollars for a shower and left. My future showers were hit or miss.

The dogs, The Cat, and I all tootled up the road, down the road, and mercifully stayed *on* the road. Meanwhile, my plans developed. In Canada's Glacier National Park, I often saw signs saying *Watch for Bears* or *Watch for Caribou*. Sure enough, as soon as I would come around a bend after seeing a sign, there would be the advertised animal. As I watched a caribou wander down a cliff off the road, I was reminded of another time, another decade, when I had been on a raft on the Kongakut River to the Arctic Ocean in Alaska.

In the 1990s, I was regaining my strength from my divorce, but I still wasn't totally good yet. I had signed up for the river trip by myself, but I was joining a group in Fairbanks. While out on the mystical journey, I was wide awake at the ten p.m. sun and told the leader that I was going on a hike and would be back later. I pointed to the area I was going to, but I went alone. That was risky because of marauding bears.

In the tussock-covered terrain, I had to go slowly so I wouldn't turn an ankle. As I reached one plateau on the hill I was climbing, I startled a ptarmigan that was changing color. Normally white in the winter, it was a spotted brown and white at this time in June and totally blended into the ground I was covering. I watched it for a long time, then left it alone.

My goal was to hike above the Dall sheep I had spotted from camp, which were grazing almost near the top of a hill several miles away. Never mind that there were grizzly bears around, most likely *hungry* grizzly bears. Fortunately there were few bears in the area, and each covered a remarkably large area of land because food was so scarce. I didn't realize that the hillsides that appeared as if bulldozers had come through had actually been dug up by bears searching for bugs and other underground creatures they might be lucky enough to catch.

I trudged onward, slowly going up the hill to the right of the sheep. My plan was to get to the top of the hill where they were grazing and look down on them. My rationale was that most predators come at them from the bottom of a hill, not from the top, so they wouldn't be startled by me. I hiked to the top of the mountain, on the side where they could not see my ascent.

I made it to the top and very slowly made my way to the area where I thought they would be. I saw them and kept creeping very slowly and very quietly, stopping every few yards. Eventually I stood still and just waited for one to see me since I was almost part of the herd at this point. It didn't take long for that to happen.

A very young lamb saw me. I was sure that these critters had never seen a human being before and wouldn't really know what to do with me. Most likely, I was correct. The youngster raised its head and started to walk toward me. It didn't come nearer than probably twenty feet, and during its walk, the rest of the herd instantly knew I was there. All eyes were on me. I stood still. After probably half a minute, a large ram with horns came toward me, trying to make sense of just what I was. It raised and lowered its head a few times to see if I would run away. I stood still.

The ram spread its legs and peed, a nice long pee. I stood still, and the sheep still didn't know what to do with me. Puzzled, the ram took another half a minute to make a decision. He somehow signaled to the herd to slowly walk away from me, not running but not eating along the way either. The herd of thirty or so left quietly, in an orderly manner, and yet quickly to get away from me. I stood still, relishing the amazing adventure.

Eventually I made my way back to camp as the sun was almost setting at two o'clock in the morning. We carried no equipment to contact anyone for rescue if any kind of incident had occurred. I checked in on the guide, watching her sleep with her rifle near her side and our food nearby on a tarp. There were no trees to hang food from, and we didn't have bear canisters, so a lightly sleeping guard with a gun was the best way to protect food from bears. Looking back, I was grateful for the independence of that trip, which helped free me from some of the weight I was feeling emotionally.

My mind jerked back to the ALCAN in front of me. On the road again in the Yukon and headed toward Anchorage, the critters and I usually avoided stopping at local joints for food, to contain costs, but there was one sign that caught my attention. It read: *Homemade Pie and Coffee, $5.* I couldn't resist, so I stopped and ordered berry pie with the locals. While I was ordering, the middle-aged woman who served me asked if I had seen "the mushroom people." *Mushroom people?* My interest was piqued. Well, no, I didn't really know what or who mushroom people were.

She continued, "Didn't you see the cars parked back there along the road?"

"Well, yes, I did, but I didn't think much about it."

"Last year we had a big fire here, and it burned a lot of acreage around here," she said as she poured my coffee. "The mushroom hunters come here to find morel mushrooms after the burns. About a year after a fire, the mushrooms come up, and everyone comes here to collect them for sale. Sometimes novices get lost in the burned forests, so it can be a real bummer."

I wasn't sure what kind of a bummer she was referring to, but I could imagine, so I didn't ask. Of course, I had to go back and talk with a mushroom hunter after I finished my pie and coffee.

SusiQ and I headed back down the road only a few miles. I pulled up alongside the other cars. There were about four cars, so I thought perhaps there wasn't a lot of opportunity to talk with one of the mushroom people. Lo and behold, almost as soon as I put the RV in park, a young man covered with soot walked out of the blackened forest. I walked up to him, hoping he would talk with me and let me know about the life of a mushroom person.

He said he lived a few hours away but made it a point to come back to this area to collect mushrooms when he thought they would be ready. He opened an aged canvas rucksack and showed me his collection of misshapen mushrooms. They reminded me of dried-up Christmas trees, black and dark gray-brown. Some were several inches tall, others smaller. He said he could get fifteen to twenty dollars per pound for them, so I was looking at a lot of money in his rucksack.

I asked him about his sooty face and how hard it is to find the morels. He laughed. "It comes with the job!" He acknowledged it was very easy to get lost in a forest in this big land since there were no roads or signs anywhere. He felt confident of his navigational skills, though, because he had been doing this for years. I laughed, smiled, and wished him good luck as I drove away in SusiQ.

Another day, I found a bunch of cars parked again, so I pulled over to see the attraction. There in front of me was a huge stream cascading down probably fifty to eighty feet to the bottom. Amazingly, on several rocks at the top of the waterfall were young men with spears. They were trying to spear salmon as the fish were jumping up the falls. Either barefoot or with flip-flops, and with only shorts on, these young men seemed to be risking their lives to catch these large fish. I was stunned and stood for the longest time to watch these talented young men. Eventually many of the men speared fish and brought them to shore. Again, I talked with one of them to find out how hard it is to catch a fish in this ancient way. He assured me that it wasn't easy and that sometimes one of them would die from falling off the rock perches. It is a developed talent to spot the fish in the raging water, spear it while it's in motion, and bring it to shore while it's writhing on the spear. Dinner depended on it. The men were as nonchalant about risking their lives for dinner as they would be about drinking a cup of coffee.

We continued down the road, my critters and me. My two dogs, Pepper and Kami, were good companions and kept me from feeling lonely or unsafe. Kami always stayed close to me, but Pepper was another story. She was a shepherd-husky mix and was prone to do her own thing at times. I guess I'm the same way.

It was a weekend day, so I found a good, safe place in the forest to camp. In the morning I opened SusiQ's door to let the two dogs out. I shut the door so I wouldn't lose The Cat, and I turned to the kitchen to heat up water for coffee and warmth. A few minutes later, I got up and called the dogs. One showed up, only Kami. Pepper was nowhere to be found. After she'd run out the door, I had seen her go downhill, in front of the RV, down a hillside with no roads or paths. What to do? All I could do right then was make a cup of coffee and wait.

I decided I would spend the night in the same spot a second night if needed for Pepper to come back. I made my coffee and sat in the RV with Kami.

It must have been about four hours after the initial escape, but Pepper showed up again, jaunting up as if nothing had happened, coming from an entirely different direction than the one she'd left from. I think she'd made a loop when she'd decided to "take a walk in the woods." After raising many dogs over the years, I had learned not to panic and to stay put so the missing critter could find its way home.

The most recent critter experience over, I could concentrate on my brother. I arrived in Anchorage, picked up my brother from the airport, deposited the dogs in a kennel, kept The Cat with us, and set off for adventures. My brother was kind enough to trust me to create those experiences.

Of course we went to Denali National Park and took the school bus to Wonder Lake. Taking the old buses into Denali was a treat in itself. While the drivers would often point out wildlife or views, they were not really tour guides. We could get on or off the bus at any point and stay for a while, and then flag down another bus to go farther into the park or return.

We were able to get tickets for very early in the morning so we could decide how far to go into the park. We drove past massive treeless areas where we could see forever, and we encountered many animals from a safe distance inside the bus. At one point along the way back, I said to my brother, "Let's get out and walk a little in this gorgeous country." He agreed, and we hopped out of the bus and started off to parallel the road on a hike. It wasn't long before I spotted a huge grizzly bear in the distance—about a mile away—and pointed it out to my brother. I was thrilled, excitedly showing it to him. He wasn't thrilled. It was huge bear, he acknowledged, but we were way too close to it for my brother's comfort. We caught the next bus out of the park and never looked back.

Talkeetna, just outside the national park, is where planes leave to drop off mountain climbers for the trek up Denali, the highest peak in North America. The next day was not pretty, and the clouds and low visibility kept the planes from taking off. We were not attempting to climb Denali, but the planes could give us a lift to see the famous glaciers. There were two other people in the office who wanted to fly to look at glaciers too, and they wanted to land on one if we could take off. I got cheap, my former modus operandi, and flatly stated, "I don't want to land on the glacier, I just want to go up in a plane to see Denali." It caused a dilemma. My patient brother stood by and listened as I made a fool of myself being a prima donna cheapskate.

Eventually the clouds lifted and we got a green light for the flight. After a quick negotiation about landing vs. not landing, we decided we would land if possible, were given a discount for the trip, and were able to take off for the mountain. The small plane flew right up a glacial path, following the white-gray-black path of the glacier for miles. Eventually Denali broke through the clouds and showed its majesty. The weather was good enough to land on the glacier for a short time. Our experienced pilot took the plane down slowly and then cut the engine and let the skis on the plane guide us to a place where the entire plane turned around. We unloaded, one at a time, and looked around. It was the most incredible adventure I've ever had, and worth every penny. The picture of my brother and me on top of the glacier is my favorite, and will forever be my favorite. He's my favorite—my *only*—brother anyhow.

After taking my brother to the airport to return to the Midwest, I collected my two dogs from the kennel and then set off from Anchorage to go south, homeward bound. On the way, I was going to meet my mountain-climbing friends Gary and Sarah in Skagway to go up the Chilkoot Trail in the Klondike Gold Rush area.

Once again I knew the two dogs would need to be put in jail for the hike, since they would not be safe on the trail. Along the way I would stop at local libraries to use their computers and look online for kennels. I called the facility south of Whitehorse, more or less en route to Skagway, and dropped the dogs off one more time. When I parked the RV, it was not hot at all, and in fact rainy, so The Cat would have the entire RV to herself for a few days, complete with litter box, open windows, food, and water. I left a neighbor with the key to SusiQ to check on The Cat. She actually did fine and was glad for the time without the dogs. Dogs in jail and The Cat in heaven, my friends and I left for a few days to backpack the trail.

I had heard tales of this hike for decades. The gold rush had drawn thousands of people into Canada from Alaska, and if they were to get into the Klondike in Canada, they were required to carry a year's worth of provisions—a thousand pounds—up the trail. Fortunately Gary, Sarah, and I had to take just a few days' worth of provisions. The thirty-three-mile hike up would take four or five days, and then there was a train that would bring us back to Skagway.

The first several days of the trail were bearable, but the last day over the boulder-strewn pass was incredibly hard. A large white fog settled around us, and despite the poles to mark the trail, we couldn't see well enough to follow them. At each pole one of us had to go to the next pole where the person would wait until the others caught up. Then one of us would go to the next pole while the other two remained at the known pole. It took a long time, was very strenuous because of the steepness of the slippery climb, and it made us wonder about the success of the miners who'd had to make many, many trips to get their gear up the pass.

I'm sure the miners didn't have the luxury of what we saw at the top of the pass. After hiking in fog all day, we were soaked. It could have been hypothermic weather, and the Canadian government knew it. From a distance we saw a tiny hut above us. As we carefully picked out the trail across the wet boulders, we slowly approached the hut. We laughed at someone waiting on the porch, hailing us to come inside. Shortly after entering the small room, we enjoyed hot tea or cocoa provided by the Canadian government—kind of a small border control or celebratory office.

My knee was bothering me by this point in the trip. I was limping, and the pain was ten on a scale of one to ten. I was going slowly, trying to imagine the problem. Heck, we had been going up a boulder field—a very steep boulder field—all day, so my knee had a right to hurt. What I didn't know at that point was that one of the four quadrants of my knee joint was bone on bone, an extremely painful condition.

After the Canadian border experience, we had to hike another several hours before camping. It was hard for me to put up my tent, but eventually it was up to protect me from any rain, which was very common there even in the summer. The next morning it was very hard for me to take down the tent, stake by stake. But it did come down, with my effort. And I kept going, step by step. My right knee constantly let me know it wasn't happy.

The rest of the hike was excruciating—I was slow, I was hurting, and I was angry that my knee hurt so much after the first several days of the hike. The first days had been brutal, yet I had done well and my knee hadn't hurt much. Today, maybe my mind was allowing me to recognize the pain.

Then two amazing things happened that day. First, I realized the wonder that I was able to get to this point in the hike, with just one more day of hiking to reach the train that would take us back to Skagway. Second, I discovered Germany's Riesen chocolate caramel candy.

I couldn't have been happier when I saw a building, the depot for the train that had been built in the Klondike to help the miners more easily get their supplies into the area. We rounded a corner, and there was a long building, which meant civilization and a train back to my RV. I wouldn't have to hike any longer.

That night we camped near the depot, and I noticed a shelter with mosquito netting on top of a small mound. As curious as my cat, I had to find out what it was all about.

I peeked inside, and a young woman looked up at me and smiled. She said she was surveying the backpackers coming up the trail, and could she ask me a few questions? I was more than willing, so I sat down inside the shelter.

The young woman had long blond hair and a beautiful sunbaked tan. Meanwhile, I was tired, my hair clung to my head, and I'm sure I smelled because of the past few days' effort.

She began, "How long have you been on the trail?"

"Five days," I replied quickly.

Next question, "What did you think of the trail?"

"I thought that the trail up the pass was rugged, I can't understand how the miners could have carried up so much gear, and the countryside above the border house is the most beautiful I have seen," I said.

That's when she handed a small piece of candy to me. I unwrapped it and, without question, put it in my mouth. It was my very first Riesen experience. After that, I felt like a dog eyeing a bone. I kept my eyes on the bag of rewards. I could answer more questions for more Riesens.

She asked me other questions such as, "Is there anything that could make the journey better?"

"Another Riesen," I replied quickly, my eye on the bag.

She obliged and gave me another candy. And so it went for another ten or fifteen minutes until I managed to squeeze a third and last Riesen from her. To die for—well, not quite.

After the train ride back, my friends left for Los Angeles, and I left to collect my old RV from Skagway and hope that The Cat was all right. She was. Honestly, I don't think she even knew I was gone. I had to leave Skagway and pick up the missing two critters, and once again we were on our way. With the physical rest, my knee was behaving once again, thank goodness.

I went home via the Cassiar Highway, then through Washington and Oregon, taking advantage of any hot springs, Lewis and Clark Expedition sites, open prairies, and free camping spots I could find. I came home to Northern California with SusiQ, The Cat, two dogs, and myself all intact, happy, and healthy.

CHAPTER 20

Africa

AFRICA WAS THE ONLY CONTINENT I HADN'T BEEN TO YET. I HESITATED about going to Africa because of my insecurity about personal safety; a myriad of mysterious diseases; killer bugs in rivers; heck, crocodiles in rivers; and any number of death-defying events that could occur. Judy had already been to Africa with a group that had climbed Mount Kilimanjaro, and she had no desire to return and accompany me. I would be on my own to figure things out. I was faced with finding a way to visit Africa that didn't send out messages of fear to others—or worse, to me.

At first, I researched trips to visit the mountain gorillas in Uganda. Seeing them was my first choice of African activities, since poachers are killing them at an alarming rate. They will most likely be gone in the wild during my lifetime. They would be magnificent creatures to see, if I was lucky enough to encounter a group during the day. I would pay $500 for the *chance* to see them. Per day. That was a bit of a risk. Additionally, the area I'd have to go into crossed into three countries: Uganda, Rwanda, and the Democratic Republic of the Congo. If the gorillas were in one country, I could research my potential safety in that country, but they live and move about in three countries, and between the poachers and civil unrest in the area, it would add to my *Worry a Lot* list.

After emailing a few companies, I truly couldn't get over the *danger* signal in my head. I thought about my choices and about the fact that I didn't feel comfortable with the information I'd been given, so I changed directions and started thinking about Kilimanjaro. Could I do that kind of a climb? Could I get in shape to do it? Mentally, I could compute in my brain what I needed my body to do: climb for seven days and get to an altitude of 19,341 feet—an altitude I had never achieved before. It would be a great challenge and would turn out to be either a victory or a failure. After the trip I could think really highly of myself, or I could be totally faced with getting old and no longer being able to achieve what I set out to do.

My mind was playing tricks on me. *Of course you can do it*, I told myself. *You know you can.*

Note to self: Do you *want* to do it?

CLIMBING KILI, AS THE MOUNTAIN IS REFERRED TO AMONG MY CLIMBING friends, would be a feat: it is the tallest mountain in Africa and therefore is one of the seven summits—each continent has a highest peak, and this is Africa's. My son had climbed it, and there was no reason I couldn't. Granted, I was about twice the age my son had been when he did it, so maybe that was a reason *not* to do it. I filed that "reason" away in the back of my head, along with others, to justify my decision, one way or another.

I researched climbing companies and found one that was reasonably priced, based in Africa, seemed to have some kind of credentialed guides, would take me up the longest route to give me the best chance of acclimatizing and summiting, plus wouldn't mind dealing with an old lady like me. Sounded like a winner to me. I didn't tell my mother I was going alone. Heck, I hated to admit it to myself.

I made the six flights to get to Tanzania in almost as many days and finally arrived at the very foreign airport. The airport was small, the weather was hot, and there in front of me, as I exited the security gates, was a sign with my name on it, held by a fellow with a very large smile. *Yeah!* I started talking a great deal, something I do when I am nervous, as the driver took me to the town of Moshi.

Moshi is a small, third-world town, but larger than the tiny villages we passed quickly on the way. It had dirt streets, people walking everywhere, and a variety of dusty cars. People were on the streets selling whatever they could to make very little money. Later I discovered that there were only a few crafts shops, and everything in the shops was expensive. Everything on the streets was cheap, unless the locals decided to charge tourist prices. Not much had a physical price tag on it.

My car arrived at a large gate after half an hour of travel. Behind the gate were lush gardens with tall green vegetation and a few small buildings, which turned out to be the hotel. A guard opened the gates, and we drove into the complex to a small reception building. I noticed several guards around, surveilling the complex for possible intruders. There would be more guards in the evening than in the daytime. As far as I knew, there were more guards than patrons. This made me wary, instantly sending up my antenna to be cautious.

The reception area for guests was painted white and paved with large tiles. A long wooden counter encouraged me to walk up and talk with the receptionist. A young girl was behind the desk, using a fan to keep the heat away. She smiled broadly and welcomed me, gave me a key to my room, and pointed down a paved pathway to a small, round building that would be my home for the night.

There were several round buildings, each with at least two separate rooms in it. There was a walkway to each building, and I followed a young man to my room as he carried my pack. I opened the door to a large bed and a clean stone floor. The room was bright and inviting, with its own fairly new bathroom. I found the roundness of the room to be fascinating and well thought out. In that moment, I felt there was nothing else to do than to lie on the bed and let a sigh of relief escape. I'd made it to Africa and was safe; therefore, one part of my long journey was over. I was totally exhausted, glad to be at my destination, and all too aware that the first day of my journey up Kili would start the next day. I fell soundly asleep on the large bed.

I woke up in time to make it to dinner, so I quickly walked to the dining room. It was massive, in my opinion, too large for the few people who were there. I walked in and sat at the table I was directed to. I noticed a young man sitting at a table by himself. After I ordered, I went over to talk with him.

Ted, the young man, told me that he was from Connecticut, was finishing college in Texas, and was off to climb Kili the next day, just as I was. He had booked the same company I was traveling with, so I assumed we could climb together even though we had two different groups of guides and porters. Ted was an amazing young man, full of enthusiasm, passion, and youth. He infused everything he talked about with wonder, as if nothing was impossible in his young world. I wasn't about to put a damper on his lofty spirit.

We were both tired after hours of traveling, so our evening was short. We had made the connection that would follow us throughout our climbing trip, keeping us laughing and teasing each other for the next week. Fortunately age was on my side, so Ted respected me and didn't tease me mercilessly about my slowness and methodical hiking mantra.

The next morning we met with the outfitter's organizer and told him that we would like to travel together. He suggested combining our groups, since we were each traveling alone and each had a support team, but I hesitated for two reasons. First, it would mean giving fewer people jobs. These people counted on their jobs as guides and porters to earn a living. Second, I wasn't sure I could follow through with the required hiking and therefore didn't want to jeopardize Ted's trip because of my age and uncertainty.

We set out in two different vans. Each van included our guide, porters, and Ted or me. My van included a large duffel bag of hiking boots and shoes that I had collected from the US with the intention of giving them to the porters before the arduous trip. I'd learned in Nepal that sturdy shoes are highly prized in mountain towns, so since that trip, I'd begun a tradition to bring used hiking boots with me on trips whenever I could to give away when I was trekking.

When I met the owner of the company, I asked his thoughts about distributing the shoes, whether to save them for the end of the trip or let the porters have them early. I was told to give them out early and to let the guides and porters decide for themselves. When we got out of the van, I spread them out and let the porters pick out boots they wanted. One very tall porter from another group came up and begged for a pair of the shoes. I looked at his feet, in very old white gym shoes that were torn and had many holes. I wanted so much to give him a pair of the shoes, but I was told no by our guides since he was not a member of our group. My heart sank, but I obeyed. I wasn't in the States.

During the trip I kept seeing various pairs of boots show up on different porters as they passed them around to try to find the best size. I didn't realize that the shoes wouldn't necessarily fit the very large-footed men here, and I should have tried to find larger shoe sizes in the States. I had to convince myself that what I had done was good and not beat myself up about the misery in this very poor country.

Note to self: You're experiencing culture shock. Feel what you need to feel, but don't react, especially not with self-criticism. You had good intentions.

IT WAS HOT. I DON'T LIKE HOT. MY SCOTTISH HERITAGE WAS COMING UP, and I knew the temperature would cool as we got to higher elevations, but the hike up Kili started in the heat of the jungle. Ted's group went past me and waited for our group when they stopped for lunch. My guide set up a tent for me to sit under and enjoy my lunch, and I appreciated having the heat off my head for a few minutes. We had fresh fruit and other food that I truly don't remember. The one thing I *do* recall, however, is that the cook did such a good job in the preparation of meals throughout the trip that I never got sick. Getting Montezuma's revenge (diarrhea) can lead to the abortion of a great trip. The universe, and the cook, were on my side during this trip.

We started out again, slowly, with me being very apologetic about being so slow. My guide kept telling me, "But, Miss Linda, it is *good* to go slowly. Like roly-poly," just like the guide on Everest had said.

The first days were painful. I was very hot, tired, and grumpy, although I usually kept the grumpiness to myself. That's the advantage of going with no one you know—you can't complain to anyone since no one really wants to hear about it, so you have to avoid saying it out loud. I complained under my breath: "Why am I doing this? I'm too old to do this. This is craziness. My children must think I am nuts. For sure, my mom does."

My mind wandered when we were walking on the rocky trail. Breaking my ankle in the mountains would be a big deal here. My mind flashed to the terrible ankle break I'd suffered years earlier, in the Nevada mountains, and my ankle twinged with phantom pain at the memory. I stepped carefully and relied on my trekking poles for extra balance and support.

We made it to a higher zone on the mountain, and the temperature started to cool. The porters always skipped in front of us, carrying all our gear including the tents, food, my backpack, plus their own gear. My primary guide stayed with me and Ted's with him during the journey.

I remember one time we were sitting on rocks with gray fog behind us. Ted got the bright idea of having me take a picture of the guides and him, seeing if I could catch them all jumping at the same time. I did. Then they thought it would be fun if I joined the picture. We commandeered someone outside the group to take a picture of the four of us jumping at the same time, and jump we did. I think it took three tries, but my feet actually left the ground a few inches while the others jumped wildly. Pictures of joy.

On day five we reached the highest camp. There were tents scattered for the climbers, with the support team camping nearby. There was little vegetation, and the wind picked up in the afternoon. The trail came very near my tent, descending between rock walls from above. My tent was ready for me, and I jumped in as soon as I got there. This is where we would rest, and then that night we'd start the final climb to the summit, come back, and rest here for a short time before starting down. After a short nap, I watched other hikers coming down from the summit.

One young woman, probably in her late twenties or early thirties, was being helped down by her guide and a porter. She looked terrible—her face was white, had no expression, and I could tell she wasn't about to say anything to anyone, including me. She was utterly spent, had nothing left to offer, and was darned lucky to have the two men helping her off the mountain. She was very slowly lowering herself down the rock walls before the campsite, staring into space, and almost completely limp as she let the guides take her arms.

Next an Asian fellow came off the mountain. He was in worse shape than the young woman. He was probably twice her age and was pale, only able to move slowly, and was being helped a lot more than the young woman. He was too sick to be scared or to know how bad his health really was. I quickly remembered my mountain-climbing friend Jennifer, who, on January 1, 2000, had climbed to the top of Kili to celebrate the new century, sat down on a rock, and died. Just died.

Jennifer had been a healthy fellow mountain climber who had arranged the group of friends to summit Kili at the beginning of the new century. She was middle-aged, sturdy, and driven to climb, just as all the members of our climbing group were. Our friends told me that she had been very slow during the trip, hours behind the group. There was obviously something wrong, but her spirit made her continue to the top in spite of the warning signs. The results were tragic.

Fear crept into my head again. So far, I had been very tired and hot, but I was holding my own and being a slug—a successful slug. At this point I was a little less fearful because I really had been doing well, so the self-doubting thoughts were not taking over my head as much anymore. Seeing the two people having trouble reminded me that I had to go slowly and be vigilant. Maybe they had taken the three-day route instead of the seven-day route. Maybe they didn't know enough about hiking or trusted themselves more than they should have. Maybe I should give myself credit for knowing what would be required of me and knowing that I could do it. I just had to plug the data into my brain and let it help me up the mountain.

My guide and the assistant decided that I would leave at eleven o'clock that night to reach the summit, and Ted wouldn't leave until one in the morning. I didn't mind being told that I was slow, and I didn't mind at all leaving before Ted. I was sure he would catch me quickly and pass me.

True to their word, the young guide and a seasoned porter woke me up at eleven so I could start for the peak. I think the first few hours were the slowest of the trip, as I barely took one step at a time. Half a step at a time was more like it. My guide kept telling me, "Roly-poly!" and he would not let me go any faster. At that time of the night, with little moonshine to help light the way, it was hard to see the trail. Plus, people had made many trails over the years, so it was difficult to decipher where to go. Until a few hours passed, when the moon came up and the main trail was clearer, it would be difficult to see anything or to go faster than our speed. As expected, Ted caught up to me and passed me on his journey to the peak. He broadcast his smile on the way by, and I knew he would make the top of the peak by daybreak. That was the prize—to see the sunrise on the mountaintop. I would miss it, but I was fine with that.

I got to the rim of Kilimanjaro's extinct volcano crater well after sunrise. I knew we were near the top. The guide, assistant, and I could now see parts of the amazing glaciers surrounding the peak and the summit far to the left on the rim of the crater. It was within my reach, and I would make it. I knew this because I had been talking all the way up the crater—something I normally can't do when I am struggling to catch my breath or climbing too fast, so I knew I was in good shape for the rest of the hike. We sat for a break, to drink much-needed water, and to eat a snack. I was offering snacks to the guide and assistant because I didn't think they had brought any food for themselves. They were carrying my daypack, and I was carrying nothing.

Then we were off again, and I was smiling because the tremendous gain was over. We had only one or two hundred feet of elevation left to the peak, although the trail was a mile or two from that point to the top. We started up, and I started smiling. I had hauled my ass up that mountain and was going to make it to the peak with no problem.

Note to self: So much for self-doubt.

The walk at this point had all been on snow and ice, but it was not dangerous or even too strenuous. I was smiling and laughing. Then Ted appeared, on his way down the mountain. He gave me a huge hug and a big smile, and it made me so very happy. This young man was witnessing my joy. He almost decided to go back up with me, but changed his mind and continued down the peak.

Reaching the peak was almost anticlimactic for me. It was the journey that was the important part, believing in myself and going slowly to ensure I could make the climb. I was in Africa, after all, by myself—hugging myself for making the peak and for having the courage to come to Africa in the first place.

The guide, assistant, and I all gathered around the Kili summit sign for pictures. There were many other people at the summit, so finding a volunteer to take pictures was not hard. We volunteered for each other. As far as I could tell, I was the oldest one on the summit that day, and I was darned proud of it.

The trip down was fun, as we got on the scree slopes and ran down. Scree is very small gravel-type terrain, and when it's very deep, you can run in it, heel first. If it is not deep, it is not possible to run because stationary rocks hidden in it can cause you to slip. This was deep scree, fun to run down, so that's what I did. Getting back to camp was a much faster ordeal than getting up to the peak, and I think I was back down to camp by eleven a.m., making it a twelve-hour hike up and back.

The plan was to move down the mountain the same day to a lower campsite so we could hike out the last day. We would descend another steeper, shorter trail. I was very, very tired, and the short break when we got back didn't allow me to sleep. I would stop often to stretch out my back. Fracturing my back several years ago was still causing me grief. I'd learned to compensate for the pain and keep my mouth shut, but sometimes the injury made me clumsy. After I fell face-first on a flat stretch of the trail on the way down, the guide slowed the pace. I stumbled into the last campsite really, really tired and hurting.

I looked for the bathrooms and saw two: one said *Visitors* and the other said *Porters*. I went to the porter one and was appalled to see how dingy and dirty this one was in comparison to the other. I used the porter bathroom every time after the first time. It came naturally to me and was probably a silent message to my group that I don't agree with the unspoken hierarchy. I see everyone as equal.

Everyone was happy to be going home after a successful trip. What I didn't know was that the last day would be one of the most dangerous ones. As we left the campsite the last morning, I started seeing large carts with huge bicycle-type wheels on them. In the front was a rail that could be used to pull the cart. There were two wheels on the cart, one on each side. I wondered what the carts were used for, and then it dawned on me. They are used to carry people down the trail when bones are broken.

The trail grew radically worse in the lower part, where the rainwater from the peak eroded it. The mud was ankle deep, slippery, and continuous. The memories of my ankle breaking in mud were all too familiar. Ted, on the other hand, was having fun slipping and sliding down the trail. He simply didn't have the background, or years, that I had on me. All this translated to yet another very slow downhill journey for me. I would plant each hiking pole in a safe spot and slowly take a step. Often I was stepping between exposed tree roots. Each of the pockets of tree roots was filled with muddy water. My feet were soaked from the roots and mud that were everywhere. I said a little prayer with each successful step and knew that I had to go quicker to get out in one day.

It took forever, but eventually the trail leveled out a bit, and I knew we were escaping from my worst nightmare. Then the mud subsided also, and the trail became more compact and less steep. I was going to live through yet another adventure, as long as I didn't let my guard down until I was in some kind of vehicle. That would be another kind of danger.

Eventually we started seeing more local people. Everyone was friendly and offering some kind of service. We were at the end of the trail, where we received a paper acknowledging that we had actually climbed the mountain, and vendors greeted us with all kinds of wares and services. People were even offering to clean our shoes for us—anything to get us to part with our tourist dollars. I succumbed to a few of them because I had been so long without spending money and was so grateful to have lived through the experience.

We drove back to Moshi, where we stayed in the same beautiful, guarded hotel. One of the maids caught me before I went inside my room and begged me to allow her to clean my shoes. By this time I had little money left because I was only in Africa one more day. I told her I didn't have much money, and she said, "Anything, just *anything* will be okay." I couldn't refuse. The shoes were as beautiful as I had ever seen them about an hour after our deal, and they were waiting for me on the step in front of my door. It was heartbreaking to give her so little money for the beautiful job.

I begged Ted to go with me in town to explore. I knew I would be safer if there was a man with me, and he agreed to go. We walked past people with all kinds of used clothing, automotive goods, used tools—everything imaginable for sale on the sidewalks of Moshi. I kept asking the locals where the market was, and people pointed toward downtown several times. After a bit of wandering, we ended up in a block behind the main street where there were vendors in stalls. Bingo—I found the market!

There were chickens in small cages, ready to produce eggs or dinner, whichever was the buyer's intention. There were dried grasses, beans, spices, eggs, fruits and vegetables I had never seen before, and a myriad of other things that were intriguing. Ted was amazed. I had seen many markets before. I was specifically looking for an aluminum teapot. In addition to fabric scraps, bracelets, and pocketknives, I've collected teapots and mirrors from all the continents. I stopped at one vendor and found one, but it was too big. By then, we had several people following us, begging us to buy whatever they had.

One young man knew exactly what I was saying when I pointed to the large kettle and motioned that I wanted a smaller one. He motioned that he would be right back with what I wanted. Ted and I looked in the small stalls at the wares. Then, sure enough, a few minutes later the young man returned with an aluminum teapot, which I bought. He wanted a tourist dollar price, though, and I didn't. We negotiated somewhere in between, and I still probably paid double what the teapot was worth. It was worth it to me, and I was glad to leave some of my tourist dollars in this poor town.

We wandered back to our hotel, tired after our trip and itching from all the dust from the roads of Moshi. I was safely in our compound once more, and it felt good. I slept well.

Having survived the Kili climb and feeling full of myself, I was in good spirits. I made it to Kilimanjaro International Airport, spending my last dollar on a tip for the van driver. I thought the flights would be a piece of cake as I easily boarded my plane to Addis Ababa, Ethiopia. We landed early evening in Ethiopia, and luckily the tourist shops in the airport remained open to catch tourists like me. Plus, they took credit cards for purchases. True to my nature, I bought a drum, a purse, and a ceramic teapot from the airport shop. The shopkeeper was grateful for the business. Once again I had to stuff more merchandise in my duffel bag or backpack. I was starting to appear like a pathetic traveler with all the stuff I was collecting. For sure, I looked like a tourist.

Next, I had a short flight to the airport in Cairo, Egypt, where yet another adventure occurred. We landed very late at night, and I was taken to a holding area with probably ten other people. It reminded me of a dungeon or prison cell, and my danger antenna went up once again. I felt as if I were totally out of control of the situation, that I had to follow the stern men who were ordering me to follow them.

I was too tired to get really upset, and I had to trust that all would be right in the universe if I didn't put up a stink or worry too much. Shortly after seating me and a few other passengers on long, cold wooden benches, the officer said curtly, "Passports!"

This was not a time to fuss. I got out my passport, and he grabbed it from me. I guessed there was a fifty-fifty chance that I would get it back. In either case, I didn't have a real choice. I was the only Caucasian, the white representative among the group, and this late at night, I started having visions of doom. *I'm going to be put somewhere and not allowed to get on the next flight because I'm American, because I'm a woman, and/or because I'm stupid.*

Across from me was a middle-aged black man. He had very kind eyes, and he glanced at me from time to time as I mentally paced. My anxiety must have been showing. He had a slight build and small stature and was wearing a suit that didn't fit him well—he seemed at a loss with the world.

Finally he smiled, looked me straight in the eye, and motioned to me with his hand, palm down, pumping it up and down a little. To me, he was saying, *It's okay. Calm down.* I nodded. He smiled and then did the hand signal once again. I smiled back, and our eyes locked for a minute. He was trying to quiet my fears, to let me know that this was a normal procedure, and that all would be okay. Funny how communication can occur on such a basic level since we spoke no common language. He smiled at me, and said quietly, "Okay." I could trust the universe, or at least this kind man. Maybe I wasn't going to be imprisoned and left for dead somewhere in Egypt.

After what seemed an eternity, the stern officers returned with a small group of passports. As they were handed back one by one, the few people who received their passports were told to follow the officers. This happened a few times, until I was in the last group to go, along with the man I had been communicating with. I followed the officers into the main airport terminal and was released to go on my journey.

God Save the Queen and anyone else, including my gentle friend who'd helped me. I'd been freed from the quasi jail cell. We entered the large airport, which was upscale and really quite nice. I looked around and decided to sit quietly in a chair along a long hallway, directly across from a prayer room. I was the only one in the terminal for a long time.

I was spending the night in the airport, something not uncommon to me. I watched the world around me as I sat in my chair. At first, a few people fully dressed in white garments passed me or sat across from me, and then the pace picked up. Several went into the prayer room and started praying and chanting. I could see them on the ground, bowing as they prayed, and I immediately knew this place was very foreign from what I was used to.

More and more people showed up, and I was getting stares that made me feel uncomfortable. I had never experienced distrustful glares before, but then I had rarely been in the minority. I finally decided to find another hall to stay in, so I got up to move. It would make me feel better, though no one else probably cared. As I prepared to leave, I smiled at a young boy with his father. The boy looked at his father, a very large man who exuded power. The man gave the youth no clue about what to do with my smile. Finally the child could not ignore my smile and smiled back.

I was ecstatic when I boarded the plane to Athens, Greece, where I would have a totally different experience.

CHAPTER 21

Greece

When I made my plan to visit Greece, my goal was to visit an out-of-the-way and less popular, hopefully less populated, island—not one of the jet-set crowded islands of Greece. I decided on Lesvos. I liked its name, and it is supposedly the birthplace of Sappho, an ancient Greek lyric poet who was gay. The term *lesbian* was derived from the island of Lesvos. It all seemed to fit into my hippie nature.

After the trip to Africa, I had made it to the Athens airport and now had to catch a public bus to the port, where I would board a ferry to Lesvos. I had come through this airport on my way to Africa, and I used that layover to research the bus routes and ferry schedule I'd need as soon as I landed here again, so I knew which bus number to catch. Although I caught the bus after landing with no problem, it was rush hour in Athens and we were moving slowly. Additionally, I was really, really tired. My fear factor was at the top level after being detained in Egypt, and I was anxious, unsure of myself, and just plain pooped.

I pushed my way onto the bus and sat on my luggage near the back, because the bus was overcrowded and people were sitting wherever they could. There was a kind man and his six-year-old son at the back of the bus with me, and although he didn't speak any English, he tried to help me. On one of my earliest trips, probably one of the Asian trips I'd taken with Judy, I'd learned to show people documents so they could see the name of where I wanted to go, or a picture of what I was looking for. In this case, I wanted to find out where the ferry terminal was, and, more importantly, *which* ferry terminal I was supposed to go to for Hellenic Seaways.

The man with the child looked at the information I had and then tried to point to where he thought I should go. Shortly after, however, he shrugged his shoulders because he wasn't sure. I knew that different ferries departed from different terminals at the huge docks. To be honest, I'm not sure I ever discovered which terminal I was supposed to go to. At the time, I just knew that my time was running out to catch the 5:00 p.m. ferry to Lesvos, plus I didn't have tickets.

The bus began to empty as it neared the end of the line, about an hour and a half after I'd caught it from the airport. I was passing buildings with graffiti all over them. This neighborhood didn't look very safe to me, and I hoped that Lesvos would be different to live up to my vision.

The father-son team left the bus with parting advice via hand signals that I should tell the bus driver where I wanted to go. I could see the water, but I was starting to see larger ships, causing me to panic. Finally I was able to go to the front of the bus and tried to show the bus driver the name of the ferry I wanted to find. He shook his head and then started saying something under his breath, which I interpreted as, *These crazy American tourists come to Greece and don't know our language or what they are doing.* I remembered my motto, "These people will never see me again."

Finally the bus driver stopped the bus and read my note. He seemed to understand enough to know that I was going to the port where the ferries were located, but he wasn't sure which dock would have my boat. In exasperation, he finally told me to get off the bus and to go back to the dock we had just passed because he thought it was the right one. I hauled my large red backpack, my duffel full of stuff from Africa, and a large pouch with more stuff to the front of the bus. He was stopped at a stoplight, so I had to jump off in the middle of the street and hope for the best.

I pitched all my things off the bus and tried my best to haul them across the street and into a large parking lot where there appeared to be ticket booths. The one with the name of the ship line I was traveling on was closed, of course. I was perspiring at this point, totally lost, and running out of time. Nothing was open, and I had half an hour before my ferry's five o'clock departure.

Finally some kind of an official told me, "Take the free bus"—pointing to a destination about a half mile away—"to Port 1 or 2. That's what you want, Port 1 or 2."

I started lugging all my stuff when a middle-aged man approached me carrying trinkets like sunglasses. He told me he had lost his job two years before and was selling what he could, and he offered to carry my gear for a price. I got out my change and gave him a two-euro coin, and he took my one-euro coin also, saying it was worth it and he needed the money. I didn't care and was grateful for the help. I didn't even have my ticket yet. He recognized the name of my boat, motioned for me to follow him as he picked up my backpack, and got me and the baggage on the free bus that would take me to the correct terminal.

Rounding a corner, I saw a huge vessel with the correct name on it. I motioned to my savior that I needed a ticket, so he took me to the ticket booth and then to the ship. I waddled onto the ship with all my stuff, tried to find out which section of the boat I was supposed to be in, found a chair, and collapsed. I was streaming with sweat in my out-of-place warm clothes, and the stares that I got from the other passengers were deserved. I had walked right past the area where I was supposed to drop off my large backpack, so there I was, the only one with all my gear right beside me. One of the ship's stewards directed me to a chair in the overflow first-class area, and I sat down until a pleasant lady came up to me and said, "I think you are in my assigned seat." I was willing to sit on the floor—anywhere—and I may have had to since the boat was packed this Friday afternoon. I left and sat in a chair right in front of a television screen with a soccer game on. Everyone looked at me and not the television. I was beside an older man who couldn't decide whether to watch the game or me.

I was totally sweating, with hiking boots on, long sleeves and pants, just a mess. I went into the bathroom to change into warm-weather clothes. I decided it was time for a beer, no matter the price. One fellow finally cracked a smile when I returned and sat down with my cold beer, and the other man who hadn't been able to take his eyes off me finally decided the game was more interesting. The boat took off about fifteen minutes after I boarded it.

I explored the boat once I got my bearings and looked less like a nutcase. It was a huge vessel, with various types of chairs, televisions, bars, food, and characters abounding. I explored the ship a bit and then was very happy to sink into a chair near my possessions and sort of fall asleep. I misread the time schedule for the ferry; I thought it was to arrive at a reasonable hour, like two thirty p.m. the following day. It wasn't until I was on the boat that I realized it would arrive at two thirty *a.m.* I was asleep, or at least relaxed, as we pulled into three island ports before finally arriving at Mytilini on Lesvos at two thirty a.m. The bus to the tiny village where I was headed wouldn't leave until one fifteen that afternoon.

Note to self: Dilemma.

ALTHOUGH THE FERRY ARRIVED IN THE DEAD OF NIGHT, THERE WAS A flurry of activity upon arrival. There were taxis, friends with cars, probably enemies with cars, and before long everyone except for me was picked up and gone. There were benches nearby, under outdoor cover, and I picked out one to sit on until I made decisions. I thought for a few minutes and then decided to wait at the ferry terminal until daylight since I didn't know where the bus station was and I felt somewhat safe at the terminal, even though two men and a bunch of stray dogs were nearby. At least I had a plan. The middle-aged man sitting across from me made my tired mind do a few flips as I worried that his whole purpose in life just then was to hurt me. Eventually I decided both men were harmless, so I relaxed a bit. The dogs were just looking for food.

After several hours, daylight came and made the entire scene less eerie. I felt safe, although totally wasted from exhaustion, but I remembered that I had to keep my wits about me since the first order of business was to get all my stuff over to the bus station. I had a book about Greece, and it showed Mytilini, including the six- or seven-block walkway to the bus station from the ferry station. I thought for a minute, contemplating carrying all my gear to the bus station, and then decided that it would probably kill me to do so. I turned my eyes up to the universe and said, "My mom would be proud of me. I'm going to find a cab or someone who will take me and all my stuff to the bus station."

Note to self: Great choice. Get over being so cheap.

I ARRIVED IN MY TAXI, WITH ALL MY STUFF, ABOUT SIX THIRTY IN THE morning. The building reminded me of a shack, and I had to find signs for any evidence that it was actually a bus station. Other folks waiting with me verified it truly was the office and then told me that it wouldn't open until 8:30 a.m. and the bus didn't leave until 1:15 p.m. I really wanted to walk around Mytilini to experience the town, but I didn't feel comfortable leaving all my stuff outside. My plan, then, was to wait until eight thirty, deposit my stuff inside the claustrophobic office, and hope for the best while I took time to explore the largest town on Lesvos. Once again, I sat outside the office and waited for it to open. Eventually the clerk rode up on his bicycle and opened the door to the tiny office. The entire bus station building was the size of my kitchen. Mercifully, I was able to leave my baggage in the office and explore Mytilini.

Mytilini is gorgeous. It is on a huge bay, and early in the morning on this summer day, all the small places to eat had umbrellas and outdoor tables inviting everyone to enjoy a cup of coffee. I found a café with computers and coffee, so I sat down to catch up on emails and let my family know I had survived the Africa trip. At these internet cafés all over the world, I could pay for a certain time period using the computer and internet. In Greece, it was about two dollars for fifteen minutes whereas in Bali, the price had been much less.

Going on the internet would be good, but I knew sometimes these cafés didn't have reliable connections or had internet that moved at a snail's pace. Another common problem was finding the @ symbol on foreign keyboards to sign in to my account. Keys are in different places on keyboards for different countries, and often the @ symbol is hidden. It's more likely for me to have to ask the storekeeper how to find it than not. There, it seemed to be a common problem because almost as soon as I got up from the computer to ask the question, the attendant was there to show me the secret on the keyboard. Shortly after sitting down, I was enjoying a cup of coffee, accessing my email, and quickly assessing if the world—or at least my world—had not shut down in my absence.

I bought a ceramic water pitcher in town and then found a small, mostly hidden hardware store where I could buy an aluminum teapot. More fortunately, I found a fabric shop to purchase a piece of material from Greece. I am truly a collector at heart. Note that I now own probably fifteen absolutely useless teakettles that hang on my walls.

Note to self: They are memories of incredible times and make you smile.

EVENTUALLY I MADE MY WAY BACK TO MY WOODEN BENCH AT THE BUS station. No one spoke English, so it was a little lonely there except for smiles from those accumulating at the station. I wanted to call the cottage I would be staying in and connect with the innkeeper, ensuring I would have a ride to the cottage once I got to Skala Eresou.

I had chosen to take the bus to the small town so I could see the countryside during the journey even though the trip would take several hours. In reality, there was no other way there. No matter that I was truly exhausted by the climb, the many flights back from Africa, the stressful ferry ride, and the lack of sleep and full meals.

Note to self: Beer is not considered a meal.

I went to a tiny food place beside the bus station and showed the owner several euros to use her telephone. She declined the money, shaking her head several times, and dialed the number for me. No one answered. This was another adventure without certainty at the other end. I tried again, and finally the innkeeper, Rena, answered. She told me she had expected me to arrive the day before, so she thought I had ditched the trip. I clarified when I was arriving, and she sounded wonderful, agreeing to meet me at the bus station about four that afternoon when the bus would arrive.

The bus took small roads, winding through the countryside. The ride showed off a multitude of olive tree groves, old men riding donkeys on the roads—as if time had stopped for them—an intermittent car on the road, and small houses along the long drive. This land seemed to me to be a collection of century-old traditions alongside tourist-inspired needs. We made stops in small, remote towns that showed off quaint main streets with tiny cafés and outdoor seating shaded by large trees. Locals were inevitably sitting at the tables drinking beer or the local ouzo, a clear liquor that, to me, tasted more like gasoline than any beverage I'd want to drink. It was the local favorite, and many men offered me drinks starting at eight a.m. throughout the day. I was getting the message that here it was common to take a break, not work too hard, and to laugh whenever possible.

Eventually I made it to Skala and tried to pick out Rena from the crowd. I spotted a woman yelling at someone else and hoped she wasn't Rena, and then I saw her. Rena was a tall beauty with a wispy long dress, bare shoulders, and a broad straw hat and scarf on her hair to shade her beautiful fair skin. She had on little makeup—heck, she didn't need any. She came up to me and hugged me, something I welcomed after the long, hard trip to get to this point. She led me to an old car, which she tried to start a few times before it jumped into duty.

Rena said her place was "just a bit" from town, which I thought meant it would be away from streets and the few tourists in the area. I was right. We went up the main road, away from town for "a bit," and then turned to the right on a dirt road. It was bumpy but very passable, and we bounced for a few more turns on the dusty road until we reached Rena's compound.

My first impressions of the compound were *Incredible. This can't be the place I'll be staying. This must be wrong.* We pulled beside the main house, a tall two-story rock building. A short distance from the large house was a smaller one-story building, likely a studio of some sort. Across the large front yard was a small two-story building, which was the cottage where I was to stay.

I dragged my bags from the back seat of the car and opened the door to the cottage. A young tabby cat scurried in before I made it in. I'd learn that Meredith, the young cat, would often be opportunistic and sneak in the door for food. Inside there was a small kitchen with a wooden table and bench, sink, stove, and—best of all—a basket of food and wine to welcome me. I had enough food to last the day, and for that I was grateful.

Rena showed me around the cottage, being sure to point out the huge tub in the large bathroom. The loft held two twin beds, but the stairway offered little protection for a nightly visit to the downstairs bathroom. It was a bit of a maneuver, with no railing on the steps and nothing to prevent a sleep walker from stepping to his or her death. The living room had a large sofa to spread out on and plenty of books. All in all, it was absolutely romantic, exotic, and just what I needed.

Rena asked me if she could show me around the next day, and I begged her to allow me to recoup for at least a day after all my journeys. We agreed to explore the following day, and my last question was if a bicycle was available to bike the several miles to town. Rena's old but reliable bicycle was leaning on the house, ready for use.

After Rena left, I drew water in the large tub and waited for it to reach an acceptable temperature and depth. I figured a depth adequate and not too decadent would work to soak out the previous adventures. Rena had left some bubble bath, and I used it, relishing in the bubbles. I soaked for an hour, with a glass of wine in my hand, of course. I went to bed early that night and woke to the sounds of birds chirping in the olive trees and a gentle wind blowing through the open windows. Rena had included a small bottle of olive oil from her trees in the food basket, and I used it reluctantly, hoping to save some to take home.

I spent the day repacking my collection of goods from Africa and then decided to bicycle into town to explore. I bumped up and down on the passable dirt road, determined to recall the right and left turns so I wouldn't get lost, as I generally went east. Eventually I came to the main road, a not-quite-two-lane road with no center line, where I tried to remember an old church-like structure where I would turn right onto the dirt road when returning home. I had no GPS, no telephone, and no real idea where I was staying if I got lost and had to ask anyone for help.

The first business I found in town, after passing several other locals on bicycles and motorcycles, was a tiny produce market. It displayed huge red tomatoes, onions, fruit, and other local produce that just plain said, *Take me—I'm fresh and local.* I bought several tomatoes and then found the local cheese market. Nothing on the planet is tastier to me than good tomatoes and cheese, preferably mozzarella. It was when I was paying for the cheese that I heard a loudspeaker announcing something in Greek. I turned around in time to see a very slow-moving pickup truck coming down the main street. In the back of the truck was a huge mound of shrimp, probably *garides*. I bought five euros' worth, a little over five dollars, from the back of the truck, and they were scooped up and put in a plastic bag for me. Now I had shrimp, tomatoes, cheese, and a very small backpack with my bicycle.

I explored more and found several seasonal cafés along the ocean. There were only a handful of food and drink places on the beach, a welcome relief to any worries I'd had about throngs of people I would have to contend with. The atmosphere was laid-back, with servers who more commonly were talking with local friends than serving any customers. Customers were few, and those sipping coffee seemed very content as they worked on computers, talked with others at a table, or just gazed at the ocean. Then I saw the rock.

The size and location of the rock was unmistakable—huge, tall, and in the ocean about a quarter mile off the beach. I couldn't help but notice it, and I made a mental note to ask Rena about it tomorrow. It seemed important.

The next day, I wandered over to Rena's house after a leisurely breakfast at the cottage. I took a cup of coffee with me and enjoyed it with her on the outside patio as I found out more about my mysterious hostess. Rena had owned a bustling business, very lucrative, in chocolates before she decided to move from Scotland to Lesvos, where one of her many sisters lived.

Rena was doing well in Greece, but as with any huge change, there were challenges and mishaps, and Rena and I talked about each of them. She talked about her red RAV4 that she'd brought from Scotland and that had to be sold for scrap, how Greece's taxes were affecting her, relationships she had counted on that didn't follow through—a lifetime of experiences. An astute businesswoman, she had her ducks in a row, but somehow the ducks had changed to a bird foreign to her. After spending the week with her, I was sure Rena would land feetfirst. I found her ability to engage so easily and deeply with a total stranger astounding and invigorating, a breath of fresh air. We met as strangers and parted as fast friends.

I mentioned the huge rock at the beach, and Rena started laughing. "So you saw our famous rock?"

"It is hard to miss," I answered. "Does it have special significance?"

Apparently the rock is the town landmark, and the primary local meaning is that anyone who swims out to the rock gets a special medal from the restaurant in front of it, Zorba the Buddha. I learned that there was a group of women who swam out and back from the rock daily, and they were always trying to induct new members into the very special swim-to-the-rock club. Rena and I stopped at the restaurant later in the day, and sure enough, there were women challenging me to swim to the rock with them the next day. I collect challenges, and this was no exception. I was in.

I asked Rena about swimming with me. She told me that she was just an okay swimmer and in the four years she had been on the island, she had never made the swim.

Note to self: This is another challenge: get Rena to swim to the rock.

THE NEXT DAY, I PUT ON MY BATHING SUIT, AND RENA AND I DROVE TO Zorba the Buddha so I could swim with the ladies. A small group of maybe ten gathered. There were all kinds, shapes, and sizes of ladies. A few were in terrific shape, but most of us weren't. Some had fins and masks, and I was able to find a set of fins to wear to make the journey quicker. I wasn't worried about the swimming bit since I had been a competitive swimmer at one point in my earlier life. Rena bowed out but said she was happy to watch me.

Swimming to the rock and back was easy, and I took my time. I didn't have to be first to the finish line. One lady came in a kayak with the group, to help anyone who could not make the journey back. One by one, we climbed out of the Aegean Sea, laughing and nodding in nonverbal triumph over the rock's challenge. There was a short ceremony, during which I got a free drink along with everyone else, and a special medal. The medal was an old, blank CD, to which a string and a label were attached, inducting me into the Skala Women's Rock Group for brilliantly swimming to the rock.

Rena took pictures and documented the event. I told her that I would swim with her to the rock the next day if she would go. As usual, she said, "We'll see." She stole my common answer.

As the end of my time on the island drew near, I took daily bicycle trips to the beach in Skala Eresou, swimming in the sea and bobbing up and down. The water temperature was perfect—like bathwater that I could stay in for hours. A small, cheap floating ring that I used to keep my head above water while I relaxed became an incredibly valuable possession. I would buy my dinner ingredients daily then come home to cook it, and it was always fresh and healthy.

The day before I was to leave was the do-or-die day for Rena to swim to the rock. Her swim was my challenge. The calm waters would be kind to us, and the wind was nonexistent. The rock was in a protected area, which made it all the more inviting. We wore our bathing suits and found a pair of borrowed fins for each of us. Rena was giggling as we waddled into the ocean with our fins. I swam beside her, and the little yellow kayak was nearby also. These were Rena's friends, and they all wanted to see her rise to the occasion. Amazingly, Rena swam slowly and methodically, putting one arm in front of the other, swimming as if she were in a large bathtub.

I slowed and stopped a few times, asking Rena if she was all right and if she wanted to continue. I never told her that I wasn't going to let her stop. She was gaining on the rock. Before she knew it, she was beaming as she climbed out of the ocean to sit on a large rock that was at the base of her destination: Big Rock. She declared, "That wasn't as hard as I thought it was going to be!" which was the response I expected from her.

She swam back to the shore to applause from her friends and neighbors as well as shouting and cheers from all directions. She was all smiles as she was greeted with a warm drink and a piece of cake from the restaurant. Solemnly, the club made a circle and inducted their friend Rena into the Skala Women's Rock Group. She and I wore our recycled CD necklaces as proudly as if they were diamonds. I treated her to a special coffee drink.

Later in the day, Rena took me to a small village where she had a doctor's appointment. I asked that she drop me off downtown so I could see what it felt like to be there for several hours. This was not a tourist town, so I'd get to see real life in a Greek island town. I picked a small café with outside tables and sat down by myself. I ordered a piece of sweet bread and a cup of coffee and then started observing those who occupied this little town.

There were a few tourists looking at the open-air markets that were strategically placed in the town, but the tourists looked out of place. A few people whizzed through town, seemingly on their way to work, but most people moved at a slow pace because the dry, warm air could do a person in. Mostly, however, there were the local folks who were sitting at the various cafés enjoying coffee and relaxing more than working.

Next to me, at the nearest table, was an older man who ordered a drink and a pastry. As soon as his order arrived, he offered me some of his drink. I insisted that I didn't want any, but he kept pushing it over my way. After several protests, I finally agreed, so I took a drink from his cup and discovered it was pure ouzo, the famous Greek liquor. In other words, white lightning. It went down fast, and went through my body quickly. One drink of it was all I would allow myself.

Rena took me back to Mytilini for me to catch my ferry back to Athens. This time the boat ride was uneventful, but I was able to see the small towns on other islands that had been dark en route to Lesvos. I watched them from the ferry, vowing to return to each of them in the future. Getting back to the Athens airport via the public bus was not an unknown this time, so the trip was quick and easy.

CHAPTER 22

Mongolia

By this time, I had been retired a number of years and, except for the trip to the South Pole, I had not worked since I retired. Grateful for that, I tried to fill my time with meaningful endeavors like traveling several times each year, strengthening my family and friend relationships, volunteering, and doing personal woodworking and other projects as they came along. The best part was that I was able to move to a small town. It afforded me the opportunity to go hiking daily and to jump into swimming holes whenever I convinced a friend to go with me. Then I got a bright idea.

"You want to go where?" Judy asked me.

"Mongolia," I replied.

"Where's Mongolia?"

"I'm not sure, but I know I want to go there." I was emphatic. I actually wasn't sure where Mongolia was either, or why I really wanted to go there. But I had heard people say, "There's nothing there," and that made me want to go. It sounded exotic, undiscovered, and like a place I wanted to see. I had also heard from others, "Go to Mongolia before it becomes industrialized—there aren't any roads or infrastructure." I wasn't quite sure what that meant.

Judy needed little persuasion, especially when I was able to book her a ticket to China from San Diego and then the same round-trip ticket as I had from China to the capital of Mongolia, Ulaanbaatar. Ulaanbaatar was the only place an international flight could fly into Mongolia. Bordered on the north by Russia and on the south by China, Mongolia is tucked between the countries and has a vast history with each country. Genghis Khan was from Mongolia and apparently gave the Chinese enough problems that they put up the Great Wall of China to keep the Mongols out of their country. It all sounded very intriguing to me.

There are really three parts to this story: one part about getting to Mongolia and two parts about experiencing Mongolia. Getting there nearly killed me. It was one of the most extraordinary events of my life, one that almost led to my demise.

Judy left on her flight to China before I did and emailed me from someone's borrowed computer: *Trouble with visas, but on my way.* That was about it, except that I also got a call from my daughter saying Judy had called her. I didn't know what *trouble* meant from the email, and we had no way to communicate. I'd find out soon enough, though.

Judy is more organized than I am. She arrives at our destinations and pulls out a neat packet of information, all in a folder. My information is usually copied from an email, pasted into a Word document on consecutive pages in some kind of order, printed, and folded several times. I had booked this trip about nine months in advance because I had the airline miles to get myself a free trip to Peking. The trip from Peking to Ulaanbaatar was a separate booking. I was to meet Judy in China and go with her on the flight to Mongolia.

My son-in-law dropped me off at the Los Angeles International Airport terminal about four hours before my flight, and I ducked inside the airport with only my backpack. I was unable to get a ticket to print from the self-serve kiosk and had to talk with a Real Person to get my ticket, so I stood in line with the other hundred customers to talk with a Real Person. This was not uncommon for international flights. It had only been a few years since computer boarding-pass machines had been initiated, and they were still for domestic flights for the most part.

I got to a desk and gave a smiling lady my passport. That's all you really need when you get to the desk—your passport. All the information they need appears once they put in your passport number. She looked up at me, still smiling. She asked for my visa to China since I was going to be arriving in Peking. My face fell. "I don't have one."

She replied, "You'll need one to get into China since that is your final destination."

"But it's *not* my final destination," I answered. I fumbled in all my folded paperwork and showed her something that said I had a separate ticket to Ulaanbaatar on China Southern Airlines.

She was still smiling, but not as much. "Where's your ticket number?"

"It isn't in there?"

"Can't find it here, although it is hard to decipher this information," she answered.

I started feeling desperate. I had no visa, and my Real Person was telling me it took three days to get it. I was scheduled to fly on a domestic airline to Chicago and then change to Air China to fly to China. Air China would not issue my ticket to fly abroad.

"Tell you what," she started saying, "I'll call over to China Southern airlines since you are flying with them to Ulaanbaatar and see if they can give me your ticket number."

I felt a weight lift off my shoulders. She called the other airline, received my ticket number, then called her supervisor to get the okay to give me my tickets and another piece of paper to document the ticket number. She was CYA (covering her ass) so she wouldn't get in trouble for letting an unvisaed passenger into China but also paving the way for me to proceed on my trip. Apparently there is a seventy-two-hour grace period in the Peking airport for people making airline transfers, so no visa needed. Fortunately, the supervisor gave the okay and I was on my way, or so I thought. I hoped to remember to write a letter of commendation for the Los Angeles Real Person.

TSA looked at the new hiking poles I'd bought to see if they were okay to take through screening. They had been advertised as the lightest poles around and had tips that were allowed in carry-on luggage for airplanes. I was going to put them to the test. Approved. After getting through the TSA checkpoint and putting my shoes back on, I sat down and started crying. In the back of my mind, I counterbalanced everything: *Don't worry, be happy, stress is not all it's cooked up to be.*

I finally boarded the LAX flight headed for Chicago, where I would connect to a direct flight to Peking. I relaxed into my window seat and tried to doze, an art with which I was becoming more familiar. All was fine until the announcement came overhead: "We are sorry, but the Chicago airport is closed to incoming traffic right now because of storms in the area. Nothing is leaving, and nothing can land. Please wait for further announcements."

My heart sank. Judy was already on her way, and she rarely looks at emails on our trips. She doesn't carry a computer or fancy telephone, and neither do I on these exotic adventures. How long was I going to be delayed, and how would I let Judy know? It wasn't long before another announcement came: "I'm sorry, but we are going to have to land in Peoria, Illinois, to await further instructions because we are low on fuel."

We landed in Peoria about ten p.m. and had been traveling for several hours by this time. We stayed on the tarmac for at least an hour and heard intermittent announcements that the airline was making decisions. Finally we heard, "Because of FAA regulations, we must take our passengers somewhere else to disembark. Peoria does not have hotel rooms to accommodate as many as we have on board. Therefore, we are headed to St. Louis, Missouri, instead." We took off for St. Louis.

The plane landed about midnight, and each of us crawled off and waited. I wasn't aware that unloading us was about as far as the airline was going to help. An extremely frustrated airline employee appeared behind the counter at the gate, and everyone swamped him with questions. He announced, "I don't know anything at this point in time." Eventually we discovered that because the problem was weather related, and not the fault of the airline, there was nothing the airline was going to do for us. We did receive paper cards with an 800 telephone number for the airline but no other help. People started dispersing one by one. My decision, as usual, was to wait in the airport until morning and see what would happen.

I walked downstairs to the ticket counter, which would open up in the morning, and waited nearby. I called the airline, and their office was not open until morning either. I texted my daughter on my ancient cell phone and told her the problem because I knew she would get up early in California, and heck, I counted on her for help. I was going to be a day late getting to Peking and needed to arrange to catch my flight to Ulaanbaatar a day later. I waited, trying to sleep a bit in the chairs that are always designed not to allow sleep.

My daughter started texting me. I could wait to call the airline directly and pay forty dollars for the change or I could go through Orbitz, where I had purchased the ticket, and make the change for seventy dollars. Not having slept much, my mind started doing backflips and getting more tangled in my decision-making. I finally decided to call Orbitz so I would be assured to get to Mongolia only one day late. I asked my daughter to email the hostel I had booked, gave her the name of the hostel, and trusted that somehow she could find it online. I also requested that she ask the manager to share the information with Judy so she would know what was going on.

With the change of flights from China to Mongolia made, my next roadblock was getting to Chicago so I could catch the flight to China. I waited in the long line of other folks who had to make changes and connections for at least an hour. Apparently St. Louis is not as sophisticated about international flights as LAX, so when I took my little strip of paper with the China-to-Mongolia information on it to the ticketing counter and spoke with a Real Person, I was told, "You don't have a Chinese visa, and I cannot issue you a ticket to China because if I do and you defect in China, I could lose my job."

I asked, "Can you just get me to Chicago?"

"No, I can't do that because the computer will only allow me to issue a ticket all the way to China. I can't lose my job," she replied.

"I don't want you to lose your job. I just want to get to Chicago," I was pleading.

She shook her head, and I had to leave.

I went back to my bed I'd made for the night (a chair) and had to think with my head, which had had no sleep the prior night. I called the 800 number and spoke with a very accommodating person who said, "Sure, no problem. We'll get you to Chicago," then booked me a flight.

I waited another hour in the line and asked for the ticket that the 800 number had issued for me. Again, I met a roadblock. I said, "May I speak with your supervisor?" The new agent looked at me and said, "I hope she's in a good mood." My heart sank because I was referred to the same person I'd spoken with initially.

I had to maintain my calm and not become angry because it would serve no purpose. Besides, my fatigue would factor in and keep me calm. I asked to speak with the supervisor again. I explained, again, that I had the e-ticket proof that I would be leaving China, did not need a visa since I would be within the seventy-two-hour grace period, and just wanted to get to Chicago to straighten everything out. As my blood pressure was rising and my hopes were diminishing, she called her supervisor in an unknown location and was mercifully granted the ability to get me to Chicago and no farther. I booked the earliest flight I could and texted my daughter to get me proof from the airline leaving China that I had a ticket to Mongolia, plus any extra information I might need such as my ticket number.

The flight out of St. Louis landed in Chicago a day later than my original itinerary. My daughter texted me that there was an airline office in Chicago for the flight to Mongolia, so I looked at the complicated transportation chart in Chicago and took two trains to the airline office. It turned out to be only a cargo office, not a passenger ticketing office, so I raced back to the main terminal. By this time, my daughter had connected with the airline to Mongolia and had scanned me a page of information. Now I just had to retrieve it somehow.

I asked an information person if there was a business office in the airport. "No," he said, "but the Hilton has one. It's downstairs and a long walk, but they have one." I sped away, following signs and escalators to the Hilton. I walked in and asked if they had a computer I could use. "Sure" was the reply from the young man caring for the office. Of course it cost money, but by this time it would be all right with me if the bill was a hundred dollars. I paid about ten dollars to get this golden piece of paper, but it was worth it. It had my official ticket number to Mongolia.

Scurrying back to the ticketing office, I kept my golden paper with me in my hand. I took up my tattered paperwork and the piece of gold to the counter, held my breath, and said, "I am booked to go to China then on to Mongolia. Here's the paperwork that I have. I need a ticket to get from Chicago to China so I can complete the trip that was interrupted yesterday."

A lovely woman, with another amazing smile, looked at everything and said, "No problem." She issued me the ticket I needed to go to China from Chicago, and I was so relieved that I wanted a big hamburger and shake from McDonald's but settled on an extremely large salad and green apple from a small booth at the airport food court. Then I bought my daughter a gift from one of the airport shops. It had been a long time since I had been so worked up, and my stress level was at an all-time high. Except for my salad, I hadn't eaten for two days, so I was hungry and thirsty. This was to haunt me later on.

I arrived at the Peking airport about ten p.m. It was empty and I was in the middle of China with no visa. I found a lone official-looking person and showed him my flight information to Mongolia, and he pointed me a certain direction several times. I clearly wasn't sure which way to go. I was afraid if I went out of the airport that I could be picked up for illegally entering China, go to jail without passing "Go," and the woman who issued me the ticket would lose her job. I would land in Chinese jail, like, forever.

I saw a young Chinese woman I had befriended on the flight, and she helped guide me. She asked the man in Chinese about my plight and was told the same information I had assumed: I had to go out of the airport on a shuttle to get to my ticketing area. I headed out while waving goodbye to my airplane friend. An employee punched my passport, so it was official. I was out of the airport.

I got on the shuttle and followed the sign to Transfers 3. I found comfort going into an office that said *China Southern*. I started asking the official-looking people there about where to get my ticket. "Tickets for China Southern?" I asked, and showed them my newly printed itinerary.

He said, "F12," and put up four fingers then pointed up.

About the same time, I felt a tap on my shoulder and heard, "Oh man, you speak English! Where do you think we go?"

As I turned, I saw a man with a huge smile who was dressed in jeans and tall work boots. He told me his name was Ricardo.

My thought was, *Thank God, another lost soul.*

He continued, "I've been trying to find out where to go to continue my trip."

I replied, "I'm lost also. Let's figure this out together."

He wanted to get a bed for the night in the airport. Apparently they were available for a few hours at a time, something new to me. I had seen a sign for a short-term bed a few shuttle stops ago, though, so now that made sense. I told him I was going to sleep in the airport if I ever found the ticketing area. I wanted to find F12 and China Southern. He had been traveling from Texas about as long as I had, but if I could do it, so could he. We became friends in this foreign country so far from our home, creating our own version of "home."

Eventually we found our way to the huge ticketing area for international flights. It is common in international airports to have a display of flights along with a set of ticket areas that open about two hours before a flight. We found F12. *Yeah!* I thought. *I'm probably not going to Chinese jail.*

My new friend and I were there after midnight, and the gates would not open until 5:00 a.m. We found a round cement pillar to sit by and wait. Ricardo was originally from Italy, was the child of an Italian father and South American mom, and had worked in Russia and many other countries trying to determine the feasibility of finding fossil fuels and natural gas in remote areas. He was headed from his home in Texas to a remote area in northern China to join a Russian team. He laughed as he told me it would be near freezing at night and he would probably sleep in a cargo van with the others.

As we were talking, a young Chinese man sat beside us and started chatting with us. He was just returning to southern China from Houston, Texas. He had solicited a company in Texas for an internship and amazingly got a two-month gig. There, he'd been able to find other Chinese folks to share an apartment with, so he'd had the best of several worlds for the two-month internship. When asked, he said Texas BBQ was his favorite thing in Texas.

It wasn't long before a young woman in her thirties walked past us and then turned around. In perfect English, she said, "I'm from Mongolia, and I hear that you are going there." She had an infectious laugh and joined the conversation. She had visited her boyfriend in Dubai for a vacation while her mother took care of her four-year-old, and she was headed back to Mongolia. From her English skills, you'd think she just came from San Diego. She had worked for several years in the office of a coal mine in Mongolia, again while her mom took care of her baby. What I would learn on this trip was that this was all very common for Mongolia—a close-knit family unit that helped each other.

My body and mind were telling me that I needed to sleep. It was well past midnight. My mind was also telling me that I didn't want to miss my flight.

Soon, a middle-aged man from Cairo, Egypt, sat down. He had three children and was on his way to Mongolia for a conference on renewable energy. I sat back at several points to listen, to get perspective on what was happening. We had collected an Italian, a Chinese, an Egyptian, an American, and a Mongolian. And we were all getting along just fine. Why couldn't this happen in real life? It was fascinating, lively, and magical.

I needed a picture of everyone, so I went out to find someone to take our picture. I found a man who turned out to be a professor from Chicago returning from a conference in Hong Kong. He was quite lively and entertaining, so we adopted yet another soul from another quite different background. The conversation turned from education to youth, finances, politics, religion, culture, work, and most any other subject with universal appeal. The talk continued all night long as my body begged me for sleep. It was just all too magical to walk away from, so I stayed. It all disappeared about five a.m. when we all dispersed for our various flights. It ended as quickly as it had begun. I was proud of myself for recognizing and embracing diversity, opportunity, and just plain magic when it came to me.

When I finally arrived in Ulaanbaatar, I was relieved to see a portly man holding a sign saying *Linda*. Underneath my name was a second name: *Paula*. He greeted me and told me we needed to wait for one other passenger. She came soon through the gate, and I was glad to see a young, slim woman with a smile that would brighten the world. Paula had come from Canada and would be staying in Mongolia for a few weeks before starting a job in the northernmost area of Canada. Originally Paula was from Belgium, but she had been working in Canada for several years and spoke English like a champ.

I immediately wanted to see if she would be interested in joining Judy's and my first trip to the Gobi Desert in the southern part of Mongolia. She wasn't sure: her backpack was missing, so she only had the clothes on her back. I told her that between Judy and me, we probably had plenty of clothes for her. She would consider it.

When we arrived at the hostel, the driver helped me put on my pack at the car and then disappeared through a large metal door on the first floor of an unimpressive building. We followed him to the second floor, went through another metal door, and found our hostel host. The host told me, "At this point in time, there are only you and Judy going to the Gobi tomorrow. Our other two participants are not sure they can go because they are getting in tonight and it may be too tiring for them." I wanted more participants because it was not only more fun with several people but also cheaper.

I tried to find Judy, but she was away from the hostel enjoying her day off before our journey. Paula and I decided to shop for clothes since I had been successful in convincing her that she needed to go on our trip. We asked about shopping and were told that the State Department Store was the best bet—it was only a few blocks away and had everything we would need. Paula focused on a few personal items. She had to pay for the items ahead of time, show the receipt for the items she wanted, and go back to the department where the items were held to pick them up. There is a lot of theft in Mongolia, and we were warned not to go out at night because gangs sometimes roamed the streets.

We went back to the hostel, where I found Judy looking for me. It was amazing to me that we could meet up so easily half a world away from home. We went back to the State Department Store to get something to eat, and I decided on only a banana from a small vendor stand. While there was a kitchen in the hostel, I was too tired to fix anything to eat. I took one Cipro pill to prevent any diarrhea that I thought might be coming.

The next morning, bread and jam were available in the kitchen for everyone. Two people were sitting there eating when I came in. I found out quickly that they were from the US and were the two people who had just gotten in last night and had decided not to go with us. It became my job to convince them to go. I was very friendly and encouraged them to join us; we were leaving in an hour. After I ate, I went to use the free computer to let my US relatives know Judy and I had gotten here and were together. I was also thinking ahead—after our first excursion to the Gobi Desert in southern Mongolia, Judy and I also wanted to head north, and of course, we wanted others to go with us to make the trip more interesting and less expensive. I put up a notice in the hostel that Judy and I would be going to the northern part of Mongolia in a few days and asked if anyone would like to go there with us for a week.

From the eating area, I could hear the decision-making ensuing from the young couple. She was saying, "I haven't even showered yet. Do you think we can do it? How tired are you?"

He replied, "This is a chance to go with other folks and save some money. We have to think about making our money stretch." He won. They decided to go with us, leaving in an hour for the Gobi Desert.

As we were waiting for our van, I saw a woman who seemed to be collecting cans to redeem them for money. She was eyeing my Coca-Cola bottle, so in our awkward sign language, I motioned for her to come over for it. She smiled and took the large bottle. Shortly after that, five of us piled into a van. The van was older and was obviously used to travel in sand and other rugged areas. It would be driven by a young man accompanied by his English-speaking wife, who would be our guide. The van had three long seats, two of them facing forward and one facing backward. It was piled high with our belongings, and we stopped at a large building with stalls of food to get our first few days' worth of supplies plus the one bottle of water a day that had been promised to us.

It was here that I had my first inkling that something was wrong. I got dizzy inside the building, told Judy, and she told me to sit down on a step for a bit until I felt better. I sat on the step for a few minutes and made sure I could stand before walking. It went away almost as suddenly as it had started, and I seemed fine. I was able to go to all the stalls and poke my head in to see candy sold by the pound, many bottles of water available, and household items such as laundry soap, sponges, and combs, as well as all kinds of food available. Our guide was nowhere to be found, but the van was still in its place and they weren't keen on losing any of us, so I wasn't worried.

We started out again in the van. After about an hour, the road turned from pavement to dirt. We were on dirt roads almost the entire rest of the seven-day journey. Apparently only the capital had paved roads, and at best, those roads were extremely slow because of untamed traffic. Traffic lights were almost nonexistent, but there were frustrated policemen trying their best to direct traffic to move in some kind of order. The buildings in Ulaanbaatar looked to me as if building codes were nonexistent. Cinder block walls were warped, and the buildings going up were many stories high. Apparently as more and more of the nomads of Mongolia were losing their ability to live in the country, they were coming to the city for jobs and warmth. It gets brutally cold in Mongolia's winters. The nomads apparently move their homes—portable *gers*, which are essentially yurts—from the barren ranching country to the small rural villages as winter envelops the country.

A ger is a round house that is completely temporary and movable. We saw many for sale, in pieces, in Ulaanbaatar. A new ger costs about $1,000 in Mongolia, and much more out of the country. When erecting the ger, the wooden infrastructure is put up first, with a painted round wooden frame at the top, colorful stakes coming from the top circle, and expandable wooden lattice-type pieces of wood made into a circle to complete the frame. The top of the ger is open to the sky, allowing a pipe from the wood- or dung-fueled stove to release fumes. The sides and top of the ger are felted pieces of wool, very thick and great insulation. The entire ger is covered with a canvas tarp to keep out the rain and to cover or uncover the open top of the ger. The door to the ger is also colorful, wooden, and short enough to bump my head on—as I would learn—but also a great size to be transported on a camel or truck.

The primary colors in Mongolia are a bright orange and a blue the color of the sky. Mongolia is known as the land of blue skies. The doors usually have shades of orange and blue on them.

We journeyed into the country along dirt roads in our van. My eyes were soaking in the sights. I started seeing many, many gers as we slowed the van for the rough roads. As we went farther from the capital, the buildings started disappearing, and the gers took over. A ger can be several sizes, from accommodating two to six or so people and beds. The gers we stayed in later usually had five twin beds in them, arranged in a circle around a fireplace. There was usually a low table with low chairs around it to eat. This was considered the tourist ger. Many of the nomads of the country had an extra ger set up for guests who might pay to stay during their journey.

Lunch was interesting. We stopped at one of three gers in a row in the middle of nowhere. We followed our guide and ducked inside. We sat on small plastic stools and were handed lunch that consisted of a soup with half-cooked meat and pasta. It was hard for me to eat the meat, so I pushed it aside and ate the other ingredients. In Mongolia, about the only food you can count on other than meat is carrots, potatoes, and sometimes onions. It's not a country for vegetarians, and luckily I am not a vegetarian. I glanced at Judy and quietly poked her to look up. Above her, hanging from the ger rafter, was a large hind leg and hip of a slaughtered animal. It nearly reached her head. It was raw and apparently ready to be sliced whenever it was needed. I didn't think the Mongolians' methods would meet any FDA guidelines.

This first night, we arrived at a tiny village after dark. Our guide stopped to ask if we could stay in a house on the edge of town and talked with the husband and wife. It was a common practice, so we were welcomed quickly. Unfortunately, there was only one bed for the five of us, so Judy took the bed and I slept, or tried to sleep, on the hard floor. We were all in one room and had no mattresses or mats for the floor. It was extremely hard to sleep, so after all my sleepless nights in airports, and now this night, my sleep record was almost nil. Thank goodness the diarrhea I'd thought I was getting had been relieved by the Cipro pill.

The next day we had bread for breakfast and started out once again. I took a second diarrhea pill for safety. It would take about three days to drive to our destination just above the Chinese border. We bumped our way up and down the dirt roads. I could see the roads sometimes disappear altogether as our driver bumped over the plains.

Apparently Ulaanbaatar is more or less in central Mongolia, and all roads lead out from there. Central and northern Mongolia get more rain than the southern area, so as we traveled farther south, the landscape became sandier and less green. The nomads in the southern area have goats, sheep, and camels to eat and to be beasts of burden to move gers. If the family was not wealthy enough to have a pickup truck, the camels would carry the gers in pieces. We began to see a few motorcycles beside gers, which made it a little easier to round up their animals. Each ger had at least one dog also, although except in a few cases, I didn't see the dogs actually work as herding animals.

It was at lunch that day that I fell apart. The van stopped in a small, dusty town in the middle of nowhere. I tried to get out of the van, but my feet slid to the ground and I stood but could not move. I tried to move my right leg, and it was unresponsive. The same with my right arm. The guide came to me, holding me. I tried to talk to her, but my mouth, particularly the right side, wouldn't move. I was sure I was having a stroke, and I was scared. I was in the middle of nowhere, without enough travel insurance to even pay for flights within the country—for once, I had not chosen the best travel insurance policy and I was only protected for a $25,000 helicopter ride if I needed help—and I was having a stroke.

The guide and Paula, who was a physical therapist, told the others to go inside and eat while we found the village's clinic by asking the locals. We drove a short distance, and I was helped into the clinic. I sat down in a large room with a bed and several instruments such as a blood pressure monitor, and shortly after, a very young woman came to see me. I couldn't imagine she had much experience, but maybe I was just old. Our guide was able to translate my symptoms: dizziness, loss of use of my right side, diarrhea pills, no sleep, and little food. Apparently the young clinician thought it all added up to high blood pressure, so I was given a prescription for blood pressure pills. I relaxed a bit and recovered my ability to walk very slowly. I remembered that stroke symptoms don't go away easily, so with this change I was somewhat relieved. Paula also reassured me that stroke symptoms are usually more long-lasting. We went to the local pharmacy (a small, dirty house with a small sign outside) and bought a few pills for me to take to reduce my blood pressure. I was able to walk better and immediately forced myself to eat and to drink a great deal of water.

I was very dehydrated, which had most likely forced my blood pressure to high numbers, plus I had eaten and slept very little, causing the dizziness. I hoped my diagnosis was correct. I could only pray it was. I was reminded about how foolish I had been not to drink more water and to have given up a chance to sleep when I had it. The good news is that I recovered.

I was most intrigued by two aspects of this Mongolian adventure: the people, both the Mongolians and our adopt-a-family in the van, and the wild and domestic camels. It wasn't long before we were into the sandier portion of Mongolia and the camels started appearing. We begged the driver to stop so we could see a small herd beside the road.

We all piled out of the van and gingerly approached the herd. Most of us were used to wild animals that would spook and run when approached. These gentle animals just looked at us and continued chewing. We walked slowly toward them with smiles on our faces. The first thing I noticed about them as I got closer was the dark brown eyes with eyelashes a woman would kill for. Their eyes were very prominent in their heads, poking out in order to see their large world. Their teeth were those of a vegetarian animal, and their jaws slid back and forth as they ate. It has hard not to notice all their hair. It appeared to be coarse and very curly, with colors ranging from a very light blond to dark brown. Eventually one of the smaller ones rose but stayed close by the herd. The others stayed as we took hundreds of pictures among us. We eventually piled back into the van and excitedly talked about the encounter. The guides knew that this was just the beginning of our orientation to the docile critters.

We asked the guide if anyone can ever touch a camel. She laughed and told us, "Oh my, they are very tame and can be petted." We found that to be true in another day or two when we were able to mount and ride camels just above the Chinese border.

After visiting long, narrow canyons with small streams and staying with more Mongolian families in their extra gers, we finally arrived at the southernmost part of our journey. The day before, we had encountered a single young Russian woman on a motorcycle. She asked our driver if she could follow us to our destination because she was losing her way on the myriad of dirt trails called roads and didn't want to get lost in the Gobi. It amazed each of us to see this beauty queen in her leather attire, completely covered with dust. I couldn't blame her anxiety about the roads. Once, when I'd been facing the back of the van, I'd asked another passenger, "Are we on a road?" He'd answered, "Define *road*."

We dispersed from the van and found our little gers for the night. Usually all five of us stayed in one ger while the guide and her husband stayed with the family or in another ger. I fell in love with a small black puppy who knew how to get into the ger by nudging the edge of the wool covering and entering on his belly through the side. It was fun to see such a young, naïve animal. In Mongolia, I'd noticed so far, the families usually cared little about their dogs but did feed them scraps.

After my "stroke" incident, I was cautious. I didn't go far on the hikes, drank lots of water, and generally was careful. I normally would have been number one in line to hike or explore, but I had to behave.

It was the camels that brought me alive again. I wasn't going to miss riding camels in the Gobi Desert with authentic Mongolian trainers. We were staying in gers just above the Chinese border. If I understood correctly, we could see the Chinese border from where we were standing.

The camels were amazingly tame and big. Touching them was a treat, with their coarse hair intermixed with very soft underhair. There was one young camel who was somewhere between a baby and a full-sized adult. I started petting it, and the camel seemed to really respond. I was petting its face, brushing its hair back and forth, particularly behind the ears, which it seemed to like. I had heard stories of camels spitting at people—well, at most everything—but this little camel was not doing that and seemed to be enjoying the touching. While stroking it, I asked a friend to take a picture. That picture, showing my love for the animal and the animal allowing me to pet it, is one of my favorites.

When it came time to ride the camels, the young one was not in the crowd, and I was glad since it seemed too young to carry passengers on its back. These camels had two humps, so it was quite easy to sit between them when I was helped on. Once the passengers were on, the camels rose on their front legs first and then their back legs, so it was a matter of holding on for dear life when they rose so far above the ground. Once they started walking, however, it was as if I was floating above the earth's surface. The graceful animals glided along the ground, with each leg clomping a large hoof in the sand as the camel followed the leader, the camel in front of it. I closed my eyes to remember the experience, all the feelings of being on the camel, in my brain: what I was smelling, touching, and seeing.

The wind was slight, the movement graceful, and the quiet of the desert remarkable. All I could see were sand dunes, everywhere. There was no pollution anywhere, and the air smelled fresh from recent rains. The long rope used for a bit in the camel's mouth was made from camel hair, and it was coarse.

In this part of the Gobi Desert, to the south of the capital, the nomads had domesticated camels, sheep, and goats. In the northern part of the country, just below Russia, there were ponies, yaks, sheep, and goats. I guess the sheep and goats were particularly adaptable.

One morning we helped the ger owner water his animals. The government had made wells across the Gobi, each a hole with a bucket on a rope. There were car or truck tires split open and placed within each other to make a long line of watering troughs. There were several of these lines leading from the main watering hole, so the animals could split up and not have to fight for a spot at one trough. The owner allowed us to lower the bucket with the rope into the well and pull it up, full. We tipped it over into the nearest tire and watched it go down the trough for the camels. Camels had priority, and they were the first to drink. As soon as the baby camels were finished, they were tied to a rope so they could not go anywhere. The adult camels roamed free, but at the end of the day, the babies started crying for their mothers, and the mothers returned without the owner having to ride his horse or ATV to get them.

Note to self: Neat, sure system. The moms always return.

AFTER THE CAMELS, THE SHEEP AND THEN THE GOATS CAME FOR THE WATER. These critters, especially the goats, climbed all over everything to get to the water. Heck, the goats climbed on their mates, on the tires, and anything else around. It was pretty funny to see all these critters come after the one essential they all needed: water.

At the mention of a hot springs, Judy and I looked at each other and asked the driver to get us there. Getting us there involved driving with no roads at all, going uphill in mud, and having our driver scratch his head once in a while as he tried to remember the route. Honestly, we were going up and down hills, the driver using nothing but intuition to get to the natural hot springs. I love hot springs so much, though, that whenever the driver started doubting himself, I encouraged him to keep going.

Eventually we saw a row of about eight gers on wooden platforms, with several other buildings around a steamy area. We pulled into the muddy spot that resembled a parking lot and got out after our rough ride. We had arrived at Tsenkher Hot Springs. Our driver questioned the owner if we could stay there for the night, and luckily there were gers available. Each had its own stove, and a very old lady, bent over from wear and tear, started lighting the stoves so we would stay warm at this altitude. She was in a long dress with a woolen beret on her head, and she smiled at us through several missing teeth. She seemed happy, having a job and seeing how happy we were to have a warm place to settle for the night.

Getting in the hot springs became a mission. Judy and I put on hiking boots and explored the area where we saw thermal springs. The biggest ones, we were told, were way too hot to go into, and they were the source for the warm water that was used in the developed pools that looked like godsends to us. The idea had been for a Mongolian resort to be established, and while it hadn't really taken off and the plan to have massages and other services had kind of died, the two cement pools were clean and good enough for me, who hadn't had a bath in several weeks. Judy and I got our bathing suits on right away and eased in, forgetting dinner or anything else important.

China is pouring a lot of money into Mongolia. At this point in time, Mongolia is just Mongolia. It's not Chinese or anyone else's country except the Mongolians'. The Gobi sand was piled up with bulldozers for roads, waiting for some kind of blacktop to preserve the piles. Detours were everywhere near the construction sites, so it usually made more sense to just make our own road. Toward China, the roads sprouted out like broad alluvial fans, going in all directions.

Once back in Ulaanbaatar, our guide took us to the Black Market. It wasn't an illegal market—as its name in English would suggest—just a huge market where huge mill vans, such as those on cargo ships, hold merchants' goods during the day. At night, it can be secured and left for the next day. If you knew where to search, you could find anything you wanted. Shoelaces, vanity mirrors, furniture, knives, fancy hats with fox fur on them, or multicolored and very expensive boots like our camel driver had. He was very proud of them, showing them off every time someone asked about them.

When we'd arrived at the hostel once again, the manager came up to me and said that I had gotten a great deal of responses from my posting. The notice I'd put up asking if anyone would like to go to the northern part of Mongolia with us for a week had worked! We were able to find seven brave souls to go on our trip, which left room for only a driver who spoke little English because the van didn't have enough room for an English-speaking guide too.

This time we were headed north, to the Russian border. Apparently reindeer herders, known as the Dukha people, are nomads in northern Mongolia who followed the reindeer, tamed them, and kept them in herds. I had always wanted to see these nomads but hadn't yet. Because they were nomadic, there was no guarantee we'd find them, but there was a chance that they were still in the area near Lake Khövsgöl in northern Mongolia. When we actually got there, however, the few people there told us that they had left several weeks before. The tourist season had dried up, and we were probably some of the last visitors of the season. Besides, we were told, it was not good for the reindeer to be at such a low elevation since their traditional food source was at higher elevations—they were brought there just for the tourists.

When we got to the lake, we were able to ride Mongolian horses, which were really more like ponies. Apparently the macho men of the area didn't like to think of their horses as ponies, but they were in fact smaller than most of the horses I've ever ridden. That was a good thing for my pitiful knees.

The next morning when I woke in the ger, I heard noise outside. I looked out the window and there, sitting on blankets on the ground, were about six men and women getting out their handicrafts to sell. I grabbed my wallet and got outside to buy the best stuff. Much of it I had seen before, and the quality was average for the crafts, but I supported several of the artists by buying a few things I probably would never need. It always amazes me how different crafts are all over the world. In some countries such as Mongolia, the artists have not perfected their craftsmanship, probably because they don't have the time to concentrate only on handicraft skills. In other countries such as Bali, people are more focused on selling crafts rather than working the land or tending to animals.

On our way the next day, I decided I wanted to buy real stirrups for a horse saddle. It became my mission. I drew a picture and showed it to the driver, who I thought understood what I had drawn and would keep his eye open for me when we stopped at small towns.

One of the small towns had a market in a set of mill vans in the middle of town. The driver pointed in there. We didn't have a long time there, so I knew I had to do quick work if I was to be successful. I walked between the containers as best I could but didn't see what I was looking for. Then I spotted a young girl with dark hair. She seemed bored at staying with her mother at her shop. I went over to the little girl and showed her my picture of the stirrup I had drawn while her mom kept her eyes on us. The little girl nodded her head and pointed down a dirt road in front of the vans. I walked a little toward the direction in which she'd pointed and then stopped because I didn't know which way to go.

Shortly after my hesitation, the young girl showed up at my side, took my hand, and led me down one of the dirt paths to a long row of mill vans. Sure enough, there was the horse shop, with saddles, bridles, and my small molded aluminum stirrups, the ones traditionally used on saddles. I was able to buy a pair for about five dollars. Today, the stirrups sit on my table with napkins in them, pretending to be napkin holders.

During our trip we were able to go in and out of several Buddhist monasteries. Whereas many had been destroyed over the centuries during invasions of warring countries, several of the temples remained. Outside, of course, vendors were all over, especially near the temples closest to Ulaanbaatar. At one temple, one vendor had a live golden eagle that Judy and I were able to hold. If we lowered and raised the arm that the bird was standing on, it would open its wings. I felt very privileged to be holding this sacred bird, yet at the same time guilty that I was interrupting its natural state. Then I reminded myself that I was a visitor in this country, should not judge by my standards, and needed to realize that the nomads captured and trained these birds to hunt. I let myself thoroughly enjoy the sacred event.

We left Mongolia without incident and with no issues with our plane ride home, thankfully. I felt as if I had been handed a gift from the country. During the trip, I recognized that I was experiencing an amazing country that was still being developed, something very few people see.

CHAPTER 23

Nepal II and III

TRIP NUMBER TWO TO NEPAL WAS TO DO THE ANNAPURNA CIRCUIT TREK. A famous route to the east of the Everest region, it was my second choice after the Everest Base Camp trip. Judy and I talked our mountain-climbing friend Lani and my kindergarten-through-high-school friend Cathy along, so there would be four of us brave souls. Lani and Cathy had no idea of what was coming. I had climbed mountains with each of them, but only going to about fourteen thousand feet high, so they had a clue about climbing but no idea about higher altitudes. The surprise ended up being how well they did and how poorly I did.

The year of the trip was challenging for many reasons. That spring, I had just returned from working at the South Pole in Antarctica, and I had several things to do before the Nepal trip. First, I had to pack up my ninety-year-old mother and move her from her house in the Chesapeake Bay area to Ohio, where I grew up. It took most of a month, with daily trips to the dump, thrift store, and antique store.

Meanwhile I was still recuperating from a fall I had taken a few months earlier, fracturing my back. There was nothing to do for my back except to let it heal on its own. Finally I decided to have a knee replacement in May before the Annapurna trip. With my decades of mountain climbing, the knee had no cartilage left and was bone on bone, causing me grief and slowing me down more than usual on hikes. I was looking forward to replacing the knee and getting on the other side of the pain. A May surgery date would give me five months to recuperate before leaving for Nepal in October. It seemed like a solid plan. But what I didn't know was that I needed my gallbladder removed too, and apparently it took priority. That knocked the time I had available to recuperate my knee down to four months.

My knee doctor counted on one hand the number of months I would have to get into shape for the trip and began to shake his head. "I don't know if you can do it or not."

I just looked back and said, "I'm going, one way or the other." My ancient stubbornness reared its ugly head.

"You'll have to work hard with physical therapy and get your leg to extend enough forward in order to make the trip. If you don't get it to extend forward enough, I will have to go in and manipulate it, which will set you back further."

I vowed to work hard, and after the appointment, I went out to buy several ten-pound bags of rice to put on top of that knee so I could push it down, helping the forward extension. After the surgery, I would sit on the couch, place my ankle on the edge of the coffee table, and set twenty pounds of rice on my knee so it was forced down. It wasn't a pleasant task, but necessary.

I immediately went into physical therapy after my surgery. One of the tasks was to get on a stationary bicycle and force the pedal to go around. I couldn't even make it halfway around. I now understood what the doctor had been telling stubborn me. It took a great deal of hard work, and the help of some friends, to recuperate, but when October rolled around, I was packed and ready to go to Nepal—four months after knee surgery.

Cathy and I flew to Kathmandu together, and Judy got there soon after. Lani's flight was the problem. Her first flight was canceled, and she had to drive many hours to get to Los Angeles to catch another flight. When Lani was finally on her way, Cathy and I went with a driver to get Lani from the airport, but halfway there as we were talking with him, he jumped out of his car, got two gallons of water from a vendor along the road, ran back to the car to open the hood, and poured water on a fire that was starting in his engine. *A possible sad forewarning at the beginning of our trip*, I thought. I tried to turn my mind to think only positive thoughts.

Cathy and I just looked at each other, laughing and shaking our heads, and got on a passenger van that our driver hailed for us. I already knew that everyone looked after everyone else in this gentle country, and I was still in awe of it. Even in small things, such as getting change for a purchase from the next vendor or finding someone who spoke better English to help in an interaction, they were kind. The passenger van took us to the airport, and we were able to meet Lani while another driver was sent to pick us up. We never found out what happened to the ignited car.

We stayed in a hotel run by the owner of the trekking agency we'd signed up with. It was the same outfit that Judy and I had hired on the Everest trip, an agency locally owned in Kathmandu, and the same guide would lead us on this trek as had taken us to Everest Base Camp. He hadn't been sure of my abilities then, and I was sure he was questioning them again.

We started out by driving to the small town of Besisaha, where our trek would begin. Once again, it was in the jungle and extremely hot and humid. I struggled, was the last one in the group, was red-faced much of the time, complained under my breath all the time, and, at times, started to cry.

Note to self: You're failing at your goal not to whine.

EVERYONE HAD HIKED TO THE FIRST LUNCH STOP, AND I STRUGGLED IN minutes later. It was all I could do to sit at the table and not collapse. My back was aching, my knee was wrapped with a brace, and I was sweating like a pig. I had been carrying a daypack, but it was heavier than I should have been carrying. My new mantra had to be to drink water or Coca-Cola or any liquid I could get my hands on.

I calmed down during lunch, lost some of the redness in my face, and trekked on for many more hours after lunch. Our first night's stop was at a beautiful long guesthouse with lush gardens, grasses, and chickens all around. The owner and his wife greeted us and showed us where to put our daypacks in our rooms. The porters, who graciously carried our backpacks, had already left them in the rooms. I dropped on the bed, totally exhausted. It was embarrassing. On top of that, I was in a bad mood because I was doing so poorly. Me, the experienced hiker, was pooping out. After a quick dinner, I fell sound asleep that night, and most of the nights that followed. I didn't give myself a curve to credit myself despite all the medical issues I'd brought with me.

Note to self: A little hard on yourself there, again. This won't be forever. Remember, nothing is permanent.

THE NEXT FEW DAYS WEREN'T MUCH BETTER, EXCEPT THAT LANI STARTED feeling badly also. Hers was more of a stomach problem, whereas mine were the two surgeries and bad back. At lunchtime one day, Lani asked for potatoes for lunch, just potatoes. The guesthouse owner looked quizzically at her but took her order. In about twenty minutes, Lani's order appeared with our lunches. We all squealed with laughter as Lani's lunch was presented to her: a plate piled about six inches high with small cooked potatoes. She offered potatoes to each of us, actually pleading for us to take some of them so we would not be wasteful with the scarce and valuable food in these remote towns.

As I ascended from the humid jungle where we'd started and the air got cooler, I started feeling and acting better. My knee, after the recent surgery, behaved for the most part, but I was sure to wear a support brace on both knees. I was eating well as we progressed and wasn't losing the weight I was hoping. The trail went higher into the mountains, and although we followed a few roads, most of this side of the circuit was a path through the villages. We eventually got to the small town of Manang, and the lower Mustang district, then mercifully had a rest day for acclimatization.

My boots had been used when I started the trip, and now the hooks for my laces on the boots were pulling off. When I got to Manang, I asked a cobbler, a man sitting along the path into town, if he could put a few more hooks in my boots for my shoelaces. He looked up and told me that he didn't have hooks but could sew pieces of leather that would hold my shoelaces in place. Perfect! I was very grateful. As more tourists came into these towns, the local people were becoming more aware of what all these strangers needed. Looking back, it seems I was plagued from this time onward with shoe problems on trips, but these boots now had leather loops for my laces, and I was grateful.

In Manang, I was able to satisfy some of my craft quest needs. I bought small souvenirs from vendors with tables out during the day, although I tried to keep the items small so I wouldn't have much additional weight in my daypack and wouldn't be tempted to put them in the backpack that the porters carried. There was a lot of jewelry, some appearing as if it were Tibetan, which made sense since that country is so close to this area of Nepal. I purchased a yak-lined hat with red patterned cotton in the back while lugging my daypack and my body up a trail. I used any excuse to stop going uphill, but now this hat is special to me because it is a very typical hat worn by the people of the region during colder seasons.

The morning we were to go over the pass, Thorong La, at almost eighteen thousand feet, we got up before daybreak. I was doing better by this point, but Lani was fading. She said she would be last and would go slowly, and I told her, "I'll be your best friend going up that pass—let's go!" We stayed at the back until Lani got her bearings, began to feel better, and slowly climbed to the top of the pass with our group. Intact and at the top, our group took a lot of pictures and celebrated with granola bars or whatever we could find in our packs.

It is true that getting to the top of a mountain or high-elevation pass is the achievement, but the way down can be more of a problem than going up. Everything in my body was starting to hurt again, and I started getting whiny. Eventually we made our way to a town where the major attraction was to climb to the top of a viewpoint and watch the sun rise on the majestic peaks in the area. The other three in the group got up and started out long before daybreak. I did too, but everything hurt too much for me to continue, so with a few words under my breath, I turned back. I was blaming people other than myself, but it was truly my problem. No one else owned it.

Note to self: No victims here.

We eventually made it to Pokhara, the second-largest city in Nepal. It was quite a bit smaller than Kathmandu, and we were able to wander the streets, avoid the cows in the middle of the streets, and become a little familiar with it. Judy and I decided to walk to a famous World Peace Pagoda, a large white structure built by Buddhist monks, on the other side of the lake from Pokhara. My Lonely Planet guidebook said the site, a UNESCO World Heritage site, was not to be missed but also warned of muggings on the more remote parts of the trails from Pokhara, so it was something to be aware of.

Lani and Cathy elected not to go, so Judy and I set out one day on foot for an adventure. Guidebook in hand, we tried to follow directions and make correct turns. Most often, however, we would get a little lost and have to stop to ask someone for help. Initially that happened a lot. After asking directions several times, we finally turned a corner and saw a sign with directions, a large trail map on a billboard-type sign, and something of a description in English. Most importantly, there was a middle-aged man from India also reading the sign. In perfect English, he asked if we were going to the World Heritage site, and we nodded affirmatively. Rajab was the first person we picked up, or he picked us up. We were grateful to have the company.

The three of us hiked for several miles near the heavily treed area of mugging concern. We jabbered as we hiked on a trail alongside a small irrigation stream. We came to another turn on the path and found two young women from Hungary who spoke almost no English. We pointed to places on my small guidebook map, and their heads started bobbing in agreement. They were also going to the heritage site, so now we had five in our group. This pattern continued until we had gathered seven people going to the pagoda—seven people from different countries and with diverse backgrounds. I felt safe.

Note to self: This is almost like Dorothy collecting strangers going to the Land of Oz.

ALL WAS FINE UNTIL I SAW THE SIGN. IT WAS A LITTLE SIGN ON A POLE above our dirt road that read *Tibetan Refugee Camp*. Oh, man, that was a sign beckoning to me, and I had to leave the group to explore it. I pointed to the sign and told the others that Judy and I were going to explore the camp first and catch up with them later. We rounded the corner and soaked in what we saw.

In order to make money at the camp, the women made small stalls that were in a square-shaped market area. Each participant had a longing look on her face and a smile. I imagined each one was praying that we would like their handmade items more than the others and leave tourist dollars with them. It was hard to watch, hard to be there. Tourist dollars were so valued in this poor country, and the refugees were at the bottom of the list to receive them. Several of the refugees were selling prized possessions they'd brought with them from home, Tibet. I promised one withered old woman that I would value her orange-and-turquoise beaded basket, something I'm sure had been in the family a long time. I could see that for them, eating had become more important than keeping such things. I bought some trinkets and the valued basket and left.

Note to self: You have a large duffel bag, and it still has room.

We made it to the huge, historical, brilliant-white World Peace Pagoda, also called Shanti Stupa, after making quite a climb and asking someone who showed us a left turn on a path in the middle of some shops. A Buddhist-style pagoda, the shrine apparently had been built with help from Japanese Buddhists in the early 1970s.

We had caught up with our small entourage and made it up the hill to the pagoda where we were able to wander around the grounds to soak in the sacredness of the site. We took pictures to show the diversity of our group, and then broke into smaller groups to follow the path back down to Fewa Lake at the bottom of the shrine. Judy and I found ourselves in yet another adventure.

Naturally, there was a place to purchase food at the bottom of the hill, but we were searching for transportation across the lake to get back to Pokhara. It would be easier than walking back. As we rounded a bend along the shoreline, we saw several large wooden boats and a boatman who apparently would row us over to the other side of the lake. The task seemed daunting to me, but heck, these were young men, even if there was only one to a boat. The fishing-type boat appeared sturdy enough even though it was fairly well aged. The trick now was to fill up the boat with other passengers so we would get the best rate across the lake.

Four of us had descended the steep path to the boats at about the same time, so we plowed into the boat that would leave next, captained by a young man who seemed as if he had enough brawn to get us across the lake. He had a big smile and seemed glad for the business.

We waited, and waited, until eventually a group of six or seven people showed up and we begged them to come on our boat so we could get the reduced fare. I can appear fairly forlorn if I have to. We finally got a full boat and were ready to cross the lake back to bustling Pokhara. To have such a tried-and-true method of transportation was amazing, making me feel as if I were in the nineteenth century.

Back to Pokhara, back to the hotel, back to Kathmandu, back to the good old USA, and this trip was done.

Several years after our Annapurna Circuit trek, trip number three to Nepal was to do the Manaslu route, which was near the Annapurna Circuit. It was something the guide for the Annapurna trip had told me I was not good enough to do. Hmm...if that wasn't a challenge for me, I don't know what is. My stubbornness got the best of me, and Judy and I signed up for the trip. This particular trip was probably the most interesting of the three trips in Nepal. It was remote, lacking tourists—and was scary for me because of its remoteness.

During one of the prior trips, we had been told that this area of Nepal was still being developed—to the point of possibly needing tents all the way because of the lack of tourist accommodations. At this time, the Nepalese were building guesthouses as quickly as they could, so we were able to stay at houses during the entire trip. This was good because it meant the porters didn't have to carry as much and the trip was less costly. We did encounter other tourists during the trip but nothing like the other trips in Nepal.

Note to self: Just as these people must embrace change, so must you when it comes up.

We decided to go with a new Nepal-based company this time, mainly because they were charging less than our other company. The difference between the two companies became apparent almost from the beginning.

They picked us up at the airport, and the hotel we stayed at was certainly adequate. I felt unfamiliar with the area because our normal hotel was not near where we were staying. I ensured that I picked up a card with the hotel's address so we could get back to it, something that could be hard to do without the address. None of this was out of the ordinary. It was just hard for my old brain to wrap around the new location.

Judy and I declined the tour of Kathmandu because we had been on two tours before, so we decided to go out on our own for the day before the trip began. We stumbled into the area in Thamal where we had stayed in the past and were proud of our bravery to wander so far. We found the local kite shop, and I stood in line for handmade paper kites. The owners were making them as quickly as they could. It appeared to me they were crossing two reeds, possibly bamboo, at ninety-degree angles and securing them with string. Then they glued lightweight paper, like the tissue paper we use for wrapping in the States, to the sticks. I waited my turn, observing the process, and finally got to the front of the line.

The owner looked to me, and I used my fingers to point to the kinds and colors of kites I wanted, and then I held up six fingers. I didn't have to say a word—I just pointed and nodded, and he wordlessly did the same. When he handed me six kites, I held out my hand with change. It meant that he could take whatever money he needed to pay for the kites. The kind storeowner took the coins he needed, and the total broke down to about a dime per kite.

I left the store and noticed many young eyes following me. I knew some of the children had been coveting my kites, and from the beginning, I had intended to give all but one away. I smiled at a young girl who was peering at my pink kite. I motioned for her to come over and then handed her the kite. She broke into a smile and ran away with it, happiness written on her young face.

Immediately, two young boys came over to me, also hoping for a kite. I smiled at them and showed them the other five kites I still had in my hand. I motioned for them to pick one out, and each studied the other colors before deciding on a blue one and a red one. Again, they ran away with smiles as the kites floated behind them. I kept one of the kites, but I should have given it away too, because it didn't survive traveling back to the States.

The following day we left for our adventure. First we'd drive to Arughat Bazar, and then we'd begin hiking. We would be following an ancient salt-trading route along the Budhi Gandaki River, which ran down a deep gorge. The adventure would go for several weeks as we trekked to Besisaha, the starting point of the Annapurna Circuit trek. I knew the highest pass, Larkya La, was over 16,750 feet high, and I was getting older and more unsure of my health. It would be a test.

We didn't have a private vehicle taking us to the start of the hike but a public bus. A Nepalese public bus was a great deal different from a US public bus. It took me a second to comprehend what we were about to embark on. Picture this: a bus that looked like it had been tagged all over with graffiti but was actually painted vibrant, primary colors—probably to make the thing more eye-catching. Well, no one could really miss it. It could have been driven directly from Woodstock in 1969. In addition, the bus was already full of people. Inside were all kinds of things hanging from doors, windows, and—of most concern—in the front of the bus. *Clean and tidy* would not have been a good description. I had to believe the items were like good luck charms, something I was beginning to feel we would definitely need on the ride.

Our guide shoved us in, taking our large packs and handing them to the men on top of the bus to secure our gear there. I held on to my daypack, which contained my trusty supply of pills and other necessary items. Judy and I were both thinking, *I can't believe this*, and could only go with the program since there were no other choices.

Looking around, I could see that the people on the bus were in varying degrees of acceptance of the journey. Some were asleep amid the chaos, some appeared weary, and some squirmed to find some kind of firm seating, or footing when all the seats were taken. People of all ages were on the bus, from gray-haired old men and deeply wrinkled women to children and babies on laps. Eventually we got on our way, with people in the seats, people in the aisles, people sitting on other people, and people who climbed to get on top of the bus, mainly men.

Once we got going, occasionally we passed other buses and could see young men on top of those buses too. I had to take my hat off to them—they were the bravest of the brave on the road. Next to me, a young boy was falling asleep in the aisle. I guided him to sit at the edge of my seat and then pointed to my daypack, letting him know he could put his head on my daypack so he would have a place to sleep.

We would stop in villages to let people and cargo off. Eternally there were people at our open windows trying to sell us water, homemade food, candy, fans, anything that anyone could possibly want. If they didn't have it, they could find it. There were tiny towns, larger towns, and medium-sized towns. Judy and I were targets for the vendors since we were the only Caucasians on the bus. It took hours to get to where we were going to start our trip, and it was turning out to be an all-day bus ride.

At one point we turned onto a dirt road. I mean a dirty, muddy, narrow road. There was only room for one vehicle at a time, and ours was super large. Here was another moment my mother—if she'd known—would have shaken her head and prayed for my safety. The universe, fortunately, was watching after us this particular day.

At several points the bus got stuck in the mud all the way up to the entrance step. Judy and I looked at each other and had to try to decipher signals from others in the bus since no one spoke English. We had to get off the bus to lighten its load and then walk up the muddy road as the men pushed the bus out of the mud—no easy task. Many of the locals smiled at us, seeming to be silently saying something like, *Well, now you know how the buses around here manage…and how we manage.*

Note to self: This is truly a gift to see these people's journey. A slice of life.

Eventually we pulled into Arughat Bazar, a town in the middle of nowhere. It had something of a street going down the middle of the wide road, with stores on either side for about a US city block. Our guide took us to our room for the night, upstairs in a modest hotel, and then he left to find iodine to put in our water to keep us safe from stomach bugs during the trek.

The night before the trek, Judy and I were able to gather most of the supplies we needed. Everyone in the town was carrying umbrellas, so after a short conference, Judy and I decided to purchase some too. The locals obviously knew something we didn't know. As it turned out, we would use them during most of the journey, both to keep the torrents of rain off and to protect ourselves from the sun in the hot, humid areas.

We didn't get started until after noon the first day because of delays in getting the required documents to complete the trip. Fortunately, our guide and porter took care of all that while Judy and I explored the town.

Judy's boot needed an immediate repair. I started pointing to the boot as I encountered locals, indicating that it needed to be repaired. One gentleman gave us a signal that I interpreted as a circle. He pointed the direction we needed to go and then made a circle with his arm. Interesting. We had no clue what he meant, but he laughed and we started in the first direction. On the way, we asked two other locals, and they did a similar thing with gestures. We got closer and asked a third older man. He pointed in the same direction, and we continued on the quest. It was then that we saw the bridge and finally understood. The locals didn't know how to tell us to go over the bridge, but because of our determination, we figured it out and laughed as soon as we saw the bridge. Once across, it was easy to ask other locals where the local shoe repair fellow was. Not too far from the bridge, we found him, sitting on the ground, working on several shoes.

We pointed to Judy's boot and showed him the problem. He indicated for us to sit down, to give him the boot, and to wait while he fixed it. It didn't take more than a few minutes for him to complete the work, and he charged maybe a dollar. We gave him two. One of the villagers asked us later on how much he charged, and they scoffed that he would let us tourists off so easily. The cobbler was a good, honest man, and we very much appreciated him.

The journey began hard for me, of course. In the heat and humidity, I was very red in the face. Perspiration poured down my head and back. It was too hot to wear a hat, so the umbrella did the work of the hat. I was miserable, and Judy just smiled in her happiness to be off work and on a journey. Then, the bad part of the journey for me began.

It started pouring rain, like a monsoon. We had elected to do this trip in early October, when the weather would usually be good, but the monsoon season lasted longer than usual this particular year. I was almost sixty-seven years old, and I was asking my body to do things more suited to a thirty-seven-year-old's body. We had been hiking a long time when the rains began in the afternoon. The monsoon rains were as heavy as I had ever experienced. Judy was doing well and was a good distance in front of me. I was in back with the guide.

Judy hiked to the place we would be staying as I struggled up and down the rocks that formed the eternal up-and-down staircases. Once we'd gotten off the bus, there were no more roads. To go into the valleys and up the hillsides from there, everyone went on foot, and that included me.

The rocks were gray, of varying sizes, and all types of distances apart. For the locals, the route was a cinch. For a chicken like me, it was hell. Breaking a leg or ankle up here would be the end of the trip, and having broken my ankle in the wild before, I was not interested in taking any risks. I was slow; I mean *really* s-l-o-w. I didn't really care what the guide was thinking or how long it was taking me. I simply knew that my boots and socks were completely wet, soaked as if we were hiking in a river. This would prove to be a problem in a few days.

It took hours for me to make it to the shelter, and I got there a long time after dark. I guessed it was all penance for my not getting into shape. The porter came back down to help me, and both the guide and porter got me to the shelter for the night. I glanced at Judy, who was not about to give me a sympathetic note, although I loved that girl for coming with me in the first place since she knew what she was getting into with me.

We continued for many days through small villages where new construction was evident all over. There were a few solar panels and a few hanging light bulbs in the buildings—electricity being a new development—plus many lumber mills and gravel makers along the way. The gravel makers were the same as we had seen on other trips. Mostly women and children, they would sit on the ground with a hammer. Taking a large rock, they would hit it with a hammer and make it into gravel by simply hitting it over and over to break it down into smaller pieces. They would do this day in and day out.

Note to self: Accept the norms of the country you are visiting.

THE LUMBER MILLS WERE LIKE AN OUTDOOR THEATER FOR TOURISTS AND locals to watch. Usually, there were two platforms, one at either end of the mill. A log would be placed between the two platforms, and one man would be on one platform and another man on the ground, with a huge lumber handsaw held between them. The man on top would push the saw down to the man underneath, and then that man would push it back up—a very slow, arduous job that would produce the much-needed lumber for building.

Just as arduous, people hand-chipped rocks to fit with each other in building foundations and even entire walls, as I had seen on the Everest trip. It wasn't until I saw the hard, repetitive tasks that it took to produce a building that I realized how the Nepalese live off the land and the raw materials it produces. There are enough trees in the area that a few can be cut for shelters. There's nothing like clear-cutting in the forests there—just a few trees handpicked from here and there. Rocks are plentiful, as is bamboo, which is used to make baskets, mats, and other useful items.

On this trek, there were so few tourists that much of the tourist etiquette had not entered the region. Take trash, for example. The Nepalese stop along their treks to eat bamboo shoots and other items the land gives them. They eat the shoot and then toss the remainder of the shoot on the ground. It is considered trash, but it will compost and go back into the soil. With that being the standard, it made sense for the guides and porters to throw other kinds of trash on the ground too.

I handed one of the porters a stick of gum I had brought with me. He seemed delighted as he opened the small wrapper and stuck the gum into his mouth. Then he tossed the paper wrapping on the ground. Judy glanced at me, and I saw her. I decided this was a teachable moment. I looked at the porter, smiled, and motioned with my hand for him to please get the wrapper and give it to me. After a few seconds, he understood. He picked up the paper wrapper and handed it to me. I put it in my pants pocket and smiled back. It was as simple as that.

I gave the same fellow another piece of gum a day later, and wouldn't you know, as soon as he had the wrapper off, he stuck it in his pocket. Yeah! It had worked, for at least one person, and maybe the idea would be repeated to another friend. I had taken advantage of a teachable moment, and it felt good to me, no matter what the outcome down the road.

It was also about this time that I had a dilemma. About day four after the monsoon issue, my lug-soled boots started delaminating. I mean, the sole that was glued to the bottom of my shoe was noticeably starting to separate from the shoe. To clarify, *both* boots were delaminating. Nothing like a shoe store was in sight—and would be nowhere in sight for weeks. What to do? I had to get creative.

I asked the owner of the guesthouse where we were staying if he had a bit of wire so I could wrap it around the boots once I laced them. He found a scrap piece, and he wrapped it around the shoes, with my feet inside and the boots tied. I, in turn, wrapped what duct tape I'd brought with me on top of the wire and around the boot. At this point, the soles were still somewhat attached to the boots, but I knew it was just a question of time and wear before the entire sole would come off each boot.

Note to self: This solution will probably last a few hours, at best.

There were no other choices in this land of few tourists, no stores, and few supplies. The guide and porters knew about the problem but had no remedies. I would have to make do until another solution appeared. I gingerly stepped with my boots on the trail, trying to avoid anything that would cut through the tape or make the wire useless. The trails in Nepal are rugged, to say the least, and they were still wet and muddy.

We hiked all day, and in midafternoon we were directed to sit at a restaurant for a short break. I had a cup of tea and was still focusing on my boots, whose soles by now had begun flapping both at the front and back of each boot. The wire and what was left of the duct tape were the only things that held the soles on. It had become an art form to walk and not to trip on the clumsy, loose soles. Then I saw just across the cobblestone walkway a store with a few odds and ends in it. I didn't need gum or a pair of socks, but I surely could use a new pair of shoes.

In the shop, I got the attention of the store owner and pointed to my boots. He nodded his head as soon as he saw the loose soles. I knew I would be lucky to find anything, but I was hopeful. By this time, the guide had wandered over and asked me my shoe size so he could translate to the store owner. The owner brought out two pairs of extremely light but sturdy tennis shoes with laces. I put each one on, and though they were a tad large, they were perfect in every other way. I chose the bright blue ones and put them on. Even as remote as this place was, the shoes were only about twenty dollars. I gave my old, heavy boots to the children of the village, who started twirling them in a circle above their heads, with their fingers on their noses and making sounds about the lingering smell of the boots.

On our journey, there were no crafts this time. Both of the other treks had been filled with all kinds of vendors who had things to purchase along the way. I am wired to keep my eyes open for locally made items, and with the lack of items so far, I was on extra alert for any potential crafts. Besides, it kept my mind off my pain and aching body parts. I was disappointed until we got high up on the trek as we were circling the eighth-highest mountain on the planet, Manaslu. I was nervous about my health and started doubting my abilities, letting my confidence level tank. To keep my mind off my physical issues, I kept looking for crafts.

At one point we were walking on the path through a small collection of houses when I spotted a woman working on a handmade floor loom. She was a petite woman, probably very young, yet she had four children running around or clinging to her skirt. We were getting into the colder environment, and she had on what appeared to be a long wool dress with a beautiful apron on it. The apron had many colors, small rectangles of vibrant colors. She was making another apron on her loom, totally handmade and taking a long time.

As I watched her process, I could see that the apron would be made in sections. Each section was woven with either earthy-colored wool or sometimes more of a display of vibrant colors. In general, the colors were deep and warm, with ivory and off-white sections added in. She was weaving each section with all these different colors, from just a few threads back and forth to about an inch of one color before another color began. Although it seemed that she was weaving and switching colors on a whim, the result was magnificent. Once there were three sections that were wide enough together to go across the body and long enough to go approximately below the knees, she hand sewed the three sections together to form the apron. She used strings on the top edge of the apron, which could be tied in the back to keep the apron on.

I was enthralled to watch the young mother work on her apron. I had seen these small handmade looms on our trek, but until now, no one had been using them. I stopped and watched her for a long time. The guide and Judy were on ahead, so I was able to enjoy the moment with the porter.

I could not speak the woman's language, and she could not speak mine. I depended on the porter, with his broken English, to ask her if I could buy the three sections she was just completing. She was wearing a fairly new apron, so I figured that she was making one for a friend, family member, or neighbor. She stopped weaving for a minute while we tried to convey the message that I was interested in purchasing the lengths. I looked at the weaving, very fine wool, with burgundy and pink accents among the browns, off-white, and blues. Once she understood what I was asking, we talked about a price. I wanted to be fair to her because the work was such high quality and she may not have known what the true value was. As we were about to leave, she took off her wool belt, and I gave her yet more money for it. She was thrilled because I probably gave her the equivalent of several months of salary. Most Nepalese live off the land, not by buying and selling goods. The exception is the store owners.

I trudged upward yet again. We had been leapfrogging with two young couples from Australia, and they were consistently surprised that we kept showing up like a bad penny. They would go in front of us, stay an extra day somewhere, and sooner or later we would all connect again up the mountain. They seemed surprised by our endurance, and eventually one of them got up the courage to ask our ages. Judy being almost seventy years old and me being right behind her surprised them immensely. One of them said, "You're my grandmother's age, and I can't imagine my *mother* doing this!"

The young couples decided to stay in the area of Manaslu an extra day, so we advanced a day in front of them and trekked to the highest town in the area. The village seemed deserted as Judy and I hiked up and down the rocky trails through town. I found it a little eerie. It was obvious that the animals lived underneath the houses, in kind of a small enclosed yard or even in a barn-type structure underneath each house. There were only a few animals around, and fewer people. One window displayed a few pieces of jewelry, and I knocked on the door. A woman answered, so I pointed to a one-stone necklace in the window. She pointed to her husband, who seemed to be in an angry mood. He was sitting on a log stool by the stove, the only source of heat and light in the tiny structure. He understood what I was asking and gave me a huge number for the pendant, more than I wanted to spend for it, and I said, "Namaste," with my hands together as I bowed out of the tiny wooden house.

The next morning, we hiked to the last structure before our trip over the pass. It was a long rock building with a large room with tables. This was the dining room. I could only describe it as cold and dark, even though it was in the late afternoon. It seemed like a tomb when I went inside and sat on the wooden benches with yak skins on them. We could get a cup of tea most any time of the day, and this seemed like the right time.

Our room for the night was small. A cord with a light bulb hung from a nail near the top of the room. The beds were simply plywood and round wooden poles with worn mattresses made of some kind of cotton. We were the only people there at this point, but the cook said that at times there were as many as fifty people there to eat. At this altitude and distance away from easy transportation, our dinner was a choice of rice this or rice that. I chose rice. Anyone expecting a lot of choices in this remote, barren area of the world would be disappointed—and most likely judgmental.

The next day, we got up at dawn and began the journey over the 16,750-foot pass. Although I had been over much higher passes, this one was taking its toll on me. I started worrying about everything, from having a heart attack and dying on the mountain, to breaking a leg, to having a stroke that would necessitate an air rescue. I had bought emergency evacuation insurance, luckily. I let all the negative thoughts take over my head, something I hadn't done in a long time. I recognized what was happening yet didn't take ownership of it to calm all the chatter in my head.

Note to self: Stay in the present, and don't worry about the future.

I CONTINUED TO WHINE MOST OF THE WAY UP THE MOUNTAIN DESPITE seeing a *National Geographic*–quality photo opportunity near what I thought was the top of the pass. The incredibly beautiful mountains to my left as we were ascending were perfectly reflected in a small lake that was totally calm. We all stopped to take pictures because the scene was one of the most incredible I'd witnessed in my life. The chatter in my head stopped for about ten minutes.

We got to what I thought *had* to be the top. Of course, like childbirth, it wasn't. The top of this pass seemed to *never* come, and my confidence level was sinking with each new hill I saw as I rounded each corner. Eventually the top appeared, and there was nothing else but to go downhill. By this time, the guide and Judy were tired of my verbal and nonverbal body language, and they were heading downhill as the rain started. One of the porters had stayed with me, and at this point, although I wasn't as afraid of keeling over from a heart attack, now I was sure I was going to twist an ankle or break a leg, so I slowed down. My new sneakers had to be adequate on these rocks and in the rain.

The downhill descent was never-ending, and I reminded myself that I was in no mental state to even do the trip in the first place. Still, my stubbornness led me to put one foot in front of the other and to continue as the rain intensified. I was off the pass and it was not snowing on me—that was good.

I started seeing buildings way off in the distance. There were several rows of small houses with seemingly new construction, ready for guests. Of course, we were staying in the last place through town. Just before I got there, the guide came to meet me and handed me a Snickers bar, which I decided to savor once I had stopped hiking for the day. I should have shown more gratitude.

I opened the door to the small room and saw Judy sitting on a bed, seemingly recovered and happy. I wasn't really happy just then, but I could only blame myself. The room was really cute, unlike most of our other accommodations so far on this trip, and had fairly new knotty pine paneling on the walls and curtains on the windows. I don't think I'd ever seen something as cute in the remote areas of Nepal. Most everything else was simple and functional. The new buildings in the entire region, however, were being completed at an unprecedented rate, and more Western amenities were showing up.

I flopped down on my bed in our room and said quite loudly and emphatically, "I'm not going anywhere tomorrow." And I didn't. *So there.*

The next night, our four friends took rooms next to us. They arrived after dinner, very tired and exhausted. I was able to greet them and then go to bed, still in recuperation mode.

It was about nine o'clock at night that I heard the first sound. It was just a little tapping on the paper-thin walls. It sounded like a person knocking on the wall, very lightly, as if he or she were packing or had knocked the wall accidentally. I paid no attention to it until it happened another two or three times. I finally knocked on the wall back, a little more loudly than their tap, and there was silence. I'd intended to relay, *I hear your tapping and am trying to go to sleep.* My knock accomplished its mission, but I felt really badly the next day.

When Judy and I were packed and ready to go, we went outside to get breakfast. It was then that I saw the neighbors from the next room to us, the ones where the tapping originated. They said they were sorry to bother us last night, but they were trying to get our attention because of a problem. "What problem?" I asked. Almost as soon as I asked, I saw "the problem."

Their eyes were almost glued shut. The other two friends came out of their room also, and the four of them looked at us with swollen eyes. I asked, "Didn't you wear sunglasses yesterday over the pass?" No, they hadn't. Apparently because it was overcast, raining or snowing at times, and not sunny, the foursome had decided not to wear sunglasses. Two of them were worse than the other two, but it wasn't something easy to deal with one way or the other.

I turned to the couple who had tapped on the wall and said, "Gee, I wish you had just said something—I thought maybe you didn't know you were tapping on the wall."

Again apologetic, he said, "I was so sorry to bother you, but I thought that if anyone would know what to do, you and Judy would."

All of a sudden I was important. Someone actually cared about some of my experiential wisdom. "Well," I started out, "I feel so honored! If anything is ever swollen, you need to reduce the swelling, so put anything cold that you can on it." End of lesson. I felt sorry for their pain and wished that their guides had made them put on shades.

In another few days, we hiked out from the area, meeting the Annapurna Circuit trail. The first night we stayed in a second-story room with a tiny balcony. We both felt lucky to have the room with a view and set two chairs out on the balcony. A balcony in the US is quite different from a balcony in Nepal. We were sitting on our tiny balcony, and I started noticing things about the balcony. For example, there was only a small string outlining where the end of the balcony was and where the street below was. We could have easily fallen off at any second. The balcony probably was just cement with no rebar or support system in it. I started imagining the worst, like the balcony, the small table, two chairs, and two old ladies falling to their deaths, or at least to major injuries in the middle of Nepal. Judy and I exited the balcony quickly, especially since no one else was outside with us.

The final day, we hiked for a long time. We saw many foreigners on the Annapurna Circuit trail sitting along the route, shoes off, rubbing their feet. Most of them were very young, in their early twenties or so. I wanted to tell them to rethink their journey because it was day one or two for them and they had three weeks more, including the almost-eighteen-thousand-foot Thorong La pass. Judy and I silently passed them, grateful we were going out while they were just beginning their journey. We arrived in Besisaha without incident and eventually got on another local bus to take us back to Kathmandu safely.

CHAPTER 24

Croatia

CROATIA WAS AN AFTERTHOUGHT. I'D ORIGINALLY BOUGHT A TICKET BACK to Athens with the plan to return to see Rena on Lesvos, but then Lesvos was in an uproar, first with the Greek financial crisis and then with the refugees from Syria and African countries. The refugee boats were coming to Lesvos because it was the closest Greek island to Turkey. I wanted to remember the carefree time I'd enjoyed there, not the turmoil of the current times, so I decided to buy an additional ticket from Athens to Croatia. I would be going by myself and had to rev up my spirits to do the trip. I was anxious about leaving my critters and making all the flights, and I had to remind myself that this was my norm before a trip.

After I booked the flights, I looked up Dubrovnik on Airbnb to see about accommodations there. Reading through the postings reminded me of using Couchsurfing.com years ago when Judy and I met Sarah in Patagonia. This would be a private apartment, so a bit different than a couch next to a cat litter bin, but I was still grateful to people who opened their homes for travelers to stay in. I found a cute little apartment near the center of town for twenty-five dollars a night. The only problem was that privately owned apartments don't typically have airport shuttles, I would be getting into town about ten thirty p.m., and I didn't want to have to find my way there that late at night from the airport. I was able to work with the owner of the apartment to send someone for me, and I was grateful. I would be picked up with a familiar *Linda* sign at the airport.

I got to my beautiful little apartment where the owner's wife met me and explained the dos and don'ts of the apartment in broken English. She was very sweet, and so was her husband when I met him a day later. I slept until noon the next day. It was important to catch up on my sleep after the long journey.

When I woke, I could see the walls of the old city of Dubrovnik below me and the ocean sweeping into the inlet. The apartment was inland and on a hill, and I could peer into the old city from above to see the historic buildings and walkways on top of the very thick fortress walls.

The next day, I had to get groceries and, of course, Baileys for my coffee. I could see that I was up on a hill with roads far below and only ancient walkways leading to the main roads. These cobblestone walkways were winding and old, and some were more narrow than others, only pathways. They seemed labyrinthine, and the first several times, I missed a turn or two and ended up walking uphill for an extra half hour with my initial load of wine, chocolate, cheese, bread, yogurt, and Baileys. Then I missed the turn to the right. It was a mistake that made me a better person, or at least that was my rationale. After the many, many trips I made up and down these pathways to the main part of town, I finally didn't get lost any longer.

This was in November, so there were very few tourists, and it was cold much of the time. That was all okay with me because it gave me more freedom to explore. While I was buying my groceries that first day, I walked into an excursion office and immediately signed up for the fifty-dollar tour to Montenegro. There was a sign right outside their office, so I knew the price and locked in the deal. I figured fifty dollars for an all-day tour, including transportation, was great. I simply had to hike down from my apartment and catch the bus at the bottom of the hill since there was no way for any transportation to pick me up.

That night I was settled in on my porch overlooking the city for a quiet dinner with my wine when I heard a couple talking on the other side of the divider between the porches. I said hello, and we chatted for a while. Turns out, they were from London, enjoyed some of my wine, and laughed at me wearing Batman pajamas. I have very little modesty left at my age. They invited me for a drink the next night, but somehow I missed them. One of the advantages of being alone is that you can reach out and meet people easier than if you are with another person. Of course, the downside is that you are alone and not sharing the experiences.

I don't often go on excursions, but it seemed a good time to do it while I was there. It truly was a good experience, and I got to see several other walled cities, such as Kotor in Montenegro. The best thing about the entire day for me was lunch. These tours know where to take you for meals. We had people from Chicago, New York, and other countries with us sharing mussels for ten dollars and beers for one dollar. It was all a serendipitous experience that would never be repeated, but never forgotten, by such a diverse crowd. Then we dispersed back to our personal worlds when we returned.

I wanted to take a public bus for a few hours and return to my starting point. It's all about getting over fear and trusting myself—and trusting that the world is not out to get me. I took an all-day ride by the water, then returned safely to Dubrovnik.

Note to self: You are not queen of the universe. No one really cares to target you at this moment, so rise to the occasion.

THE NEXT DAY I DECIDED TO GO ON A KAYAK TRIP ALONG THE COAST AND to a nearby island. I would be part of a group and had to show up at the docking area in the early afternoon. I could do this. When I got to the area a few minutes ahead of time, all I could see were two-person kayaks, paddles, life vests, and men—or rather, young men in their late teens or early twenties. Great, I would be the poorest paddler in the group and probably wouldn't be able to keep up.

Note to self: That would be another *poor me* thought here.

It wasn't long before I realized I was one of three outsiders who were going with the group of young men on our kayak adventure. The other two were a couple in a boat together. Then there was me. The leader let it be known that I was "alone" and looked at the boys to see who might take me along. There were no takers. It felt like the last kid to be picked on a school sports team. I truly understood the situation and didn't take it personally—or at least too personally. At last one kid said he'd go with me, and I could see some of the smirks on his friends' faces. Poor fellow. In addition to everything else, he spoke French and only very little English, and my French was about nonexistent. So, I was in deep water with a guy I had never met and couldn't communicate with.

Turns out, these young men were all from Paris, France, and were garden workers. Their boss had brought them all on the trip to Croatia, and they seemed to be having a blast. The best news was that most of them had never kayaked before.

Note to self: Linda, one point for you. Enjoy your advantage.

We all started out, getting into the kayaks. I let my partner choose if he wanted the front or back, and luckily he chose the front so I could follow his strokes. Getting into the kayak was a trick for most of the fellows, but no one got dunked, mercifully. It was truly kind of comical, though I didn't laugh and kept my thoughts to myself as I watched them and slid into my kayak.

Once in the boats and on the water, these fellows had no clue about what to do. They kind of flailed around with paddles missing the water, only catching wind, and not coordinating anything at all. My partner didn't know what to do either, and I couldn't communicate to tell him what to do. All I could do was what I knew best: follow his lead by doing the same strokes he did.

My partner started paddling more evenly, and I matched his stroke, pulling the water as I did so. I was able to correct our position from where I sat, whereas he was doing the power strokes. He didn't really know what was happening, but he knew that we were out in front of the whole pack. We were going smoothly and learning to stroke slowly and powerfully. He turned back to look at me one time with a huge smile on his face and started waving to his buddies as we were leaving them in the dust—well, water.

It didn't take long for the other fellows to learn some of our tricks and catch up, but the boys all started poking fun at me and asking what questions they could about America. I smiled back at them and even entered some of the water fights they had once their confidence in kayaking emerged. The fellows apologized for getting me wet when we returned, and I just laughed, letting them know that I'd had a terrific time and wouldn't have missed it for the world. My thrill of the moment was when they said their grandmother would never do this! The world can be such a friendly place if I just let it be.

I took the memories from the afternoon with me as I headed home the next day.

CHAPTER 25

Driving in Italy

When my friend Kate agreed to go to Italy in 2016, we talked about who was going to drive the tiny rental car that was included in the deal. The deal I'd seen for $1,500 each was fairly good financially and included the plane tickets from Los Angeles, car rental in Italy, and four-star hotels in Tuscany. I coaxed Kate into the deal, and as she continued to ask questions, I could tell she was nervous not only about going to Europe for the first time but also about going with me.

I'd met Kate through Barb. She was Barb's best friend and became one of mine also. She was reliable, was able to take things in stride, and had the ability to laugh at odd situations that arose. Besides, she was one of my only friends who had the money to travel like I did.

To say the least, Kate was a great sport. I can be easy to travel with, but when my stress level goes up, my patience drops down and defensive armor comes on. Just getting the car after we landed was an adventure in itself. We waited in line with several other weary travelers. In general, I had not done much driving in Europe. What I had done was fairly uneventful, though it was usually out in the country with very few ways to get into trouble. Italy would be different.

We landed in Milan and picked up the rental car. The information from the travel agency stated that it would take about three and a half hours to get from the airport to Tuscany. It took us seven hours. Traffic was totally stopped, plus we encountered toll gates along the route and learned that the drivers in Italy were crazy. I mean, there had to be something in the water to make the locals drive crazily on the roads. It was my job to learn to deal with it for a week. It wasn't *Mission: Impossible* where I could decline the job at this point.

On that first day Kate and I were both tired, and the freeways were crowded—not a great setup. It was a Friday, so people were trying to get out of town, and everyone was driving fast when they weren't stopped. I noticed a lot of cars with scraped paint and small dents. What didn't help ease my mind was that I had run into another car recently in the US and had caused a few minor dents but thankfully no injuries.

Note to self: Keep alert.

WE FINALLY MADE IT TO TUSCANY, WHERE WE WOULD ENJOY AN INCREDible two-day hike along the coast, including starting the hike on a Friday afternoon and trusting that we could find a place to stay for the night in one of the small towns, as Judy and I often did.

That day, I drove down a very steep, winding road to the village, toward the starting point of the hike, but we came to a gate. When another car with a permit opened the gate, Kate yelled, "Go on through!" I did and was instantly sorry. This area was obviously for locals only, and it stated that at the entry. Now, I would have to turn around in a very tiny, one-way parking area and try to get back out.

I asked Kate to get out and see if someone would open the gate from this side, hoping to get out before any other traffic appeared. She ran to the people at the gate and begged someone to open it. Meanwhile, our car was facing uphill with a manual shift and I didn't want to stop for fear of how hard it would be to get started again. When the gate opened, I revved up the car and moved forward, yelling out the window to Kate, "Get in!"

She said, "Well, stop the car!"

"I can't!"

She fretted a second then jumped into the car as it was moving forward. We started laughing hysterically as I drove back up the hill to find a remote parking place. We had to walk an extra distance to get to the trailhead.

We started on the hike about two o'clock in the afternoon. We'd be hiking on an alternate route because the main route was closed for some reason. Turns out, the alternate route is really kind of gnarly, going straight up and straight down. In the next town we hiked to, Kate bought a pair of hiking poles to help her survive without injury. It hadn't occurred to her to bring poles even though she knew we would be hiking.

About seven at night, in the dark, I asked Kate if she was prepared to sleep in a doorway in the small town we were approaching. Who knew if there would be rooms left? I was only partly joking.

"Oh, sure, we can be homeless for the night if there's no alternative. It's a Friday night, by the way," she replied.

Yep, we were prepared to stay anywhere. I asked a group of three middle-aged men standing outside a small restaurant if they knew where the hostel was or if they knew of a room available in the village. The oldest, most rotund of the men seemed startled, thought for a second, and then waved his hands vigorously, saying, "No, no rooms. The town is totally sold out."

I shot a glance at Kate, whose mouth was open with shock. I had no expression on my face as I tried to digest what he'd said. The jovial fellow couldn't help but burst out laughing almost immediately. He was teasing us, and we had taken the bait, hook, line, and sinker. He asked the fellow beside him, "Do you have any more rooms available tonight?"

His friend looked at him, and then at us, then said, "Do you need the room for just one night?"

I nodded. "Yes."

"Then I have a room for one night for you—follow me and see if it is okay for you."

Thank you, universe, I thought. We were going to have a shelter for the night and avoid sleeping in a doorway.

The next day, we finished the hike and went to the train station to catch a ride back to the area where the car was parked. Getting a train ticket was exasperating, to say the least. We got in a line with ten other people trying to purchase tickets from a machine on the first floor. We tried and tried but couldn't get the machine to work. Worried about taking too much time while others waited, we finally went to the back of the line to wait and try again, still unsuccessfully, to get a ticket. Finally we decided to go upstairs and see if there was another way to get a ticket. Upstairs there was no ticket machine but a Real Person selling tickets, so we did it the easy way and bought the tickets we needed from him. From there, we easily got back to the town where we'd started our trek and drove several hours back to our hotel in Montecatini.

What would become known as the Famous Last-Day Car Ride began slowly enough. After breakfast, about eight thirty in the morning, we would have all day to get to Milan. We had to negotiate the one-way streets in Montecatini and find a gasoline station, a priority. The little Renault with the ring on the gearshift got good enough mileage, but between the cost of the gasoline and tolls, the costs were adding up. I usually pulled into the gas station on the wrong side and had to turn around to get the correct side with the gas cap toward the pump. That was a minor nuisance compared to everything else on the ride.

We had rented a GPS device to help us with directions throughout Italy, but we didn't totally trust it. We needed it to get us from Montecatini to the large town of Lucca and then to back roads in the mountains, back to Genoa, then to Milan. On paper, it sounded great. Just getting to the toll road was an adventure unto itself. We had to backtrack several times through towns because I kept missing the exit from the roundabout and landing on streets going ninety degrees out of the way. I tried to dismiss my frustration.

I drove, and Kate navigated as best she could given the maps we had. While they included all of Italy, they were not particularly detailed. Plus, sometimes the town names we expected were spelled differently or went by the last of three names for the town—like Florence appearing as *Firenze* on the map. Then we had trouble getting on the correct road to go the alpine route in the mountains. Once in a while, though, we were reassured with road signs that had correct road numbers.

We went through many towns with very small city centers—some were so small, we wondered if they really were villages at all. When leaving a town, sometimes there would be a sign with the name of a village on it and a red stripe through it. Interpretation: *You are now leaving such-and-such village.*

We stopped in one or two villages and welcomed the free parking. Most everyplace else we had been required paid parking. At the top of a beautiful hill looking to the other side of the mountains, we pulled into a lookout that had a restaurant underneath it, almost built into the hillside. There were several young folks in the tiny restaurant, but they shook their heads when we opened the door—not open for lunch yet. It would have been a beautiful place to eat, but they told us there were more places down the road.

About fifteen more minutes down the road, we saw an old building made of gray and brown rocks at the corner of an intersection. A small road led down the valley to the left, so we stopped at this point to see if this beautiful old stone building had a restaurant or not. A familiar beer sign was swinging in the wind, so it was a good bet they had some food too.

We went in, and a man directed us to sit at a table off by itself. There were men collecting in another room around a larger table, and apparently the restaurant wanted to keep us separated. Shortly, a blond woman came in, welcomed us, and asked if we wanted beer, wine, or water for lunch. Kate got the wine—no choice of type, just red. I was driving so had water, although I did sneak a bit of wine from Kate. The server brought us a bottle of wine with no label and a cork on the top, plus my glass of water.

The server, obviously an owner of the establishment, asked if we wanted spaghetti for dinner. I asked her if I could have a menu. She laughed and told me, "I serve you what we are having for the day." In other words, there were no choices. While Kate was in the restroom, I told her that Kate would have spaghetti and I wouldn't. I knew there would be more food coming, and I could pass on spaghetti.

Not long after that, the homemade spaghetti appeared, and Kate got back from the restroom just in time to enjoy it. She plowed through it without knowing there were other courses. We could hear the men, who seemed to be locals who took their noon meal there, laughing and asking for food as it was being passed around. They sounded like a good-hearted group.

There were three small pieces of white meat with a sauce that looked like hummus. Very strange. I cut them up and started eating them, telling myself that they were really delicious. Then I examined them more closely, looking at their particularly round shape, and finally decided they were probably cow intestines or stomach lining. I tried not to think too hard about what I was eating because, really, it was quite good.

To round out the meal, the server brought us bread, a huge chunk of cheese, and fresh fruit—a whole apple and pear—for dessert. When we got up to pay, we had no idea how much the bill would be. The cashier, who was also another server, asked how many drank wine. I sheepishly admitted, "Well, one of us drank more than the other."

He walked over to our table, picked up our unlabeled wine bottle, and brought it back to us. He spoke little English, something not uncommon with the older folks. He took the bottle, filled it back up most likely with local Chianti, and handed it to us. Our mouths dropped open. We weren't sure just what was happening, but it appeared that we were going to get the entire bottle for the lunch, and we could take it with us.

The fellow wrote us both out a bill for ten euros each, which was about twelve dollars for the large meal and the to-go wine. We took the wine back to the car as if it were a present from God almighty, putting it carefully between soft suitcases so it would make the trip safely. We left the establishment about one thirty p.m., with the next destination of Genoa.

From Genoa to Milan would be all expressway. I knew where the airport was on the map, so we started out. I expected traffic and crazies all around me again, so I asked Kate to tell me about all the weird people and situations in her family so I had something else to think about. She thought for a minute then started. I was riveted. She began with tales of her children, then went to her family of origin, and from there to her own life, basically covering all of her world. I asked questions once in a while and begged for more. As we got closer to Milan, I told her I appreciated all the entertainment with such amazing stories.

We started seeing signs for Milan. Kate yelled out for me to make the next turn on the roundabout because it said *Aeroporto*, but a bus was there almost blocking the exit, so I continued around the roundabout until I could exit. That's when things really went south. I should have known that I needed to explore that *Aeroporto* sign more and to listen to the GPS that was constantly telling us to make illegal U-turns.

I was getting frantic. I had no idea where we were, didn't trust the GPS even though we had dialed in the address of our hotel near the airport, and was heading for a meltdown. I decided to have the meltdown when we stopped at a gasoline station somewhere in the middle of Milan. I drove in, stopped the car, wrung my hands a little, and said, "I have no idea where we are or where we are supposed to go!"

Of course, Kate didn't either. We were on a tree-lined boulevard in a tiny gas station on the right side of the road, and I was starting to cry—like, really hard. I asked, probably *told*, Kate to get out of the car and to ask anyone who could speak a little English to get us headed in the right direction. She went into the office, then immediately turned around to the person at the pump. I could see them nodding once in a while, hands pointing away from us, and general agreements.

She came back saying they suggested we follow signs to *Linate* ahead, taking us to the airport. I questioned it again, ripped the Milan page from the Lonely Planet guidebook, and left to talk with the men myself. At this point, they were annoyed that we didn't trust the advice they'd originally given to us. I wasn't sure about my own *name* at that point.

We left the gas station and started down the large street with landscaped areas in the middle of the road. I would see a *Linate* sign and try to follow it, but it would disappear or I was in the wrong lane or I would miss it. At one point I tried to turn around. I turned to my left, drove where other cars were parked, and started to make a U-turn. The car scratched bottom as we went over a large curb to get down and into the lane I wanted. Kate's face turned white, and then she broke out in laughter. I could do no less, so I broke into laughter too, with hope that the rental agency wouldn't see any scratches on the car upon return. I told Kate that I had looked at the map and would follow my nose at this point.

Shortly after the laughter, disaster struck again. We ended up in a bad area. We could tell because the bars didn't seem upscale, and neither did the people nearby. I tried to see if I could hail a taxi that we could follow to the airport. No luck. Then I saw two women and thought, *Maybe two women would help two women.* So I tried to pull myself together and ask them if they could help with us a map so we could get to Linate.

They did stop and eventually said they would hop in the car and help us get on track since it was difficult to explain. I started crying again because of their kindness. Meanwhile, Kate was saying, "The GPS has it—I think we're okay!" The women conferred with Kate a minute, and then they smiled and waved goodbye. Our saviors were leaving, and I still wasn't sure about where we were. There was never a chance to see the street signs, even if you could find them quickly enough.

We drove farther, and I got lost again. I was beyond tears at this point. I saw a lady on the street and decided to ask her directions. I pulled into a street as if I were turning onto it. Immediately a car behind me started honking like crazy. The woman we were talking with gave them the finger and then stopped traffic. I can't make this stuff up; it's too amazing. She tried to get us back on track again, but it was still bewildering.

Kate and I wandered around a lot, found a few signs to follow, and after hours of travel, pulled into the Linate Airport and returned the car. The car rental place didn't look like the place where we had picked up the car, but at that point, anything could have changed. We took everything out of the trunk and set it down on the ground. The fellow dealing with returns looked over the car, agreed that it had no scrapes, and gave us the final contract as we gathered our things quickly and were off to find a shuttle to our hotel.

Once outside the actual airport, we put everything down again and tried to find someone to ask about hotel shuttles. Kate found a young man who was getting off work, and he tried to help but couldn't. I decided to go on a bus and ask a young woman sitting in the bus about our plight. I showed her the name and address of the hotel. She shook her head, saying there was no shuttle. I had hoped that the hotel would have a shuttle, but I hadn't expected it. Then she started saying something that scared me.

When I finally understood her, she was telling me that we were at the *wrong airport*. We had come to Linate Airport, the one I had seen on the map, and we really needed to be at the Malpensa Airport, *about seventy miles away*. It took me a minute to recuperate from that news. It was about eight p.m., and Kate and I were at the wrong darned airport.

I was astounded. I didn't know what to say or do, but just for a minute. I went back to where Kate was talking with the young man and told her the news. She didn't say a word, very unlike Kate. My wheels went into gear and I asked the young man if there was a bus he knew about that went from one airport to the other. No, he didn't think so. I asked about other means of transportation. He said that we could take a bus into town and then the train to the airport, but it would take a long time.

Kate re-awakened. "*No way*," she began. "We are *not* taking buses and trains to the other airport. We are taking a taxi, and that's the end of it." We hailed a taxi and were off, with no idea of the fare. The little box with the fare displayed just continued ticking away, and we didn't care—or maybe I cared a little.

The meter got over one hundred dollars and kept going. We were all talking on this lengthy trip, as Kate seemed to be settling into the knowledge that we would soon be at our hotel. I was not as settled as Kate. I kept my eyes on the road since it was dark and there were still scary drivers out there. As the driver and Kate were talking, I saw something strange on the freeway ahead of us. It looked to me as if cars were stopped in the middle of the freeway. When I could see it better, there actually were three cars stopped, and we were heading right into them.

"*Stop!*" I yelled to the driver. "*Look ahead,*" I said as I pointed. He put on the brakes and then maneuvered forward between two cars on our left that had just had a collision with a third car on our right. All three cars were stopped on the freeway, and people were just starting to get out of their cars. The accident had just happened, and we were the first of the cars following them to come across the scene. The driver decided stopping would be too hazardous, so going forward made sense. Kate and I were both grateful to the driver for getting through the accident with no further problems, and without hitting anyone or any other car.

Kate and I were speechless and couldn't think of anything else that could go wrong that day. There was too much to remember, to consider, to be grateful for.

We eventually got in the vicinity of the hotel where we had reservations, and it took all three of us to keep our antennae up and spot the place. Once we arrived, Kate gave the driver her credit card for the $150 ride, and it didn't work. We each rolled our eyes, and I gave the nervous driver my card. It worked. We brought in all our belongings, registered at the hotel, and got up to the room to enjoy the almost-free bottle of wine we had brought so far during the day. It wasn't there. We looked through everything, and then surmised that it had to have been left at the first airport—the wrong airport—and the car rental place probably enjoyed it. Bummer.

We went downstairs to the reception area where there was a bar and ordered two glasses of wine. We told our story to a few people who would listen, took our glasses upstairs with us, and had those two glasses of wine. Because it was late, we went to bed soon and started reliving the tale for a few minutes.

Kate started giggling as we recalled brief moments of the journey. "I couldn't believe that woman gave the finger to the driver!" Laughter. Then she said, "Who would have believed that trip would take so damned long?" More laughter.

I replied, "It wouldn't have been so bad if I didn't drive through Austria to get to Milan." We laughed so hard, I worried we might get a phone call about a noise complaint. Minutes and minutes of belly laughs, so very good for us.

We took the hotel's shuttle to the airport the next morning. I waited with our luggage as Kate walked around the airport. She came back with an excited expression on her face, saying, "I just met a guy at the bar who said we are the famous women who drove to the wrong airport! He said we were on television!"

I shook my head. I knew no idiot would believe such a story and make it newsworthy and that Kate was most likely talking with someone at our hotel who had heard about the whole encounter. Secretly, I started looking on the web for a news story about two crazy US women.

As a fitting ending, four months after the trip, I had a Visa charge showing I had gotten a traffic ticket somewhere on our fateful driving trip, because a camera caught me. A year later, the actual ticket arrived at my mailbox.

CHAPTER 26

Spain—The Camino

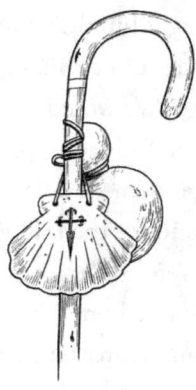

WALK FIVE HUNDRED MILES IN SPAIN? NO WAY. **WHILE THE CAMINO DE** Santiago was on my mind, it was inconceivable to me to walk that many miles at once. I watched the movie *The Way* with Martin Sheen again. *Well, maybe I could walk that far.* My mind was playing tricks on me now. I had never hiked five hundred consecutive miles at one time, so of course, the challenge became a mission.

Judy was in as soon as I mentioned the trip, but then we both balked at the amount of road walking there would be. We were used to trails and off-trail hiking. But the Camino kept creeping back into our thoughts, especially after Judy experienced losses close to her heart. Hiking the Camino has traditionally been a spiritual pilgrimage. It would be a spiritual journey for her because of deaths in her family the previous year. It would be a spiritual journey for me—well, I needed to find out why on the trip. The trip was on—we'd leave in just a few months.

Judy had a high school graduation to attend, and I had a fiftieth high school reunion to go to, so our dates were set between those events. The trip would be from mid-June until later July in 2016. We would have five weeks to do the hike, including two emergency days in case we needed them. We never knew what would come around the corner and cause two seventy-year-olds—well, one seventy-year-old and one almost seventy—to miss a step, or two or three. We had a guidebook that suggested about that many days to hike the eight hundred kilometers, approximately five hundred miles. It would average out to hiking about fifteen miles per day, if we were up to the challenge. We would be on the French Way, the one starting in France and ending in Santiago, Spain. This is the most common route, and I wanted to experience the real deal, both so I could understand what a pilgrimage is and also to see the traditional cathedrals, paths, and people along the way. If we were able to continue the walk all the way to the ocean, Finisterre, it would be a bonus, but the main goal was Santiago.

Friends said, "Oh, that sounds great. You can do it!" even though their shaking heads were saying, *No way!*

In order for me to make the trip, I would have to get mentally and physically prepared. I had admitted to myself after the Manaslu trip that I was definitely mentally and physically out of shape. It was hard for me to accept the concept of getting older and questioning my abilities. Before this point in time, I had been more sure of myself—more *everything* about myself. It had been easier to get into shape quickly for trips when I was younger, or to make it through trips without getting in shape. It was becoming more difficult each year going forward. It was a challenge I wanted to face squarely.

We would fly to Paris, where we would take trains and buses to the starting point of the trek in southern France, and our return ticket would take us from Santiago, Spain, through Istanbul, Turkey. Our path was set. We decided to make no other reservations.

Now I had to determine if I could physically do the trip. I figured information about my body and physical condition would help my mental state. Most of whatever I had achieved through the years had been based on my mind getting data and then preparing my body for what I was mentally asking it to do—the mind and body acting in unison. In this case, I wanted to know about my heart, my knees, my cholesterol, and my general health.

Note to self: Be your own advocate.

IN SHORT TIME, I ARRANGED A LOT OF DOCTOR APPOINTMENTS. ONE BY one, the doctors told me I was fine. My knees were good, and the doctor recommended a drug to help alleviate any discomfort from a cyst in my knee and the injury in my back that still lingered. An angiogram showed that my heart was fine for the most part, and my cholesterol—well, shall we say, it still was high through heredity. I was advised to double the dose of my statin drug, but when I tried to do that, the painful reactions in my joints were too much, so I kept the dosage the same as it had been for years, since I was going on such a strenuous trip. Hiking five hundred miles would obviously help my cholesterol levels. I would double the dose after the trip, if it was still necessary.

I added hearing aids to my list of things to do/check out/get. One ear registered much more hearing loss than the other. The technician was concerned and said there could be an explanation for the difference. I was sure it was because one ear canal was more twisted than the other and therefore plugged up with earwax more often, but she said it could have been because of a former stroke, or possibly a brain tumor, or some other issue—all scary possibilities, especially after my "stroke" scare in Mongolia—so she referred me to a specialist. After a battery of tests, including an MRI to see if I had ever had a stroke or currently had a brain tumor, I was told all was absolutely fine with my ears and, more importantly, with my head.

I had nothing to worry about and had a really clean bill of health at my age. Now I had to plug that information into my head and believe it so my mind could make my body do what I was asking of it. Not easy, but necessary.

Note to self: Remember your Buddhism. Nothing is permanent; suffering is optional. Rise above all this and get on with living.

The day we were to leave, my son-in-law was kind enough to take us to LAX. Judy and I got out of the car, and I said, "We look like we're homeless, don't we?" He rolled his eyes, gave us hugs, then left us as he was shaking his head and silently laughing.

Judy said, "The last words out of Dave's mouth when I left were 'Don't do anything stupid!'" Her husband knew we had a tendency to get into trouble, especially when he heard about things once we returned. Judy and I had long joked that this was Dave's Stupid-O-Meter. We were sure it would have registered when we went into the bordello in Patagonia and also when we hitchhiked all over Corsica one year, but of course he never knew any details until we got back. Judy would sometimes whisper to me, "I'm glad Dave doesn't know about this!" On this trip, we would imagine the meter's alarm sounding several times.

Day one, we flew to Paris directly from LAX. Arriving there in the morning, we had several hours to find the train station in the airport. I had purchased tickets to Bayonne, where we would have to stay the night before the 7:45 a.m. bus to Saint-Jean-Pied-de-Port, our starting point in the Pyrenees. It was in Bayonne at ten thirty p.m. that Dave's Stupid-O-Meter came into play for the first time on our trip.

If possible, we were going to stay overnight in the train/bus terminal once we got to Bayonne. Apparently another young man was also thinking of staying in the station at night, because he started spreading out gear. All three of us settled down in chairs near the front window.

It wasn't long before I heard a dog growl. Judy and I woke and glanced at each other, then at the young man who was on the floor. I slowly turned to look over my shoulder and saw a man in a uniform appearing rather gruff, holding a large German shepherd with a big black muzzle on its snout. The dog was not happy with us, held back only by this officer. We asked if the station remained open all night. A simple "No, you must move" was the response. With the dog ready to attack us, all three of us quickly gathered our things and walked out the front door as he locked, chained, and barred everything behind him.

Dilemma. Where would we stay the rest of the night? The third man in our little group glanced at us and then ambled off to another area, where we saw him claim a bench. There was another person or two, probably homeless, wandering around. We weren't homeless, just without a home for the night. By this time it was after eleven p.m., so Judy and I talked quietly to each other.

"Well, what do you think we should do?" I asked Judy.

"I don't know." That was about as truthful as you could get.

I thought for a minute and then glanced back at Judy. I cracked a smile as I saw she was starting to quietly relocate all her money from her waist pack to a pocket in her shirt, to a lower pants pocket, to inside her bra, to any hidden place she could find. I started doing the same thing.

Finally I said, "This is registering on Dave's Stupid-O-Meter, ya know."

She smiled and said, "You're so right. I don't want to stay here overnight. There's no place to sit, it's too scary to sleep, and we'll be zombies tomorrow."

We decided to walk a little bit and search for a hotel. Generally, hotels near train or bus stations are sketchy at best, but this late at night, we had few choices. We walked about two blocks and saw nothing, even though someone had told us the hotel was "right there." We walked back to be sure we wouldn't lose sight of the train station. There were a few restaurants still open, and we peered into one of them.

Just then we saw two women walking. I remembered them from train rides earlier in the day. We smiled at one another, and the older lady said, "We keep seeing you on the trains. Are you doing the Camino?"

I nodded. "Yes."

She said, "My daughter and I are here to do the Camino also. Wouldn't you know, we were able to get the last hotel room?"

I looked at Judy, and she gave me a brief nod. "Well, we just got into town, too, and were going to stay overnight in front of the depot, but we're a little frightened and wonder if you might consider letting us share some of the cost and stay in your room tonight? We'll sleep on the floor!" The request was simple enough, and we held our breath, as we were almost out of options. They agreed and told us they would let us in the room and then would be going out to get something to eat. We just wanted the bed, floor, or anything safe.

We talked with the hotel receptionist, paid a little bit more for the room, and then gave our saviors money to cover our part of the hundred-dollar room. It was probably the largest room payment we made on the trip, except for two very special hotels. We slept great, had our own beds, and put Dave's Stupid-O-Meter away for a while.

The next morning, Judy and I boarded the 7:45 a.m. bus for Saint-Jean-Pied-de-Port along with other hopeful Camino pilgrims. Once we got off the bus, we were official *peregrinos*, "pilgrims" in Spanish. I was drawn to all the tourist shops that lined the streets, and Judy had to gently remind me that all the crafts we were seeing would be at the end of the trip also. She knew that the heavier my pack was, the slower I walked. For the most part, she was right; however, we were in the middle of Basque Country. This was a special region of southern France and northern Spain that truly considered itself a separate country. Graffiti on walls proclaimed, *You are NOT in France*, and *You are NOT in Spain*. I had wanted to visit this area for a long time because of what I'd heard about the food, never-ending wine, and camaraderie among the people of the region. But Judy was right—we needed to be on our way.

One of the first hiccups in our trip occurred before we even really started the trail. Judy tried to get money from the local ATM because she had no euros since we had not exchanged money at the airport. Traditionally, the ATMs will give a better exchange rate and have fewer fees than the foreign currency exchange booths at airports. It really didn't matter because as many times as Judy tried, she was unsuccessful and the screen kept flashing *Contact your bank*. Neither Judy's nor my phone would call the United States from Europe, so we would have to beg someone to let us pay for a call on their phone. At this point, though, we were anxious to get on the trail and felt we had enough to get by to begin with, so that would be a matter for another day.

We bought a few things to eat. I bought one or two very small items, and then we were off to find the Pilgrim Office. As soon as we started questioning people, everyone pointed up the hill and said, "Thirty-nine." I didn't want to go up a hill since I knew we'd be facing climbing the Pyrenees for the next few days, but it was the thing to do—the office to start in—so we headed up the hill. Soon we learned to start keeping our eyes out for the scallop shell symbol of the Camino, and there it was on a wall outside building number 39.

Judy and I went inside, and I started scouring the office for trinkets. Not disappointed, I picked up a scallop shell from a pile and asked how much it was. "Nothing," I was told. "The conch shells are free, a gift to start your trip." I took one and asked Judy if she wanted one for her pack.

Judy tilted her head, which I thought said, *Not really, but I'll do it.* She said, "Just pick one out for me."

We each tied one on our packs and were more or less ready. We had a great time talking with the receptionist who helped us. She was incredibly pleasant, knowledgeable, and very kind—maybe because we seemed so old compared to the younger crowd. It was amazing to me that she could talk with pilgrim after pilgrim and keep her friendly demeanor. We were able to get our first credential, a folder that could be stamped along the way, showing that we had actually walked everywhere and didn't skip any sections by taking buses. She proudly gave us our first stamp in the small booklet.

We started hiking about noon, much later than anticipated. The map showed uphill terrain, but we were near a road that a car could navigate, so it wasn't that hard a climb. Still, even with training, the backpack was heavy, the trail was uphill, and I tried my best not to whine.

We made it to the last hostel on the road. From here to the next village of Roncesvalles—and the next hostel—for the most part, the trek would be a trail over the Pyrenees. This hostel was inviting, so we stopped for a beer on the outside deck. Because it was about three thirty in the afternoon, we knew we couldn't make it all the way to the top of the mountains and down to the hostel at the bottom without fighting darkness. We decided to stay at the hostel for thirty-five euros for a bunk bed, communal dinner, and breakfast.

The dining room had long tables with everyone seated on benches, making the meal feel very communal and comfortable. The dinner was typical Basque food—soup, meat, beans, an amazing cake, and all the wine we could drink. I mean, they just put bottles of wine on the tables and we could have as much as we wanted. Considering what we had done to get to this remote place, I wanted a lot of wine. After the meal, we were told that it was their practice for pilgrims to go around the table introducing themselves with their names and destinations. Of course we were all on the Camino, but not everyone had the goal to hike the entire trail at one time. I proudly got up and told the group that we were going to Santiago and then on to Finisterre, to the ocean. That was the goal, anyhow.

The room got louder as the wine bottles were emptied. Someone spotted a rainbow, and we all went outside just in time to see a double rainbow, which I interpreted as an indication that we would be successful on our journey. The group dispersed to go to bed early, and I fell asleep easily because of the wine. According to Judy, I snored a great deal that night and battled demons enough to say, "Oh shit!" once.

The next day, we easily crossed the border into Spain as we went over the Pyrenees. The trails were mercifully not too wet this day, and although a lady just starting the Camino had recently fallen and broken her wrist on this stretch, it was an easy though slow journey for us. The highest elevation we reached was at Col de Lepoeder at about 4,700 feet, not very high by Judy's and my standards. We descended into the tiny town of Roncesvalles, where the most popular place to stay was a monastery converted to house the hundreds of peregrinos who walked the French Way—this particular path for the Camino de Santiago—daily. Judy and I had two bunk beds, and the place was amazingly clean, with many people available to answer questions for us novice pilgrims. We signed in and were asked if we wanted dinner that night. Apparently the town is so small that the two restaurants in town need to know the number of people who will order dinner so they can ensure there's enough food to go around.

This time, instead of long tables with everyone seated on benches, this dining area had tables for four, so Judy and I were joined by a couple who spoke no English. Sign language of some sort became the order of the day. Dinner was the peregrino meal, one that we became very familiar with. It would always include a choice of soup, salad, or another appetizer; a main meal of fish (often trout), chicken, pork, or another meat with vegetables; dessert of flan, ice cream, or another choice; and water *or* wine. Wine flowed like water, and I got used to drinking about half a bottle most nights. I cut myself some slack on the trip since I was hiking fifteen or more miles per day. Occasionally I would eat an entire bar of milk chocolate. It didn't take us long to get the hang of the journey.

As my euros started to run low, the mission of calling Judy's bank was becoming more important. I started scanning the crowd of young people sitting at tables in the large self-serve kitchen to see if I could spot an American with the capability of calling the States. Additionally, the "target" had to look friendly and seem as if he or she would feel pity for us older folks. I saw a woman who fit the description.

I pointed her out to Judy, and we sat down beside the beautiful young girl. Rather than going through small talk, I just plain came out and said, "We're having trouble with Judy's bank, and she can't get any money from the ATMs. Do you have a phone that will call the US, and if so, can we pay you to make a call to her bank for us?" We learned her name was Kathy, and she was really the first friend we made along the trail. It would prove to be an amazing encounter with an amazing young lady who was hiking the trail with her mother.

Since we were not sure how to make the phone call in a foreign country, Kathy made the call for us, and when connected, she handed the phone to Judy. Judy pleaded with her bank to help her overseas. Although it seemed like hours before the problem was resolved, the call was probably only twenty minutes and the young person at the other end did some true magic to make the card work the next time Judy tried to get money. It all came down to passwords.

As we made our way to Pamplona, about fifty-seven miles into our journey, it rained. We'd brought our rain jackets, but most people were using ponchos to cover their packs and themselves. I wanted one. We stopped in a *tienda*, a small shop with many things that the villagers could use under one roof. The store usually had fruits, vegetables, cheeses, bread, a variety of packaged goods, and of course, chocolates. Often they also had things that people passing through might be searching for, such as plastic ponchos. Judy and I purchased a couple for about six dollars each and put them on as the rain started to fall more heavily. We had brought umbrellas also, but with the wind, they were likely to collapse, so we voted for the ponchos instead. Besides, the umbrellas were more effective against the hot sun than rain.

We hiked on, and the rain continued. The trail became more muddy and dangerous, and as we passed a trailer offering coffee and other drinks, Judy asked if I wanted to stop to get something. I said no, walked on a few steps, and then stopped. "Well, yes, I do," I told Judy. "I would love a cup of sangria." When walking past the vendor, I had spied a sign for one-dollar cups of sangria. We ordered two and downed them quickly. It seemed to make sense to the other folks stopped there, and soon they were drinking too while we were on our second. We became the Sangria Mamas while our new friends were smiling and taking pictures during the downpour.

On day four, we hiked into Pamplona, the most famous city for the running of the bulls. A beautiful, old walled city, it seemed there was history wherever we turned. At one shop, I stopped and asked, "On which streets do the bulls run and chase all the idiots?" The shopkeeper looked up at me in amazement and said, "You're standing on one of them, the main one."

I had left my water containers at our previous night's hostel, the same place where I'd left my brain that day. I had a choice of buying a plastic bottle of water or buying a bota bag, since Pamplona was famous for them. I voted for the bota bag, and after buying a cheap one that the store owner most definitely assured me would hold both water and wine, I got the deluxe one made in Pamplona by the Las Tres Z.Z.Z. company for twenty-five dollars. I was annoyed at myself for settling for the cheaper version originally. I deserved the best I could get, and I had to let my cheapness go.

Again, I was assured that the bag would hold either water or wine, not just wine that the most expensive bags hold. However, I was cautioned to go online for instructions to take care of the bota bag, because if handled right, a good bota bag can be handed down for many generations.

By this time, Judy and I were tired of our backpacks. They were heavy, and we still weren't used to carrying them. People were telling us about different possibilities to handle the situation, and we learned that we could have the packs transported for us. We could put five euros in an envelope and attach it to our packs. We would leave the packs at our hostel, and whichever agency we used would pick up the packs and transport them to the place we indicated on the envelope. We'd hired porters in other countries, so why not get help with our bags here too? The problem with this system, though, was that we had to be sure of where we would be staying for the next night because if we didn't make it, we'd have no supplies. Someone else told us about an option to take a box of stuff we wouldn't need to the post office in one of the larger towns and send it to ourselves in care of general delivery in Santiago, near the end of the trek. Apparently there was a special rate for pilgrims. We opted to have our packs shipped on a daily basis.

Because of our age, it wasn't easy for either Judy or me to climb to the top bunk bed when we were issued one. Besides, we had to go to the bathroom at night occasionally, and it could be a death-defying feat with the sketchy or nonexistent stairs to the top bunk. We agreed to take turns with the top bunks, but that meant I would have to do things such as use my pillow to whack Judy in the face to ask her to get a chair so I could get down to go to the bathroom in the middle of the night.

One time I tipped a hostel greeter and asked for two lower beds. She took us up several flights of stairs, which was the norm, but then she unlocked what seemed like a jail cell at the top. Inside, she motioned to two lower beds that we could use. It was a jail cell because it was where all the supplies were kept under lock and key. Apparently we appeared old enough and wiped out enough to receive mercy and be trusted with the supplies.

We found mercy throughout the trip. Many of the hostel owners and greeters would assign us lower bunks, especially once I learned to give them a forlorn smile when asking about the beds.

I started seeing signs for a winery along the trail. I didn't know enough Spanish to understand all the details until I finally saw a sign in perfect English that said the building we were passing near Los Arcos was a true winery. Even then, I didn't have any idea what was coming around the corner. There, we saw over a dozen people with cups or bottles out to catch the free wine coming out of a fountain. Understandably, everyone was extremely happy.

CHAPTER 27

Camino, Continued

DAVE'S STUPID-O-METER WENT OFF AGAIN WHEN WE WERE HIKING INTO Logroño. We had hiked about 120 miles by then. Even though we did all the right things, the heat introduced a danger. We got up at six a.m. and started hiking by six thirty a.m., which was good, especially for me. The problem was that the day was hot—very hot—and we had a long way to go to get to the large town. As we descended into the town, the weather got hotter. At one point, we saw a police car pass us on a dusty dirt road, and I imagined his duty was to either pick up dead bodies or give water to those who really needed it. The ones needing help would be the ones who hadn't really understood the effect of blistering heat, or the ones who didn't care about it when they should have. In our case, we were experienced but miserable. Then Judy decided to tell me that her mother had had a heat stroke and had never been right since. I understood her very real concern. I was worried for my own safety too, and was hydrating as much as possible. The expensive bota bag and I became close friends.

The hike to Logroño was very long, and the trail took us on a sandy path under the main roads. We, like scared little rabbits, ran from one underpass to the next one because they were the only places we could find shade in the hundred-degree heat. It was a good thing we had the underpasses because they were major rest places during that hike. We would get to one and drop, exhausted, onto whatever curb or piece of cement we could find. Then we would shake our heads in disbelief at the heat. It was the first time we started wondering if we could do the rest of the hike if the heat continued. It was three in the afternoon, and Dave's Stupid-O-Meter was again brought to mind.

Eventually we made it into town and found a church. Almost instantly when we entered, the temperature dropped at least ten degrees, and we just sat on a bench inside the church to cool our body temperatures. These churches were mostly made of large stone blocks, plus there were few windows inside, so they were much cooler than any other place. Whenever the temperatures were rising, it became our mission to find the local church.

We found the Logroño hostel and booked our two beds, then asked about our backpacks that had been shipped. "No, they aren't delivered here," we were told. Apparently they were all delivered to a central spot and we had to hike to that spot to retrieve them. It wasn't a difficult walk, but it was another kink in the works. That was the same night that we had a glass of wine and a big dish of ice cream with chocolate chips on top for dinner in the large downtown plaza.

Note to self: You so deserve this. Good for you for treating yourself.

THE NEXT DAY, WE WERE UP MUCH EARLIER AND STARTED OUT TO BEAT the heat as much as possible. We couldn't begin in the dark, though, because it would be too easy to get lost, particularly in the big cities. It had been confusing to get into Logroño, and it was just as difficult to leave the city. We dropped our packs at the place we'd picked them up, hoping they would be collected and arrive at our next destination unscathed. Fortunately, they would.

All the way, we were meeting new people. There were Kathy and her mother; the two crazy South Carolina ladies; the purple-highlighted-hair mom named Kelly and her fifteen-year-old daughter, Alexa; and mom Dana and daughter-going-to-college Rhena. We'd pass each other on the trails and see each other at hostels along the way. One day Judy and I rounded a corner, and there, sitting at the local bar and restaurant, were the Southern ladies, Kelly and Alexa, and Dana and Rhena. They were just enjoying the afternoon, having coffee, and gabbing.

We didn't have far to go, so we sat down and joined them for an hour, which turned into two hours and then three hours. We had such fun talking and enjoying the day. Still, though, I felt guilty for sitting there for so long. I had to remind myself that our days were supposed to be like this and I needed to enjoy it. During the encounter, I tried to take myself out of the situation so I could really soak in the experience from a distance to get perspective. Eight dusty, dirty, healthy, amazing women from the US were sitting together, laughing together, and strengthening bonds in a small town somewhere in the middle of northern Spain.

I thought back to that little bedroom I'd grown up in and the fear of the world I'd held on to for so long. Although it felt familiar, it was so far from my experience of the world now, it was almost foreign.

Note to self: Your world doesn't have to be big and scary. Sitting and laughing with friends is *what life is all about.*

A FEW DAYS LATER, JUDY AND I CAME INTO GRAÑÓN, A SMALL VILLAGE with a very special parish. We had hiked about 147 miles now. I was told later that this parish was one of the most popular places to stay on the Camino. I looked at my list of hostels in the town and saw that it didn't give a price for a room there, but it did say *donativo*. I learned it meant that you gave what you could for the room—in other words, a donation. I was excited about the experience, and Judy was always game.

We got to the church and walked inside. There was a service going on, so we started to back out of the church but the parishioners encouraged us to stay. The church was so crowded that there were people standing in the back, where we'd entered. The priests were conducting communion, coming down the aisle our way. I was grateful for the experience but decided not to block the doorway any longer and exited the church.

Outside I asked several people where the peregrinos hostel was, and everyone kept pointing to the back of the church. We made our way there and found a large wooden door totally open, and inside we could see the exposed large rocks that made up the building. The entrance looked more like a dungeon to me than a church building, but we saw a small sign on the outside wall that said this was the correct building. As we entered, there were two huge sacks of potatoes, much like you might envision a large garbage bag of leaves, with our backpacks on top. Another day of success with the forwarded packs.

We rounded the corner with our packs and went up a spiral stone staircase. The staircase continued my feeling of being in a dungeon, but it was all darned intriguing. We saw that many hiking boots had been deposited on a ledge halfway up, understanding by now that we were to take off our shoes when entering many buildings to help keep the trail dirt out. We went up the steep staircase to the third floor and were greeted warmly by a smile from a young Canadian woman. This was totally off the chart for us.

She explained that she had completed the Camino the prior year and because it had been so life changing for her, she had decided to donate two weeks a year to the hostels that needed volunteers. She had ended up in this one in Grañón, and she was grateful she was here because it was one of the best she had stayed in the prior year. She told us about making a donation, that there were mats to sleep on on the floor—no bunk beds—that we were expected to help with dinner, which was provided by the money deposited the day before by pilgrims, and to wash our dishes. She went on to say that we would go to the church's second story by a secret doorway and talk about our Camino after dinner, that there would be a celebration of chocolate that night, that all the local children would be out building bonfires, and lastly, that breakfast would be available before we left in the morning. It sounded like a bargain to us, plus quite an experience.

We set our packs down in the area to rest and take it all in. About five p.m., a man with a small guitar walked in and was greeted warmly by the Canadian hostess. She whispered to me, "He's been coming here the past three days and playing his music. I don't understand why he's staying so long!" The Frenchman came in and started talking with the pilgrims gathering for the night. We had people from Hungary, Germany, the US, Montenegro, Croatia, and more. The Frenchman wanted to know what kind of songs he could sing for the group. He had a small computer, like a tablet, and was able to locate music and lyrics from all the countries with it. He became an instant hit, and we all gathered around to start singing. For the US folks, he sang John Denver's "Take Me Home, Country Roads," a song that I couldn't get out of my mind for weeks after that.

During the singing, which went on for three hours, Judy and I chopped onions, potatoes, and anything else the staff handed to us. We stayed out of the small kitchen because it only needed one or two people in there at one time. In the meantime an amazing stew was simmering in a huge kettle. It reminded me of a witch's brew, complete with large stirring stick. About eight p.m., as promised, we had a salad and stew. By this time we were all laughing and having a great time because of the hours of singing. Yes, there was wine with dinner also.

Note to self: You received a gift tonight. Welcome it.

SHORTLY AFTER DINNER, THE GROUP DID THE DISHES IN A LONG ASSEMBLY line. Judy and I kind of backed out of the duties since we had cut up so many vegetables. Shortly after the last dish was dried, we went through the secret entrance to the second story of the church. Candles had been lit, and the balcony looked out into the church. We were asked to pass a candle around to each other and say something about the Camino, if we chose to. While many were silent, I said that I was very happy to have my best friend with me and that I was proud of myself for going so far at this point.

When we got to one of the next hostels, our packs were MIA. We'd learned by then that the hostels weren't always the delivery location—they were usually taken to a central place, like a bar, much like they had been in Logroño. When we went to the bar, there was a note in Spanish on the door. As much as I could make out was that the owner was on vacation and wouldn't be back for several days. That left a huge question for just where the packs had been delivered, if they'd been delivered at all. It meant I needed to find another kind soul who would loan us their telephone to see if the main operator could figure out what had happened to the packs.

Eventually I asked someone to call the office, and the person there told me that the packs had been delivered to a different hostel where they could be picked up. We made our way to the place and then watched as many pilgrims, including us, retrieved packs while the owners looked on, hoping someone would want a room. None stayed at their place for the night. I felt bad for their hurting business when they'd done a service to let our bags be delivered there, but we'd already paid for our beds in another hostel. There were so many places to stay, and we couldn't stay in them all.

Note to self: Sounds like undeserved Midwestern guilt on your part.

THE NEXT DAY, AS WE STARTED TO WALK, I THOUGHT ABOUT PLANTING A seed in Judy's thought process. I started slowly, "I was thinking…we could get a box and send the stuff we don't need ahead to general delivery in Santiago. That way we can carry our packs and not worry about where they are. We need to do it in a large city, and we're heading right for Burgos." Judy jumped right on the bandwagon. Getting the bags to Santiago would still be on the way to Finisterre, if we had time to hike there.

So our next mission was to find a box and get to the post office. Boxes were available all over the large, beautiful city, so we collected two. We wanted to see the city, so we stopped hiking about noon that day to allow time to get the shipment off, check in to the new municipal hostel, and see the city.

We got to our assigned beds, mercifully both lower bunks. Our next task was to spread out somewhere to go through our packs and take out items to reduce weight. I went outside on a bench to start the process and immediately wished my box was bigger. Judy and I jointly decided not to camp, so our pads and small tent went into the boxes, along with my two-pound sleeping bag. I was able to find one that weighed only a pound at an outdoor store we passed in Burgos. I also bought a very red rain jacket, much better than my blue poncho, that fit over my pack. Little did I know Judy wanted one also. It took us another few weeks to find another one for her.

We filled the boxes and started for the post office in Burgos. One problem was that we weren't really sure where the post office was, but I knew it was a long way from where we were staying, and I took my map. We were told that the post office is normally open twelve hours, from 8:30 a.m. until 8:30 p.m.

The boxes were heavy, so we had the challenge of carrying awkward, large boxes a long distance, plus the boxes were open because we had no tape for them. Judy had more trouble than I did because she is much shorter than I, which meant that the box was larger and more awkward for her. I would take a few steps until I heard, "Hey, I'm stopping. I can't carry this thing anymore for a minute."

If it hadn't been so hard to carry the darned boxes, and if it hadn't been so hot, and if it hadn't been so far, it would have been a piece of cake. As it turned out, it was a lively, hot, slow, and darned funny trip. We overran the post office, and luckily we were smart enough to stop and ask some people where it was. They pointed out a building about a block back, where we had just been. Judy gave me a glance, but that was my only punishment for the overshot.

We made it into the post office and took a ticket number for service. There were no other customers in the building, so we were surprised when it took another fifteen minutes for our number to be called. When we got up to the window, the first thing I asked for was to buy tape so we could complete taping up our boxes before sending them off.

"I'm sorry, but we don't sell tape for boxes," the customer service rep told me. Hmm—that thought hadn't entered my mind. She said there were places around the office that sold tape, but that they would be closed until 5:00 p.m. It was about three o'clock. I told Judy I would search for a store that had tape if she could wait with the boxes. She agreed, so I took off. I stopped at every store I could find, asking where I might find tape. I walked to two markets that were open, but they had no tape. I asked a delivery person who was taping up a box. I wanted to buy an extra roll from him, but he didn't have an extra roll and needed the one he had. Darn.

I finally went back to the post office where Judy was still stationed. Out of sympathy, one of the clerks had come up to talk with her, and she was able to ensure the shipping forms I had completed were correct. I asked her where I might purchase tape, and she assured me the store next door had the tape. I still had to wait another half hour until the store opened, but I found the tape and purchased it—as soon as the store's cash register computer glitch was fixed—and got back to Judy. We taped up the boxes, cut the tape discreetly with my small pocketknife, and pulled another ticket to wait in line to mail the boxes to ourselves to Santiago. It was about fifteen euros per box, which was a bargain since we still had another few weeks to hike. Life would be good after this decision. By this time, we had hiked about 192 miles. We would have less weight on our backs, and I was feeling good and in condition. Surprisingly, it was Judy and I who were helping the younger folks with blisters and motivation not to quit.

A few days later, Judy and I had one of the most unique adventures of the trip. We started out in the dark, leaving a little before six a.m. The way out of town wasn't too hard to find, although we did use our flashlights to verify our route. Judy kept me in view, at least until we had some daylight. By that time, it was a clear shot to our destination of the day, so she moved on ahead, as she often did when we trekked. At that same time, I had to go to the bathroom—not just pee but poop.

Pooping along the trail would always be tricky, but even more so when the trail was along a main road like this one was. Judy was way ahead of me, but I figured she would wait for me after a while. I found a place for my mission and took another ten minutes out of my day. Shortly, I got back on the trail and looked for evidence that Judy was still ahead. Because we had started so early, there were few people on the trail at this time, so I plodded ahead alone and hoped to eventually find Judy.

I came to a fork in the road. I could go over a little bridge to the right and follow the scallop shell markers for the trail, or I could stay straight with other shells. There were two cement blocks in front of the route straight ahead, and I took them to be barriers. I followed the markers to the right and wandered into a small, older town. I noticed one pilgrim in front of me wandering through the town also. I wasn't able to catch up to her, but I didn't expect to. Usually Judy would wait for me before going through a town so we were sure to both come out at the same place, but she wasn't anywhere to be seen. I wandered through the town, following shells, and she wasn't at the other end of town either. I remember the sense of loneliness, fear, second-guessing, and uncertainty I felt. I didn't know what to do. I was missing my right arm, my Judy.

I decided to keep going, following the trail. At one point the trail petered out, and I stopped to ask an older lady about the Camino. She pointed to a trail a few yards away. I had missed the trail beside the stream, and she helped me get back on track. The support from locals was phenomenal the whole way. Any time we had a question and asked someone, they helped us get back on track. Sometimes someone would come up and tap me on the shoulder to correct a wrong turn. But no one could give me directions to Judy.

After hiking another half hour and seeing no one, I finally ran across a young man from Tennessee I'd met earlier on the trail. I asked him why we weren't seeing more of the usual crowd, why there were so few people on the trail. He told me, "That's because we are on the alternate route, not the popular route." My face fell.

I didn't know what to say. All of a sudden, it all made sense. He told me that the most used trail continued straight, along the main road, where I had turned right. I looked at my guidebook and saw my mistake. I recalled the two cement posts that I thought were blocking my route. They had to be, in fact, beacons to the most popular way. I had totally misread the message and was on my own journey—kind of taking the road less traveled. He was kind enough to tell me that the trails would come back together in another hour or so.

I thought for a while and then decided I had to continue forward and get back on the main trail. Certainly Judy would be there, waiting at the junction, because she would have figured out the problem. If we'd missed each other at the first junction, then surely we would connect at the second junction.

Not so. I got to the main junction, where my secondary trail joined the main trail, but no Judy. What to do? I started thinking, *What would Judy do? Maybe she went back to the hostel we stayed in to see if something happened. Ah, that would be sweet, but not what Judy would do. I have to go forward, to where we talked about staying tonight.* And that's what I decided to do, continue.

I maintained my pace so I could continue to the next town. When I got to the outskirts of town, I followed the shells to stay on the trail through the town. As I got closer to downtown, I searched for a place to stop and wait in the shade if I could find some. By this time I was feeling the hole in my stomach, hoping to find my friend again since we had to make other decisions going forward. Last night, I had kind of mentioned the place where I thought we should stay in this town, but I wasn't sure Judy had heard me, and we hadn't come up with alternate communication plans in case this situation happened.

Note to self: Always make backup communication plans.

I MADE MY WAY TO SOME SHADE AND SAT DOWN BECAUSE I WASN'T SURE what to do. I figured I should just stay here since the place I wanted to stay in, a monastery, was nearby. I wasn't nutso yet, still just trying to figure out what to do.

What I didn't know was that Judy had taken her own journey. Judy is more of a point-A-to-point-B person, someone who doesn't stop much between destinations. When she gets on a straightaway, she takes off like an Olympic athlete. I'm the one who wanders and stops when something interesting comes my way. I'm sure it drives Judy nuts.

By this time, I had figured out that Judy had stayed on the main path and I had taken the less popular route. I thought I would have run into her by now, though, and yet I was sitting here alone. I decided just to sit, maybe get out my remaining chocolate bar and eat the entire thing. Chocolate always made me feel better, and eating was the thing to do. At least, I hoped it would make me feel better.

I was chomping on the third level of chocolate when I saw her. She was waving her umbrella, coming toward me from the trail ahead of me, all smiles. Maybe she had gone up through town to see if I was already at the other side. She kept getting closer, and I got up from my cement wall, chomping on the fourth level of chocolate. As soon as she reached me, we hugged each other and smiled broadly. It was great to be together again, and to second-guess each other's decisions.

Judy had put on her blinders for this leg of the trip and figured I wouldn't get lost since it was a straight shot along the main highway. She hadn't waited for me at all, just kept going for the next night's stop. I tried not to look too disappointed.

What I didn't know was that she'd overshot the goal. She had been going so fast and straight that when she got through what was supposed to be our final town for the day, she kept going. When she was at least two miles outside of town, she happened to run into another hiker and started talking with her. The friend told her that there were no more towns with places to stay for another eight miles or so, and she might think about turning around. It was then that Judy realized she had overshot and had to race back, retracing her steps to try to find me before I picked out a place for the night and disappeared.

Once we found one another, the stories were great, but they didn't really matter. We were together again and had learned a lesson—*that* mattered. I remembered saying a day or two prior that we should wait in the destination town if we got separated. The only problem was that my guidebook and the map the Pilgrim Office had given to us sometimes differed on recommended destination towns. Going forward, I tried to be sure that we discussed the place we were aiming to stop in before leaving each morning. Two mistakes had autocorrected, gratefully.

Note to self: It's wonderful to hug your friend again.

I made it to the local store and brought back dinner plus a ninety-three-cent bottle of wine, splurging over the other sixty-two-cent box of wine. Judy was pooped but was able to eat—and to drink cheap wine. A great way to finish an unusual day.

Along our path, we kept meeting unusual people. There was the seventeen-year-old from Tennessee who hiked one trail nude because it was so muddy. There were two young women, one from London and one from Spain, hiking together. In Leon, we celebrated the Londoner's birthday as well as that we'd hiked about 307 miles by now. At another bar stop, we sat down with them again, when the Spaniard looked at me and laughed. "You eat Oreos, Kinder Chocolate, and ice cream. What a diet!"

At earlier points in my life, I might have become self-conscious from comments like this, worried about my weight and diet. But by now, I'd let all that baggage go, accepted my love for chocolate and ice cream, and focused solely on my health in terms of my ability to adventure, not on my weight. I smiled at the Spaniard and replied, "I'm closer to dying than you are." That was the kind of humor that followed us throughout the trip.

Our chests even puffed out once in a while when we heard comments from youngsters like, "I can't wait to tell the people back home that we hiked with seventy-year-olds!" Or, pointing to us, "Those are the ones who helped me with my blisters!" From others, we heard, "You are legends on the trail." *A legend in my own time—who would've guessed?* I think that compliment was the apex of my journeys.

ALGFO (a little girl from Ohio) had broken her own boundaries and arrived at her destiny. I didn't have to be a Mother Teresa to leave the planet with something important and big. I could be a mentor by example, albeit on a small scale. It felt good, being of value to someone.

At one point, Judy said to me, "You know, most seventy-year-olds have stopped dreaming." When I stopped to think about it, I knew she was right, but I would have added that most seventy-year-olds have stopped *playing*.

Then I said to her, "Do you know how silly we look, especially you with your Gomer Pyle–style hat?"

She looked me straight in the eye and said, "I don't give a shit."

The trip continued with large towns and small towns in our path. We got stronger and stronger as the trip progressed, and the packs felt manageable and lighter on our backs even though the weight was the same. We laughed together, conferred about our route, made sure we knew the end destination daily, and eventually found that large sign that said *Santiago de Compostela*. It was the official end of the pilgrimage. Everyone was taking pictures, and so did we. We had hiked every step of the five-hundred-mile journey and were darned proud of ourselves.

But the day's journey wasn't over. We were trying to get to the cathedral in the old part of Santiago, to the Saint James monument, in time for the noon pilgrim mass. We had left early in the day, before sunrise, stopped for breakfast, and were going as fast as we could to get to the church on time. Judy snapped at me a few times to hurry, but I couldn't keep up with her.

She finally said, "I take three steps to your one because I'm short, and you can't keep up! What's your problem?" We had been hiking daily for five weeks, and it was definitely time for a break.

We finally got within shot of the church with fifteen minutes to spare, so we looked for a hostel to stay in for two nights to drop off our packs. We couldn't take them into the cathedral service, and didn't want to leave them outside near the church in case the packs were ripped off. We stopped and asked someone in front of a hostel sign, and she told us to go up another half block where we would find a better place. We raced back to find it.

I went in to ask if they had two lower bunks for two nights. Yes! We took them, dumped our packs, and ran to the church—where we immediately got in line. After a few short questions, we realized we were in the wrong line—this one was for the museum and store—so we went to the other entrance where we could see the noon mass for us, the pilgrims arriving today.

We went inside, only to discover the cathedral was full and there was no seating, so we sat on the base of a large pillar. It wasn't long, though, before we got a tap on the shoulder and a middle-aged man we had been hiking with motioned for us to take his and his wife's seats on the bench. I couldn't believe it. I guess we looked older than they, and besides, we were *legends*. We gratefully took the seats and listened to the service. The act was touching and opened my mind to whatever was supposed to come next. I told myself, *Okay, mind, open up. What am I supposed to learn today?*

Although the service was in Spanish and I couldn't understand it, it was beautiful. I felt the presence of all those who'd come before me and felt gratitude that I was able to walk the entire distance at my age. What a blessing. Judy was crying.

Before we'd started, I had known that the Camino walk would be for my benefit in some way, although I'd told most people that I was accompanying Judy because of her losses. We had deposited her sister's ashes along the path. Quietly, the message came to me as I sat on the cathedral bench. My quest on the Camino was to find balance in my life, balancing all those things I love so I could be content. I needed to learn to accept what integrated my head, body, and heart as a unit instead of allowing them to battle each other. I needed to ask for help instead of always needing to appear so self-sufficient. It was all very cathartic to go on the journey in the first place, learning about monotony, self-discipline, generosity, resting, and finding friendships. Coming to peace with my weight, letting go of caring so much about my appearance at the expense of my health, and *feeling good* became a motto—the balance I was searching for. All along the Camino, I'd lit candles in churches for my father, Aunt Bertie, and of course Helen—my mentors. I knew the people I had lost were all smiling on me right now, and I could sense their warmth.

Note to self: Continue seeking balance, peace, and harmony, and accept that nothing is permanent. If you can't be happy, be content. More importantly, embrace spending time with friends and family, the essence of life.

WE WERE FINALLY ABLE TO VISIT THE TACKY TOURIST SHOPS IN SPAIN and buy stuff. We wandered in and out of shops, finding a bota bag like mine for Judy and other stuff for me.

That night, I looked at the news. There was a coup attempt in Turkey, in Istanbul, and the airport there was closed. *Closed?* In my ever-enthusiastic desire to see different countries, I'd booked our flight home to go from Santiago to Madrid, then through Istanbul to home. We had two days before we were to leave, so I asked Judy what she wanted to do, and she reminded me of Dave's Stupid-O-Meter.

Through spotty messages to my daughter on the other side of the planet in California, we asked for her to get us two new tickets from Madrid to LAX. She didn't have all our passport data, so she had to beg for it from the company that had initially issued the tickets. Long story short, she was able to get us two tickets from Madrid to LA through London so we could avoid Turkey. I often think she is the older, wiser, more centered person in the family. Meanwhile, I was adding to my reputation as the nutcase in the family.

We didn't have time to hike to Finisterre, so we took a bus there for a day trip. I must admit that eating a large seafood dinner without having to hike to it was a real treat.

On our last night in Santiago, Judy and I elected to stay in the *parador*. A parador is a government-run hotel that typically is a historic building that has been converted to a hotel. In some cases, it was an old hospital or monastery, or perhaps both during different times. In this case, it was originally a monastery and had fulfilled different roles over the decades, including being a hospital during the World Wars. It was pure luxury and rated a five-star hotel. We had stayed in one in Leon, so this was our second one, in Santiago. We both looked forward to the breakfasts, a feast for our eyes.

The day we were to leave, we had extra time and arranged a taxi ride with others to help keep costs down. We went to breakfast, and I dug in. Two mimosas with good champagne, an espresso, fruit, yogurt, pastries—just about anything you could possibly want was available. I overate. It wasn't long before I started not feeling good.

We made one more round of the tourist shops, and as we came out of one, I told Judy, "I don't feel too good. I'm going back to the hotel." I ran to the bathroom and tossed up most of breakfast. Too bad it didn't stop there. I made it out to the taxi with all the other people and threw up again beside the taxi. There was nothing I could do except let everyone in our small world see me puke on the street. I had a plastic bag with me in case I needed it during the ride. Oh, man, what an ending to our trip.

We made it to the airport without any more incidents, but I would double over often as my stomach cramped. I tried to make it through the lines to the waiting area—I had to do it because I didn't want to miss that flight. The first flight was from Santiago to Madrid, then London to LAX. We would be spending the night in the Madrid airport, so hopefully I would have time to recover before the international flights.

I made it to the waiting area with Judy's help, and there I kept the bag close to my mouth. I retched a few times, sure that several people's eyes were glued to me. I kept my eyes on the floor and bag next to my mouth. Judy, sitting several seats away from me, confirmed my suspicions that several people were watching me with a lot of interest. I prayed they didn't think I had Ebola or some other horrible disease and kick me off the flight. Someone could report me, and I would be doomed. I was sure they were debating it.

By some miracle, I got on the flight. Getting off in Madrid wasn't easy, but we did it. Judy parked me in a spot with our stuff and asked if I wanted something to eat. "*No!*" I replied. It wasn't until morning that I ate anything, a piece of toast, and was grateful that it stayed down.

In London and on the flight home to LA, I got better and better. To ensure my safety, I found the barf bags in each of the seats I occupied and was again grateful that I didn't need them. So much for Istanbul, but London was great. When I returned, my mother expressed amazement at my achievement. With a huge smile, she said, "I'm so proud of you!" Darn it, I was proud of me too.

Note to self: Remember this.

HIKING TO FINISTERRE, AND THEN TO MUXIA WHERE THE EARTH WAS thought to end, from Santiago would wait another few years, when my beautiful daughter would hike it with me and help deposit some of my mother's ashes in the ocean.

Epilogue

AT FIRST, I THOUGHT IT. THEN I ACTUALLY WHISPERED IT TO MYSELF: "I think I'm happy." It wasn't until I said it aloud to a friend, "I think I'm happy," that I knew it to be truth. No, not eternally happy, like in Nirvana, but *content* with life most of the time.

My memory can take me to the good places, and I control my thoughts as much as possible not to take me to the negative places of my past or future places of fear. When I'd returned from working at McMurdo in 2005, I stopped working. I was able to leave LA and move to a much smaller town north of LA where there was space to breathe, and where I could see some of the wildlife I love. I think that rural life, and calming down from the Los Angeles pace, was one big factor that helped me get to this point. Instead of eternally trying to escape my daily life by running to totally foreign places, I can be content sitting still. I can allow myself to not be productive and to value having a cup of tea with a friend.

It only took me most of seventy years and excursions on seven continents to get here. I'm not trying to please a partner, to fill a hole, or to keep eternally busy. I'm content in Hawaii, in Los Angeles, in Mongolia, in a small town, even in a cardboard box for a short period of time.

I'm not constantly fighting to go upstream. I think we are all trained to swim upstream, to work hard at all costs, when truly, it is easier to go downstream with the flow. It surely makes for an easier life. It just took me a lifetime to understand that I didn't have to give up my unique personality to go downstream.

In accepting that I am going with the flow now, I'm trying to embrace that I am still one of a kind, a "maverick." Sometimes it takes reminding, but I've established myself as my own person, and no one can change that or shake that except me. But that doesn't mean I don't need people in my life. I hang on to my personality and spend my time with people who actually like me rather than with people who expect me to please them or who want something from me.

In other words, I'd been on a pendulum most of my life. On one end, I learned to hold on to my self-sufficiency as a badge of courage. *Look at me. I don't need anyone or anything in my life. I have myself,* I thought. On the other end, I was too dependent on others, changing my life so I fit into theirs. Luckily everything comes full circle in life, and with age, I allow myself to lean more on others, to ask for help, and to give it, without giving up who I am. It's all about trying to bring that pendulum of life to a place of centeredness instead of going to either extreme.

I've always loved walks in the forest with the dogs, by a stream, tossing sticks into the water for them. The dogs have always been a common factor that has given me great joy. Now, in addition to the dogs, the cat sleeps by my feet, clinging to me after a week's absence. The simple pleasures they give me become more valuable, and the primary lesson is that I am able to see it.

I watched my ninety-seven-year-old mother struggle with life, and I understood when she said, "I want to be with Don," my dad, the love of her life. The scary thing is that I see myself as more than three-quarters through my own life, just as she was at my age. I asked my sweet mother once what I should learn from her, what she would tell a new person on the planet. She thought for a minute and then said with a smile, "Don't take life too seriously. It will be over before you know it."

My dear friend Helen had told me once when I asked her what I should learn from her, "Have no regrets." Well, I kind of went overboard on that no-regrets thing. I made sure I have traveled everywhere I wanted to go and have done most of what I wanted to do so I have no regrets as the years close in. I am sorry that I no longer want to tackle eighteen-thousand-foot passes and nineteen-thousand-foot mountains, but I achieved those things so I have no regrets about them. It's okay for me to go downstream and not have to do those things any longer. It's okay to have a cup of coffee with a friend and count it as time well spent.

The Linda and Judy Wild Adventure Trips came to an end in the Swiss Alps a few months before I turned seventy. In the US airport before we left on the trip, two ladies came up to us and said, "Oh, you look so *great!* Where are you going?"

"To the Swiss Alps," I replied quite proudly. We had on our hiking boots, pants, and shirts, looking very much the part.

"Well, you are both our heroes!" they said as they left.

We were in a refuge high in the Swiss Alps above the timberline when I looked out on a severe rainstorm hitting the moonscaped terrain and high, rocky passes. I had a meltdown. My head was jumping up and down with thoughts. According to my body, the Alps were too hard, too remote, and too scary for me now. My body was no longer willing or able to do what my head asked of it.

Judy and I had a heart-to-heart talk, and I asked her to put on her business-coach hat to help me work through it. We decided to abandon the Alps and head for a tamer, more achievable trip in France. The Linda and Judy Wild Adventure Trips became the Linda and Judy Tame Adventure Trips. And eventually, we knew, they would become the Linda and Judy Lame Adventure Trips, when we would have to hire someone to push our wheelchairs.

Note to self: No regrets.

Acknowledgments

ALONG MY PATH TO WRITING THIS BOOK, I LISTENED TO TIDBITS OF ADVICE from friends and family. To those people, I cannot thank you enough. To Roy Ferguson, my high school English teacher and mentor, thank you for believing in me. A special thanks to my book editor, Ali Shaw, for being a kindred spirit and believing in me, making this book as good as it can be. To my son, James McDermott, who completed the drawings in my book, I am honored to have your support. To my daughter and son, who lived the journey, and friends who have continuously supported me in all my quirky endeavors, I am eternally grateful for your love. May this book encourage people everywhere to grow, to embrace change, and to recognize how amazing our planet is.

About the Author

LINDA MCDERMOTT SPENT HER CHILDHOOD IN THE CINCINNATI, OHIO, area where she developed a lifelong love for nature and a deep curiosity about everything outside of Ohio. After raising children and completing a career in human resources, she started traveling the world in earnest. Now in Tehachapi, California, Linda hosts Pacific Crest Trail hikers from all over the world and continues to travel, both domestically and internationally.

www.ingramcontent.com/pod-product-compliance
Lightning Source LLC
Chambersburg PA
CBHW052009070526
44584CB00016B/1679